Silence and Voice in the Study of Contentious Politics

The aim of this book is to highlight and begin to give "voice" to some of the notable "silences" evident in recent years in the study of contentious politics. Specifically, the authors offer agenda-setting chapters on the following important, yet underrepresented, topics: emotion, temporality, the spatial dimensions of contention, leadership, threat as a stimulus to contention, religion, and demographic and life-course processes. In doing so, they also provide a partial synthesis of various literatures that have grown up around the study of non-routine or contentious politics. As such, the book not only undermines conventional disciplinary understanding of contentious politics, but also lays out a number of provocative new research agendas.

Ronald R. Aminzade is Professor of Sociology at the University of Minnesota, St. Paul. His publications include *Ballots and Barricades* (1993), winner of the Contribution to Scholarship Award of the Political Sociology Section of the American Sociological Association.

Jack A. Goldstone is Professor of Sociology and International Relations at the University of California, Davis. Among his numerous publications is *Revolution and Rebellion in the Early Modern World* (1991), winner of the American Sociological Association Distinguished Scholarly Publication Award.

Doug McAdam is Professor of Sociology at Stanford University and Director Designate of the Center for Advanced Study in the Behavioral Sciences. His numerous publications include *Freedom Summer* (1988), cowinner of the 1990 C. Wright Mills Award, and *Dynamics of Contention*, coauthored with Sidney Tarrow and Charles Tilly.

Elizabeth J. Perry is Henry Rosovsky Professor of Government and Director of the Fairbanks Center for East Asian Research at Harvard University. Her most recent publications include *The Politics of Chinese Labor* (1993) and *Proletarian Power: Shanghai in the Cultural Revolution* (1997), which she coauthored.

William H. Sewell, Jr., is the Max Palevsky Professor of Political Science and History at the University of Chicago. His many publications include *Work and Revolution in France: The Language of Labor from the Old Regime to the Revolution of 1848* (1980), which won the 1981 Herbert Baxter Adams Prize from the American Historical Association.

Sidney Tarrow is Maxwell Upson Professor of Government (and also of Sociology) at Cornell University. He specializes in European politics and social movements and has most recently (with Doug Imig) completed a collective volume entitled *Contentious Europeans*.

Charles Tilly is Joseph L. Buttenwieser Professor of Social Science at Columbia University. His many books include *Durable Inequality* (1998), for which he received the 2000 Distinguished Scholarly Publication Award from the American Sociological Association.

Cambridge Studies in Contentious Politics

Editors

Doug McAdam   *Stanford University and Center for Advanced Study in the Behavioral Sciences*
Sidney Tarrow   *Cornell University*
Charles Tilly   *Columbia University*

Ronald Aminzade et al., *Silence and Voice in the Study of Contentious Politics*
Doug McAdam, Sidney Tarrow, and Charles Tilly, *Dynamics of Contention*

Silence and Voice in the Study of Contentious Politics

RONALD R. AMINZADE
University of Minnesota, St. Paul

JACK A. GOLDSTONE
University of California, Davis

DOUG McADAM
Stanford University

ELIZABETH J. PERRY
Harvard University

WILLIAM H. SEWELL, JR.
University of Chicago

SIDNEY TARROW
Cornell University

CHARLES TILLY
Columbia University

CAMBRIDGE
UNIVERSITY PRESS

CAMBRIDGE UNIVERSITY PRESS
Cambridge, New York, Melbourne, Madrid, Cape Town,
Singapore, São Paulo, Delhi, Mexico City

Cambridge University Press
32 Avenue of the Americas, New York, NY 10013-2473, USA

www.cambridge.org
Information on this title: www.cambridge.org/9780521001557

First published 2001
Reprinted 2013

A catalog record for this publication is available from the British Library.

Library of Congress Cataloging in Publication Data

Silence and voice in the study of contentious politics / Ronald R. Aminzade . . . [et al.].
    p. cm. – (Cambridge studies in contentious politics)
    Includes bibliographical references and index.
    ISBN 0-521-80679-8 (hardback) – ISBN 0-521-00155-2 (pbk.)
    1. Social movements. 2. Revolutions. 3. Democratization. 4. Ethnic conflict.
    I. Aminzade, Ronald, 1949– II. Series.
    HM881.S535 2001
    303.48′4–dc21   2001018440

ISBN 978-0-521-80679-4 Hardback
ISBN 978-0-521-00155-7 Paperback

To Fresh Voices:
Lissa Bell
Pamela Burke
Jorge Cadena-Roa
David Cunningham
Manali Desai
Robyn Eckhardt
John Glenn
Debbie Gould
Hyojoung Kim
Joseph Luders
Heidi Swarts
Nella Van Dyke
Heather Williams
Kim Williams

Contents

Preface   *page* xi

1   SILENCE AND VOICE IN THE STUDY OF
    CONTENTIOUS POLITICS:
    INTRODUCTION   Sidney Tarrow   1

2   EMOTIONS AND CONTENTIOUS POLITICS
    Ron Aminzade and Doug McAdam   14

3   SPACE IN CONTENTIOUS POLITICS
    William H. Sewell, Jr.   51

4   IT'S ABOUT TIME: TEMPORALITY IN THE
    STUDY OF SOCIAL MOVEMENTS AND
    REVOLUTIONS   Doug McAdam and
    William H. Sewell, Jr.   89

5   LEADERSHIP DYNAMICS AND DYNAMICS
    OF CONTENTION   Ron Aminzade,
    Jack A. Goldstone, and Elizabeth J. Perry   126

6   THE SACRED, RELIGIOUS, AND SECULAR IN
    CONTENTIOUS POLITICS: BLURRING
    BOUNDARIES   Ron Aminzade and
    Elizabeth J. Perry   155

7   THREAT (AND OPPORTUNITY): POPULAR
    ACTION AND STATE RESPONSE IN THE
    DYNAMICS OF CONTENTIOUS ACTION
    Jack A. Goldstone and Charles Tilly   179

ix

| 8 | CONTENTION IN DEMOGRAPHIC AND LIFE-COURSE CONTEXT   JACK A. GOLDSTONE and DOUG MCADAM | 195 |
| 9 | HARMONIZING THE VOICES: THEMATIC CONTINUITY ACROSS THE CHAPTERS DOUG MCADAM | 222 |

| *References* | 241 |
| *Index* | 267 |

Preface

The publication of *Silence and Voice in the Study of Contentious Politics* marks an end to one aspect of a unique collaborative project that began in the early 1990s and stretched into the new millennium. Ultimately, the project came to involve twenty-one core participants and a host of others who attended one or more of the nine miniconferences that structured the project. In form and function, the project resembled nothing so much as an extended, collaborative conversation concerning the nature and dynamics of "contentious politics."

Motivated by a shared concern that the study of social movements, revolutions, democratization, ethnic conflict, and other forms of nonroutine, or contentious, politics had grown fragmented, spawning a number of insular scholarly communities only dimly aware of one another, the project was committed above all else to exploring possible lines of synthesis – empirical and theoretical – that might transcend some of the scholarly conventions that still largely divide the field. Among these conventions are: persistent theoretical divisions between rationalists, culturalists, and structuralists; putative differences between various forms of contention (for example, social movements, revolutions, peasant rebellions, industrial conflict, and so on); and the longstanding assumption of area specialists that any general phenomenon – such as contentious politics – can only be understood in light of the idiosyncratic history and cultural conventions of the locale in which it takes place. While respectful of these conventional distinctions, the project has been committed to exploring their limits and embracing promising new approaches and topics in the study of political contention.

A bit of history: The project began in 1993 with a casual conversation between Sid Tarrow and me, in which we found we shared a deep ambivalence regarding the proliferation of work on social movements. On the one hand, we were delighted that a topic long regarded as peripheral by political scientists and sociologists alike had come to be seen as a legitimate subject of so much academic work. On the other, we were concerned by the increasing narrowness of the field and its disconnect from other "proximate" fields of study. Wouldn't it be great, we mused, if scholars from these separate fields could together explore the possibilities for synthesis across these nominally distinct subfields? In turn, the conversation led to a concrete suggestion: Why not submit a proposal to the Center for Advanced Study in the Behavioral Sciences to convene a one-year Special Project devoted to the kind of exploration and synthesis we had in mind? Why not, indeed! After enlisting Chuck Tilly as a third coconspirator, a proposal was drafted, ably vetted by Phil Converse and Bob Scott (then Director and Associate Director of the Center), and in 1994 approved by both the Center's Advisory Committee on Special Projects and its Board of Trustees.

Having secured the Special Project, the enterprise then took a fateful and felicitous turn. Knowing how ambitious – yet amorphous – our aims were, Bob Scott encouraged us to seek the additional monetary support that would allow us to stretch the project over a longer time frame. At his suggestion, we made application in 1995 to the Mellon Foundation's Sawyer Seminar Series seeking support for a three-year seminar series organized around the broad topic of "Contentious Politics." To our delight, Mellon granted the request.

The challenge now centered on finding the right core faculty around whom to build the ongoing conversation. Eventually, we were lucky enough to attract four other colleagues who are our coauthors on this book. In Ron Aminzade, Jack Goldstone, Liz Perry, and Bill Sewell, we could not have asked for more qualified and generous conversationalists. (Speaking personally, the opportunity to interact with all six of these colleagues over the life of the project has been one of the most rewarding experiences of my career. None of them can possibly know just how much I have learned and continue to learn from them.)

Though neither our Center nor our Mellon "sponsors" required us to do so, the seven of us agreed immediately that we wanted to involve graduate students in the project. Who better to offer fresh perspectives on important topics than promising young scholars not wedded to disciplinary boundaries and subfield conventions? The model we hit on for facilitating student involvement in the project was a yearly competition to select five Graduate Fellows drawn from applications solicited nationally from across a range of social science disciplines. The results of our first competition confirmed the approach. The voices of the five members of that first graduate "cohort" – Lissa Bell, Pamela Burke, Robyn Eckhardt, John Glenn, and Joseph Luders – blended so seamlessly into the conversation that, in the end, they forced us to revise our plan to limit the Fellowships to one year and to approach Mellon for funding to enable us to retain all Graduate Fellows for the life of the project. Mellon came through for us a second time. Nine more talented students – Jorge Cadena-Roa, David Cunningham, Manali Desai, Debbie Gould, Hyojoung Kim, Heidi Swarts, Nella Van Dyke, Heather Williams, and Kim Williams – joined us over the next two years, bringing the total number of Graduate Fellows on the project to fourteen. It is to these fourteen that we have dedicated the volume. It was their many interventions, provocative queries, and fresh takes on familiar topics, as much as anything, that inspired the exploratory focus and tone of this volume. We thank them collectively for their innumerable contributions to the book and broader Mellon/Center project.

There are many others we need to thank as well. To do so, it will help to know something about the way the broad project was structured. In each of the three years of the Mellon project (1995–96, 1996–97, and 1997–98) we organized three two-day miniconferences, each focused on a specific topic relevant to a general understanding of contention. Among the topics explored in these sessions were: religion and contention, emotion and contention, the globalization of contention, identity and networks in contention, and the like. Besides the grad fellows and core faculty, each of these conferences featured participation by two to three "invited experts" on the specific topic of the gathering. We owe these colleagues a deep vote of thanks as well. Many of the ideas pursued in these chapters benefited from insights gleaned from this or that "conversational guest." A complete list of these distinguished colleagues follows: Mark Beissinger, Craig Calhoun, Bill Gamson, Jeff Goodwin, Roger Gould, Susan Harding, Michael Hechter, Lynn Hunt, Jane Jenson, Arthur Kleinman, Hanspeter Kriesi, Marc Lichbach, John Meyer, Ann Mische, Aldon Morris, Maryjane Osa, Gay Seidman, Kathryn Sikkink, Verta Taylor, Mark Traugott, Paul Wapner, and Timothy Wickham-Crowley.

In addition to the three miniconferences held during year three of the project, four of the core faculty – Ron Aminzade, Sid Tarrow, Chuck Tilly, and I – constituted a Special Project on Contentious Politics while in residence at the Center. Besides meeting extensively as a closed group, we also organized a general seminar on the topic for interested Center Fellows. Once again, we were lucky to attract the attention of an unusually large and talented group of our colleagues. These Center colleagues included: Jerry Davis, Jenny Mansbridge, James McPherson, Rob Sampson, Carol Swain, Ed Tiryakian, and Katherine Verdery.

A fourth group of colleagues intervened more directly in the content of the volume. These were friends who read and gave us generous feedback on one or more chapters of the book. These academic samaritans included: Neil Brenner, Kathy Simon Frank, Scott Gartner, Debbie Gould, John Hall, Clyde Hertzman, Stuart Hill, Lynn Hunt, Howard Kimeldorf, Bert Klandermans, Theodore Kemper, David Laitin, Erik Larson, Barbara Laslett, Richard Madsen, Mary Jo Maynes, Jennifer Pierce, Ed Tiryakian, Mark Traugott, and Lisa Weeden. Another colleague, Yang Su, labored long and hard to discharge a host of editorial matters connected with the volume. I owe him a personal debt of gratitude for all his help.

We have reserved two very special institutional acknowledgments for last. We refer, of course, to our two institutional sponsors, who responded creatively and generously to our requests for support. To the Mellon Foundation, and Harriet Zuckerman in particular, we offer a very sincere vote of thanks for their creative stewardship of the project. Without Mellon funds we simply would never have been able to undertake such a unique and ambitious project.

And then there is the enormous debt of gratitude we owe the Center for Advanced Study in the Behavioral Sciences. It was the prospect of a Center Special Project that set us in motion in the first place. It was Bob Scott's vision of a longer-term project that motivated us to approach Mellon for support. It was the consistent support of two Center Directors – Phil Converse and later Neil Smelser – that sustained the project over the long term. And, we are convinced, it was the special quality of the Center experience that allowed the larger Mellon group to grow so close over the life of the project. We therefore salute the entire Center staff for their critical role in the success of the enterprise. More prosaically, much of the work on the volume was carried out at the Center, either as part of the Special Project or in connection with the various miniconferences held there between 1995 and 1998.

It remains only to say a few words about the volume itself. How did *Silence* come about? Interestingly, I had drawn up an outline for a volume of that same name a year or so before the start of the project. Reflecting the same concern about the increasingly narrow focus of most social movement scholarship that motivated the project, I had in mind a volume in which I would devote chapters to a half dozen or so neglected topics in the study of social movements. But early on in the broader Mellon/Center project, I realized that the collaborative conversation in which we were engaged afforded the perfect vehicle for a much more interesting version of the book I had in mind. Why not collaborate in identifying and giving voice to a set of consequential silences in the study of political contention? That is what we have tried to do. The ground rules for the volume were simple. All core faculty proposed silences, but at least two had to endorse the topic and agree to serve as coauthors for it to make it into the volume.

This does not, of course, mean that these are the only relevant silences in the study of contentious politics. Our own initial list of candidate topics ran to fifteen or so. No doubt there are many more than this. Nor should our thoughts on any of the seven silences be taken as the last word on the topic. In the exploratory spirit of the overall project, we offer these chapters as little more than provisional agenda-setting efforts. By doing so, we hope not only to motivate scholars to think more systematically about these seven topics, but to identify other silences that deserve similar treatment. We will count the volume as successful to the extent that it stimulates a still broader conversation on the dynamics of contentious politics.

Doug McAdam
Menlo Park, CA
September 20, 2000

1

Silence and Voice in the Study of Contentious Politics: Introduction

Sidney Tarrow

A Strike at Siemens[1]

On the morning of April 2, 1993, a small group of labor organizers from the West German metalworker union, IG Metall, stand shivering in the dark outside a Siemens plant in the East German city of Rostock, passing out leaflets to the morning shift as it enters the plant. Siemens' West German management and other firms in the East have just tried to renege on an earlier promise to increase wages by 26 percent, claiming that they can no longer afford increased wage costs due to the disastrous conditions of the East German economy. That was the official story; but with 40 percent unemployment and massive job insecurity in the East, with no history of western-style collective bargaining, and with membership in free unions new and untested, the employers hope an aggressive united front against the union will win them reduced labor costs and more wage flexibility (Turner 1998:3).

It seems – in Lowell Turner's words – like "an employer's dream labor conflict" (p. 4). The business community and the business press urge restraint from the union, while the *Economist* titles its article on the coming conflict "Mass Suicide" (p. 3). On that chilly morning in early April, it is by no means clear that the union effort to fight the wage freeze will succeed. And the stakes are high: Should it fail, the future of social partnership and unionization are uncertain – not only in the eastern *laender* but in Germany as a whole. Union leaders have planned only a "warning strike" for this day, but no one knows how the East German workers, after sixty years of Nazism and state socialism, will react. "Listen, I don't know

---

[1] This incident is summarized from Turner (1998).

1

what will happen. I only know that we have our backs to the wall and have to fight," says Manfred Muster, a West German IG Metall leader who has come over from Bremen to head the strike effort (p. 5). The stage seems set for a "heroic defeat" (Golden 1997).

Political scientist Lowell Turner, who was there, later recalls what it was like on that cold April morning:

Since this was a Friday, the plan was for everyone to walk off the job, march down-town for a rally at the shipyards, and then take the rest of the weekend off . . . A strong showing would bolster the union position heading into a full-fledged strike, as well as increase the likelihood of a favorable settlement. A weak showing would cut the ground from under the union position. (p. 6)

As daylight rises and the Siemens works councillors mill about uneasily, union leader Muster jumps onto a van, circles the building in it, and turns on the loudspeaker. "This is IG Metall speaking," he says. "Today we are going out on a warning strike. 11:00 A.M. This is our right under Article 9 of the Constitution" (p. 7). Faces appear from behind the curtains of the offices. He drives around to the other side of the building and repeats the message. More faces at the windows. But by 10:45, writes Turner, "the lawn in front of the building was still empty except for a few anxious works councillors." When two squad cars approach, Munster cheerfully greets the police officers who emerge as "colleagues" who have "arrived to join the warning strike and escort us into town" (p. 8).

"And then," recalls Turner, "something quite surprising happened." At 11:00 A.M., as punctual as the German trains, the white- and blue-collar employees of Siemens streamed out through the main door. There were twenty, then fifty, then a hundred, two hundred, and still the numbers grew. . . . Along the route, small crowds from several other workplaces waited to join the march. . . . An IG Metal youth group joined at the front of the march with a wide red banner calling for wage solidarity East and West. . . . Columns approached from other directions, the workers had already spilled out from the shipyards, and there they were, about five thousand eastern workers . . . milling around in the crisp sunshine in front of a lashed-together stage, participating together in this history-making event: the first legally sanctioned collective bargaining work stoppage in eastern Germany since 1933. (p. 8)

The April 2 "warning strikes" were only the opening salvo in a cycle of work actions and negotiations that would spread across East Germany in erratic progression through April and early May, bringing into the con-flict workers from other eastern regions, other manufacturers' groups and the government, and western workers in solidarity with their eastern comrades (pp. 9–10). On May 12, 400,000 workers demonstrate throughout Germany in support of the eastern workers; on May 14, another 50,000 eastern metalworkers go out on strike (p. 10).

Mediated by *land* Prime Minister Biedenkopf, on May 14, a settlement is reached in the state of Saxony. This leads to agreements throughout the East. Though the union is forced to compromise on the timetable for the 26 percent wage increase, it wins a symbolic victory when the commitment is briefly reinstated retroactive to April 1. But much more important, the offensive against unionization has been stopped, East–West union solidarity is established in the face of western diffidence toward *Ossie* reliability, and Germany's system of social partnership is firmly extended to the East (pp. 15–16).

Silence and Voice

We have begun our collection of essays on silence and voice in contentious politics with the story of the successful warning strike in East Germany for several reasons:

First, though far from a typical site of capitalist contention (ex-Socialist East Germany had been merged with the German Federal Republic for less than three years), and not even a "social movement" in the classical sense, the story echoes a number of familiar themes from the "voice" of western social movement literature;

But, second, the story cannot be fully understood with the inherited tools of western social movement theory alone – there are some major "silences" in that body of theory;

Not only that: third, the typical recourse of social movement scholars who cannot explain a case with their existing toolkit – to trade it in for a new one – will help us even less. Familiar voice and muted silences need to be combined to provide a theoretically driven and empirically satisfying account. Let us briefly sketch what the Siemens story tells us:

- *Familiar Voices:* The unions in the story – like social movement organizations elsewhere – employed their organizational resources to attract followers and confront opponents. They offered strike funds, brought in experienced organizers, and took advantage of institutional opportunities – like Article 9 of the West German constitution – seeking the intervention of sympathetic, or at least neutral political forces like the Prime Minister of Saxony. The incident

3

evokes familiar voices from the canon of western social movement theory.

- *Loud Silences:* But these familiar aspects of social movement mobilization as developed in the West since the 1960s will not take us far enough. For a start – in focusing on movement *actions* – it too often excludes the crucial *inter*action between actors and their antagonists. And in focusing on opportunities, the existing canon too easily ignores both the threat to the unions and the leadership strategies of unionists who either take advantage of opportunities or risk missing the boat. Moreover, in its preoccupation with resources, the traditional canon too often ignores the key factor that brings frightened and uncertain people into the street – their emotions. "Worker mobilization in this case was fueled by extraordinary passion," writes Turner of the April 2 strike (p. 14). Agency, emotion, and interaction have for too long been muted in social movement theory.

- *Combining Voice and Silence:* Nor can we explain the outcome of the successful 1993 strike wave in East Germany by substituting such "new" elements for familiar ones. For example, although union organizer Munster exercised leadership skills – a muted voice in existing social movement theory – when he greeted approaching police officers in a friendly manner, his gesture would have meant little had he been facing the police of the ex-German Democratic Republic. Also, had he lacked IG Metall's resources – well-known refrains in social movement research, his efforts would have been stillborn. And had the passion of the angry East German workers not been channeled by the organizational routines refined by the union over decades of strike practice, it might have led to violence and defeat or been buried in internal resentment. We need to find ways of filling the silences, but also combining them with familiar voices in social movement theory to provide a rounded account of so fleeting an incident as the strike at Siemens.

That is the goal of this volume.

Dead Silences: What We Will Not Do

Let us begin with what will *not* be claimed here. At first, when planning the volume, we thought mainly in terms of "silent concepts" – that is, areas of research in which scholars of contentious politics have been completely mute. But so rich and varied has been the development of this field since the 1960s that one would be hard-pressed to find subjects that have not been studied by some scholar somewhere or themes that have not been broached in doing so. Following to the emergence of a new wave of movements since the 1960s, scholars turned to the concepts of the resources, opportunities, frames, and repertoires of contention, drawing on organizational sociology, political science, social psychology, and history. Impressed with the conceptual richness of this field of study, we quickly climbed down from the idea of constructing a new and better social movement mousetrap.

Nor did we find that the field has been overly focused on single types of movements. Take, for example, the range of movements that have been studied in the United States: From the Civil Rights, New Left, student, and antiwar movements of the 1960s, scholars moved in the 1970s into the study of ecological, women's, gay and lesbian rights, prochoice and prolife, and animal and disease victims' rights, before refocusing on the peace, sanctuary, and new religious right and right-wing movements of the 1980s and 1990s. Similar lists could be composed for Western Europe. The breadth of single-movement studies in both Western Europe and North America is truly impressive.

Nor do we think the field of social movement studies is methodologically impoverished – though the self-flagellation of many of its practitioners might lead one to think so. From the 1970s on, to the organizational and ideological studies that have been traditional in the field, social movement scholars have turned to survey methods, analyses of contentious events and event histories, discourse analysis, theoretically grounded historical studies, and comparative methodologies. Several rich studies of social movement methodologies are currently available and others are in progress.[2]

The current need of the field lies not in implementation but in the conceptual placement of social movements. We propose to advance toward this goal by,

> first, exploring aspects of contentious politics that have not been given sufficient attention by scholars of western social movements;
> second, employing concepts from areas of social science that have not been prominant in social movement studies;

[2] Among others, see Diani and Eyerman 1992; Rucht, Koopmans, and Neidhardt 1998; and Klandermans and Staggenborg forthcoming.

and, third, attempting to integrate or confront these new aspects and concepts with those that have shown their worth by stimulating empirical research or producing new theoretical insights in social movement theory over the past two decades.

For example, to the inherited canon of research findings on "opportunity structure," Jack Goldstone and Charles Tilly add an often-lacking and complementary focus on threat. To the canonical emphasis on the instrumentality of protest, Aminzade and McAdam will counterpose an increased emphasis on emotions. To the largely secular focus of most social movement research in the West, Aminzade and Perry will add an examination of religion and religious motives for contention. To the prevailing organizational definition of movement resources, Aminzade, Goldstone, and Perry will join the importance of leadership. Temporality – a dimension of contention that has mainly been limited to the study of "cycles" in the movement literature – is the subject of McAdam and Sewell's chapter on "temporality." Orthogonally, Sewell will explore the dimensions of spatiality and scale that are often ignored in – but are seldom absent from – contentious politics. Finally, Goldstone and McAdam will attempt to bring together a microfocus on the life course with a macrofocus on demographic change surrounding episodes of contentious politics. In his conclusions, McAdam will summarize four areas in which we hope to have made a synthetic contribution to the study of contentious politics and social movements. Let us begin with the connections between these two key terms.

Bridging Silences: From Social Movements to Contentious Politics

In one sense, our effort *will* attempt to break new ground – or at least to fill in gaps of what other groups of scholars have already etched: Social movement research has too often been cut off from the study of other forms of contention. Like the IG Metall union in the story that opens this chapter, many subjects in contentious politics do not reduce to classical social movement organizations. The same is largely true of revolutions, ethnic conflict, nationalism, democratization, and war (McAdam, Tarrow, and Tilly 2001). In recent years, scholars specializing in these forms of contention have made substantial advances in describing and explaining each of them. But on the whole, they have paid little attention to each other's discoveries.

6

Introduction

We think the study of all these areas of conflict will profit from being examined within the common framework of what we call "contentious politics," which we see as broader than social movements but narrower than all of politics. Three of us have defined contentious politics elsewhere as:

> public, collective, episodic interactions among makers of claims when a) at least some of the interaction adopts noninstitutional forms, b) at least one government is a claimant, an object or claims, or a party to the claims, and c) the claims would, if realized, affect the interests of at least one of the claimants.[3]

Thus defined, contentious politics sometimes overlaps with a regime's *prescribed* forms of political participation (for example, military service and payment of taxes), often falls into the area of political expression *tolerated* by the regime (for example, electoral campaigns and pamphleteering), and under specifiable circumstances adopts forms of action (for example, assassination and armed rebellion) the regime *forbids*. Prescribed, tolerated, and forbidden identify three modes of governmental connection with the forms of public politics. Collective making of conflicting claims identifies the special territory of contention within the broader zone of public politics. We focus mainly on transgressive contention, first because this is where most of the attention of scholars lies, and second, because it has had the most impact on social and political change.

Some readers may object that *all* politics are contentious, and to some degree, they would be correct. But much of politics is ceremonial or routine; or is processed in the internal relations among the same claimants, or is authoritatively authorized. The contentious politics that interests us is episodic rather than routine; occurs in the interactions between makers of claims and their opponents; affects or potentially affects the interests of at least one of the claimants; and brings government in as a mediator, target, or claimant. We see social movements as a particularly crystallized, sustained set of interactions between challengers and authorities around long-standing claims and identities – but they are not the only ones.

We use focused, structured comparisons between and within various types of polities to search out the common mechanisms and processes that are nested within different environmental conditions. For example, in

---

[3] For the development of this definition and the "political process model" it grows out of, see McAdam 1982; McAdam, Tarrow, and Tilly 2001; Tarrow 1998b; and Tilly 1995b. For a stimulating critique, see Goodwin and Jasper 1998.

examining religious phenomena, Aminzade and Perry will not only contrast the secular/religious division of western societies with the imbrication of religion and secular politics that they find in many nonwestern ones; they contrast politicized religion in Africa with sacralized politics in China. In comparing temporality in France and the United States, McAdam and Sewell find both commonalities and differences between revolutionary time and social movement time. In turning to the role of space in contentious politics, Sewell shows its relevance to social movements, guerilla organizations, and revolutionary mobilization alike.

Through these and other observations, we aim at studying how similar mechanisms concatenate differently in different kinds of contention in different social and historical settings. While we cannot reach into all important areas of contention – for example, industrial conflict or ethnic nationalism will be missing from these accounts – we hope that broadening our focus from social movements to other forms of contention and from western to nonwestern polities will stimulate others to go beyond the social movement canon and cross these bridges too.

Hearing Different Voices

In addition to broadening the range of forms of contention we examine, we have also striven to mine veins of social scientific research that are poorly represented in the study of social movements. Paradigms are variable-finding devices; but by the same token, they are sometimes scholarship-blinding ones. While we are unsympathetic to the view that each new variable uncovered allows the scholars who find it to dismiss the research of the last wave of scholarship, several areas of research suggest examining dimensions of contention that have been poorly explored in social movement research in the past.

Consider emotion: No sensible social movement scholar would exclude emotion from the repertoire of factors that induce ordinary people to pour into the streets, risking danger or arrest from opponents or the forces of order. But the emotions of participants in contentious politics have too often been reduced to stylized feelings of solidarity or collective identity. The feelings that bring people into the streets, cause them to face superior forces, and link them to people they hardly know and may never see again are various, elusive, and often empowering. As Aminzade and McAdam write in their contribution,

The uncertainty that characterizes contentious politics serves both to generate heightened fears and hopes regarding the future ... *and* to render the normative ... behavioral routines that normally structure social life increasingly irrelevant.

In their chapter, Aminzade and McAdam mine the literature on the sociology of emotions as a source of hypotheses and insights to help them suggest ways in which emotionality can be analyzed in the context of contentious politics.

The sociology of religion is another area that offers fruitful intersections with the study of contentious politics. Since Max Weber, social scientists have intuited that some kinds of authority are "charismatic." Following Weber, David Apter explored the concept of "political religion" (1960). Anthropologists like David Kertzer have examined how religious ritual informs contention and provides sources of nonrational authority for insurgent movements (1988). But until recently, the sociology of religion has remained largely distinct from the study of contentious politics.

In their contribution, Aminzade and Perry draw from African and Chinese materials to show how the intersection of religion and contentious politics assumes quite different consequences in the two areas – and different again from "the church–state separation and attendant freedoms of religion that are taken as hallmarks of liberal democratic politics". They go beyond the role of religious organizations in the mobilization of various movements to "ways in which the cultural dimensions of religion inform secular claims-making." Though focusing on two major nonwestern areas, their explorations may help to encourage the reexamination of the relations between religiosity and the supposedly secularized political systems of the West.

Research on the life course has made significant strides in sociology and human development in recent years. While students of movements were traditionally interested in the importance of generational factors in triggering the emergence of new movements (Heberle 1951), it is only in the last decade that they have moved sufficiently beyond the time-compass of particular movements to examine the effects of social movements on the life course. But even these studies exaggerated by oversampling on the life courses of veterans of particular movements or movement families; they seldom specified how movement cycles could influence the life course of broader publics. In their contribution to this volume, Goldstone and McAdam make just such an effort.

All of these chapters will attempt to bring voices from other sectors of the social sciences into the concert of social movement research.

Variations on Themes

In addition to accessing areas of research new to the study of contentious politics like emotion, religion, and the life course, we will try to transfer insights from one area of contentious politics into others. We begin with the hunch that robust analogies exist between mechanisms and processes in one setting or form of contention and others. We do not conclude from this that identical results will follow; we think that mechanisms interact with environmental factors and with other mechanisms to produce markedly different outcomes.[4]

For example, revolutionary leaders' personalities, their ideologies, and their strategies are part of the familiar stock-in-trade of revolutionary studies. But in the social movement field, leadership skills, predispositions, and outcomes have been submerged beneath organizational and opportunity factors. In their chapter on leadership, Aminzade, Goldstone, and Perry attempt to bring leadership factors into the study of contentious politics in general.

Like leadership, temporality is a concept that has been employed in some areas of contentious politics research but less so in others. For Crane Brinton, each major revolution goes through detectable and near-identical stages (1965). But there are long-term change processes through which largely anonymous social trends are transformed into profound transformations in patterns of contention. McAdam and Sewell do not deny that these cyclical and long-term change patterns are important in the dynamics of contention; but they propose paying attention to two additional forms of temporality: the influence of single events and of cultural epochs on contentious politics. Of the opinion that "sociologically oriented analysts of social movements and revolutions have left events to historians," McAdam and Sewell see events as "unique happenings, full of accident, contingency, and sudden, unexpected transformations." Their chapter focuses on the importance of particular events like the fall of the Bastille in July 1789 and its impact on both subsequent events in the French Revolution and on the very meaning of the concept of revolution.

[4] This argument is elaborated in McAdam, Tarrow, and Tilly 2001.

Various units and forms of temporality – events, cycles, cultural epochs of contention, and long-term change processes – intersect. For example, as Aminzade, Goldstone, and Perry point out, events can be crucial turning points within a larger cycle of national independence movements, as occurred in Tanganyika when Julius Nyerere chose to participate in racially based elections despite his personal disinclination to do so.

If temporality is a familiar concept with various dimensions, so is spatiality. Numerous scholars have focused on contention across space, and have involved different territorial units. But accounts of space are often underspecified, ignoring the fact that space structures both contention and repression; that contention is often *about* space; and that public spaces often structure the way contention unfolds and is remembered. Geographers like John Agnew (1987) have recently explored these aspects of space, but they have seldom been treated as parameters of contentious politics. In his chapter, Sewell explores these various dimensions of space, turning again to the French Revolution as a major site for spatial contention.

Point/Counterpoint

Since much of the research on social movements has been carried out in single countries, little use has been made of the comparative method. Of course, it is possible to compare different movements in the same space–time continuum, or to compare the same or related movements over time in the same polity. But even these studies have tended to focus narrowly on social movement organizations, squandering the possibility of examining the mechanisms that produce contention of different kinds in different settings. Comparison can help to isolate the factors in the political opportunity structure of movements – both favorable and threatening ones – that produce success in one case and failure in another and that lead to different strategies and repertoires of contention (Klandermans, Kriesi, and Tarrow 1988; Kriesi et al. 1995).

An important feature of many of the chapters in this book is that they focus on contentious politics in widely varying settings. This strategy makes it more difficult to narrow the range of variables to isolate the causes for outcomes of interest; but it has the compensating advantage of allowing our authors to test the boundaries of theories that have been developed in one kind of setting and identify robust mechanisms that power contention in widely differing environments.

Harmonizing Voices

Much of the promise of the classical social movement paradigm is that it shies away from single-variable explanations, attempting instead to search out combined causation for mobilization and movement trajectories (McAdam, McCarthy, and Zald 1996; Tarrow 1998b; Tilly 1978). But while sets of variables like "political opportunities," "mobilizing structures," and "collective action frames" are much closer to people's decisions to participate than such distant causes as "mass society" or "relative deprivation" were, few mechanisms were adduced to combine these factors with one another or to link them to broad change processes in society.

Combining broad macrosocial processes that produce the conditions for the emergence of contentious politics with the microlevel processes that produce recruitment into movements is a major task in the study of contentious politics. In their chapter on demography and the life course, Goldstone and McAdam seek such a juncture: For example, linking the biographical sources of activism in the American New Left to macrodemographic processes like the growth in higher education, prosperity and optimism and the propensity to take risks, and generational identification and the sense of efficacy it supports.

The political environment in which mobilization occurs is another area in which broad environmental processes need to be combined with the proximate causes of mobilization. For example, while Tilly's original polity model emphasized both threat and opportunity in the environment (ch. 3), most scholars look at the political environment since then have focussed on the latter concept – including some of the coauthors of this volume. In their chapter, Goldstone and Tilly make a stab at both rectifying this gap and conceptualizing the relations between threat and opportunity more clearly. They regard opportunities as factors that conduce either to lower costs of collective action or greater chances of success. They operationalize threats as changes in conditions and/or state actions that harm a population from which protectors may be drawn.

Coda

In the chapters that follow, we attempt to combine silence and voice in the ways proposed above: broadening our focus from classical social movement studies to contentious politics in general; drawing conceptual machinery from other areas of social science research; applying themes from familiar areas of contentious politics to other areas or research; comparing contentious politics across borders and types of policy; and combining motifs that have frequently been dealt with in isolation. The reader will have to decide to what extent we have succeeded.

We should not claim too much – certainly, we do not claim to have produced a new general covering law for contentious politics. And there is much that a single collection of essays by a small group of scholars cannot attempt – let alone, accomplish. Just as there is no hegemonic paradigm in the study of contentious politics, we make no claim to produce an integrated vision. But working together on the Mellon/CASBS project on contentious politics for the past four years has revealed commonalities in our approaches and produced intersections that sometimes surprised us (it also revealed differences of viewpoints, which we happily expose in this volume). If there is a single goal in our effort, it is to examine how an expansion of the boundaries of our field from the narrow social movement paradigm of the 1960s–90s to a more general examination of contentious politics affects what we study, how we can best study it, and what our efforts can produce in the way of new research on contentious politics.

2

Emotions and Contentious Politics

Ron Aminzade and Doug McAdam

In all fields of study, dominant theoretical perspectives tend to obscure as much as they reveal. By highlighting specific dimensions of complex empirical phenomena, leading paradigms render other aspects of these same phenomena more or less invisible to scholars. This is no less true of the study of contentious politics than it is of other fields of inquiry. Focusing only on the more narrow literature on social movements, we find that the recent dominance of what might be termed "structural environmental" perspectives (for example, resource mobilization, political process, and so on) has tended to focus attention on the environmental facilitation or suppression of movement activity rather than on internal characteristics or dynamics of the movements themselves.

In this chapter we want to take up one especially notable "silence" in the social movement literature as it pertains to internal movement dynamics. We are referring to the mobilization of emotions as a necessary and exceedingly important component of any significant instance of collective action.[1] Our aims in this regard are modest. Given the lack of systematic work in this area, we hope simply to: (1) Highlight this "silence" for other researchers; (2) parse the literature on the sociology of emotions for insights relevant to the study of social movements; and, (3) in a nonsystematic way, describe, what to us, seem like some of the critically important aggregate level emotional processes/dynamics that shape the ebb and flow of protest activity. More specifically, we argue that the mobilization

---

[1] There are a few exceptions to this general rule. William Gamson (1991; 1992a; 1992b) has certainly made references to emotions and emotional processes in his work. But perhaps the two scholars who have made emotions most central to their scholarship on social movements are James Jasper (1997; 1998) and Verta Taylor (1995; 1996; 1997). We have benefitted greatly from the many insights contained in all of the above work.

14

of heightened emotion is necessary, but not sufficient, for an episode of contention, identify certain emotions as central to movement emergence, growth, and decline, explore how emotion work and feeling rules shape public expressions of certain emotions during different points in the trajectory of movement development, and suggest certain emotional dynamics operative during different phases of a movement. Before we take up these topics, however, there are three preliminary issues that need attention. The first concerns a necessary delimitation of our subject matter; the second, an explicit discussion of what is to be gained by engaging the topic and; the third, a brief exegesis on definitional matters. We take up each of these issues in turn.

Delimiting the Topic

The relationship between emotions and contentious politics is so complex and multifaceted that we cannot possibly hope to do it justice in a single chapter. Moreover we do not think the current state of knowledge concerning the relationship between emotions and contention is sufficiently developed to allow for the construction of any systematic theoretical framework. Our more preliminary aim is simply to highlight those concepts and dynamic processes out of which such a framework might emerge.

Space constraints force us to delimit the topics we will address here. But in the spirit of the volume, we want, at the very least, to flag a host of related issues that we will not take up here, but which we feel are deserving of attention in their own right. These topics include:

1. The complex relationship between individual emotions and their collective aggregation and expression. In our remarks we are going to focus overwhelmingly on the latter topic, highlighting public collective expressions while leaving aside the critically important issue of the genesis of subjective emotional experiences in conscious and subconscious processes and the role these experiences may play in constraining/facilitating individual activism.
2. The role of emotions in motivating the actions of other parties during unfolding episodes of contention. We will artificially confine ourselves to a discussion of the emotional dynamics of movement groups/actors, while ignoring the complex interactive processes that mobilize the emotions of others during periods of struggle. An illustrative accounting of the emotional dynamics that characterize other

parties to such conflicts will give the reader a sense of the potential richness of the topic. Think only of the role of: (a) fear and anger in helping to account for the actions of social control forces during confrontations with challenging groups; (b) anger and, in some cases, shame at official abuses of power (for example, as in the mobilization of the Philippine middle classes in the anti-Marcos movement of the mid-1980s) in transforming "bystander publics" into engaged partisans, and; (c) fear on the part of authorities as a key ingredient fueling the by now familiar dynamic of the "radical flank effect" (Haines 1988).

3. The transformation of emotion rules, resources, and repertoires in response to large-scale and long-term processes of change, such as state formation and capitalist development. Although we acknowledge the need for more comparative/historical research, of the sort pursued by Norbert Elias, space constraints prevent us from doing more than identifying a potentially rich agenda for future research on micro-macro linkages.

4. How the structural dynamics of emotions themselves generate changing collective experiences and expressions of emotion. These dynamics, such as shame about anger or guilt about jealousy, modify and displace emotions and testify to the ambivalent, unstable, and processual character of emotions and the problem of reducing emotional change to either actors' strategic manipulations or the force of cultural rules (Barbalet 1998:23).

What Is to Be Gained by Studying Emotions?

In taking up the silences addressed in this volume, we, as authors, had to wrestle with the thorny issue of the "value-added" importance of our chosen topics. Any complex social phenomenon – such as contentious politics – has many features. But the presence of any particular feature tells us nothing about its explanatory centrality to the phenomenon in question. One might, for example, argue that the intense emotionality of episodes of contention is merely epiphenomenal and therefore not worth studying. It is therefore incumbent on us, not simply to note a silence in the literature, but to, at least, provisionally assert its importance. Let us do so with respect to the topic at hand.

We want to make two strong, if provisional, claims about the explanatory significance of emotions and emotional processes as they relate to the

16

emergence, development, and decline of social movements and revolutions. The first claim concerns mobilization at the collective level; the second, the onset of activism at the individual level. Both, in our view, are keyed by emotional dynamics.

At the aggregate level, we think the onset of an episode of contention is associated with, and partially dependent upon, the collective mobilization of heightened emotion. This is not to say that the mobilization of strong emotions "causes" movements or revolutions, but that otherwise favorable environmental circumstances (for example, the presence of established organizations, expanding political opportunities, population pressures, and so on) will not produce a movement in the absence of heightened emotions. Or perhaps more accurately, the various facilitators of mobilization familiar to scholars of contention may well operate, at least in part, through the emotional dynamics they set in motion.

The second claim concerns the role of emotions in motivating individual activism. Much has been made in the literature of the daunting "free-rider" problem, which allegedly impedes collective mobilization by making it irrational for any individual to expend time and energy pursuing collective goods that s/he would receive in any case if the movement or revolution succeeded. Many objections have been raised regarding the nature of and predictions that derive from the "free-rider" problem. For example, a good many critics of the perspective have argued that the formulation is too narrowly economistic in its identification of the "selective incentives" that are held to overcome the free-rider problem. This may be true, but, in our view, there is a more basic problem with the formulation of both the free-rider dilemma and its hypothesized solution. Quite simply, the formulation ignores the power of emotions to shape both the assessment of potential gains and costs involved in any line of action the individual might take and perhaps to motivate action directly quite apart from any instrumental calculus of risks and rewards. Intense fear can motivate action, even in the face of extreme risks and seemingly no hope for payoff. Take, for example, the little known case of gentile wives who took to the streets in Nazi Germany to protest the detention and threatened internment of their Jewish husbands. Given the extraordinary risks they ran in challenging such a brutal regime and the seeming hopelessness of their plight – to say nothing of the presumed rationalist appeal of the free-rider stance – it is not at all clear how one can understand this "movement" without invoking the power of emotions to trump or, at the very least, shape rational calculus.

One should not read our remarks here as suggesting some kind of essential opposition between rationality and emotionality. We reject the conventional approach that opposes rationality and emotions, treating the latter as inherently irrational. A number of scholars have argued that emotions support rationality by providing it with salience and goal formation and guiding rational action in situations where there are uncertainties or high costs for procrastination (Elster 1998). Others have gone even further, viewing emotion and reason as continuous and arguing that emotion does not just guide reason but that reason is constituted by particular emotions, including a feeling of certainty about the future. (For a discussion of these perspectives, see Barbalet 1998:29–61.)

Consistent with this latter view, we see episodes of contention typically involving both heightened emotions and an increase in rational, instrumental action. The uncertainty that characterizes contentious politics serves both to generate heightened fears and hopes regarding the future (among a host of other strong emotions) *and* to render the normative (read: nonreflective) behavioral routines that normally structure social life increasingly irrelevant. This undermining of behavioral routines forces people – both individually and collectively – to subject their actions to more conscious, purposive decision making. It is in this sense that we associate collective action with an increase in both emotionality and rationality.

The Definition of Emotion

Any viable definition of emotions must, in our view, incorporate five key components. Peggy Thoits (1989:318) identifies four of these components as follows: (1) thoughts/cognitions (appraisal of a situational stimulus or context); (2) feelings (changes in bodily sensations); (3) actions (a display of expressive gestures); and (4) interpretation (a cultural label applied to constellations of one or more of the first three components). Together these four components constitute emotions, which she defines as "culturally delineated types of feelings or affects." In highlighting a deep sense of engagement of the actor's self, Michelle Rosaldo adds a crucial fifth component to our definition of emotions. Emotions, she writes, "are embodied thoughts, thoughts seeped with the apprehension that 'I am involved.' Thought/affect thus bespeaks the difference between a mere hearing of a child's cry and a hearing felt – as when one realizes that danger is involved or that the child is one's own" (1984:143).

18

Although our discussion highlights the social structural and sociocultural, rather than psychological or biological, dimensions of emotions, we assume that all emotions have cognitive, temporal, and somatic dimensions. All emotions presuppose cognitions, but some emotions may highlight cognitions about "what is" while others may emphasize moral aspirations and norms about "what should be" or stress the counterfactual dimension of "what could be." Whereas hope, regret, and relief emphasize what could be or could have been, sympathy and anger highlight what should be. Although they are less episodic than feelings, emotions also differ in their durations, in their socially expected durations (Merton 1984), and in their temporal orientations. Some emotions, such as hope, are directed toward the future while others, such as regret or relief, are oriented toward the past. The different temporal orientations of cultures toward the past, present, and future (Aminzade 1992) are likely to lead individuals to value or devalue certain emotions. For example, in cultures strongly oriented toward the future, activists often regard expressions of regret or prolonged expressions of grief as distractions from the tasks ahead. There is also a physical, or bodily, dimension to socially defined emotions, such as the release of adrenalin or hormonal changes, that gives them their power, but some emotions, such as hope, may be less likely to involve bodily symptoms than others, such as fear or anger. Emotions also have characteristic observable physiological expressions, such as crying, laughing, blushing, or frowning, which serve as signals to others (Elster 1998).

Thus far our consideration of definitional matters has skirted a key debate within the literature on emotions. Culturalists typically downplay the universalistic physiological roots of emotion and stress instead the variability of culturally constructed meanings and feeling rules. For example, certain basic facial expressions may be culturally universal (Ekman 1982), but the meaning of, and patterned responses to, the bodily changes accompanying emotions varies across cultures.[2] Culturally specific languages and beliefs about emotions shape their content and consequences, producing very different emotional responses to the same stimuli. The display of animals or humans in circuses and sideshows, for example, may generate anger, pity, or joy, depending on the observers' interpretation of the situation, which is informed by culturally based emotional beliefs.

---

[2] For a discussion of theoretical debates in anthropology on the relationship between emotion and culture, which focuses on the tension between universalist, positivist approaches and relativist, interpretive ones, see Lutz (1986, 405–36).

Structuralists, on the other hand, emphasize the role of general structural properties in producing the same emotions crossculturally, even if the expression of that emotion takes different form in different settings (Barbalet 1998; Collins 1987; Kemper 1978). Kemper, for example, argues that certain emotions are provoked by circumstances – for example, structural relations of power and status – and experienced as inclinations or dispositions to act. Thus, power relationships resulting in dispossession will produce anger, which may then be acknowledged and expressed in different ways across cultures and subcultures, from individual weeping and private guilt about the unfeminine emotion of anger to aggressive behavior and collective action.

This enduring split in the field may, however, be more illusory than real. In a recent article, James Jasper (1998:401–402) offers the interesting suggestion that the structuralists and culturalists may actually be highlighting emotions with very different temporal properties. The culturalists (or "constructionists" as Jasper calls them) typically focus on "emotions that represent temporary responses to events or information" which he labels "reactive emotions." The structuralists, on the other hand, focus on what he calls "affective emotions," deeper, more enduring feelings such as "love of one's family. . . . [or] a sense of identification with a group and loyalty to its members." While we remain agnostic about Jasper's resolution of the structuralist/culturalist debate, we find his basic distinction useful. Our own stress on the cultural construction of emotions may appear to privilege "reactive emotions," but we also acknowledge – and indeed will later touch on – the role of "affective emotions" in the initial mobilization of collective action.

Rationality and Emotions in the Study of Contentious Politics: A Brief History

Studies of collective behavior recognized the importance of emotions and highlighted the expressive dimensions of crowd behavior. Some theorists contended that heightened emotional arousal was a basic feature of collective behavior and classified forms of collective behavior in terms of an episode's dominant emotion (Lofland 1981). But work in this tradition was limited by a number of problematic assumptions and silences. Scholars typically treated collective behavior as irrational and/or emotional responses by alienated or anomic individuals and assumed that emotions and rationality were incompatible (LeBon 1960; Smelser 1962). They regarded protesters as abnormal, irrational, and emotional deviants who threatened social order. As a result of these assumptions, collective behavior theorists failed to ask a number of critical questions. For example, the assumption that emotions were closely connected to sudden outbursts, irrationality, and illegitimate behavior led to a focus on the emotions evident in ephemeral crowd behavior, such as hostility, joy, and fear, and silence about emotions that may sustain a movement over time, such as pride, love, and hope.

Reacting to questionable assumptions about irrationality which devalued the movements in which many of them had actively participated, proponents of a resource mobilization approach were typically unwilling to incorporate emotions into their analyses. Highlighting the continuities between social movements and conventional political behavior, they correctly insisted that protest contains rational elements but ignored or downplayed the expressive and spontaneous dimensions of social protest. Like most collective behavior theorists, they problematically equated rationality with legitimacy and emotions with irrationality. Thus, in order to legitimize protest movements, with which they were largely sympathetic, they ignored emotions and implicitly accepted the assumptions of rational choice theory, embracing the false dichotomy of emotions and rationality. While problematizing the process by which grievances were translated into collective political action, they assumed that grievances were ever-present and widespread. This assumption meant an unwillingness to analyze the emotions that often impel people to engage in collective action and the emotional dimensions of the process of constructing movement identities. It precluded an analysis of how oppressed racial or sexual minorities come to revaluate their identities by replacing shame with pride and publicly proclaiming that "black is beautiful" or "gay is good."

Rationalist assumptions led scholars to "normalize" collective protest and thereby ignore the emotional energy required for, and generated by, disruption, rule violations, and collective political violence (Piven and Cloward 1992). An analysis that ignores the emotional dimensions of attachments and commitments is incapable of explaining activists' determination in the face of high risk and their willingness to endure suffering and self-sacrifice, including torture and death. Emotions are central to the process by which people affirm oppositional values and lifestyles. "From direct emotional experiences . . . ," writes Ferree (1992:43) "people acquire their own perspectives and learn either to challenge or to respect the definition of value provided by the hegemonic (patriarchal, racist) order."[3]

Scholars of revolution have highlighted threats, opportunities, and alliances in their explanations, but failed to analyze the emotional dimensions of threats, opportunities, and the bonds of trust that make or break alliances. Zolberg (1972) acknowledges the qualitatively different emotional climate that accompanies periods of revolutionary upheavals and sudden political transition, characterizing these "moments of madness" as times when people believe that "all is possible," when "the wall between the instrumental and the expressive collapses," and when "emotions are freely expressed. . . ." However, sociologists of revolution have not attempted to trace the shifting emotional climate of a revolutionary movement during the course of its trajectory or explore how emotions, such as resignation or hope, shape the way people respond to violence and structured inequalities.

Culturalist theorists have been more attentive to the noninstrumental dimensions of contentious politics and to processes of meaning construction and identity formation. Those working in this tradition do a much better job of connecting institutional and personal change and exploring the symbolic and expressive dimensions of social behavior. However, much of this work is informed by an overly cognitive understanding of culture that reduces emotions to a consequence of cognitive processes and treats movements as forms of cognitive practice (Eyerman and Jamison 1991) or an instrumental perspective on culture as a toolkit used to construct strategies of action (Swidler 1986). This leads to silence about the emotional dimensions of culture and contention and the emotion complexes that characterize different cultures and movements.

Studies of movements have noted that emotional investment is required in the definition of a collective identity (Melucci 1995), pointed out the importance of "hot cognitions" in the creation of injustice frames (Gamson 1992b), and acknowledged the use of emotions, such as fear of the abnormal, to assert stigmatized identities, cross boundaries, and disrupt labels (J. Gamson 1991). Scheff's (1994) research on aggressive nationalist movements highlights the role of pride and shame as master emotions, but fails to acknowledge that affirmations of, and affronts to, cultural conceptions of masculinity are key sources of collective shame and pride in nationalist movements. In general, scholars have inadequately addressed the question

---

[3] See also Passerini (1996) and Kaplan (1997).

of how emotions, or emotion-generating behaviors such as rituals, help to create the energy needed to forge collective political identities and sustain the cultural boundaries that maintain them (Laslett 1990). They have made little effort to systematically explore the gendered emotional impacts of movement symbols, frames, and rituals, the emotional power of ideologies, or the role of different emotions over the life course of a movement.

Why the Silence?

There are at least four factors that help to account for the silence about emotions among scholars of contentious politics, including the gendered character of academia, the assumptions of western culture about legitimate political behavior, the concept of the political deployed by most analysts, and the relative illegitimacy of certain research methods. The gendered character of academic inquiry appears to be a factor, given that most scholars of movements and revolution are North American men who have been socialized by their culture to downplay or repress emotions in their personal and academic lives. Feminist scholarship, which has led the way in critiquing rationalist assumptions that disconnect reason and emotions and highlighting the emotional dimensions of rationality, has made relatively limited inroads in this branch of the disciplines.

Second, in the United States and Europe, which has produced the vast majority of studies of contentious politics, the dominant culture tends to identify emotions as irrational and illegitimate in political decision making, where dispassionate deliberation and legal rational authority should hold sway. In contrast to cognitions, notes Catherine Lutz (1986), emotions are viewed in western cultures as uncontrollable and involuntary and devalued as primal, precultural, and biological. The norm is to seek legitimacy by presenting one's enemies as irrational and one's own position as highly rational, to value self-control rather than impulsiveness, and to treat reason and emotion as diametrically opposed. Given the widespread sympathy of most scholars with the social movements and revolutions they studied, this produced a tendency to portray movements as rational attempts at change and to ignore their emotional dimensions.

Third, a state-centric understanding of politics inhibits the study of arenas of political contestation where different emotional repertoires, valuations of emotion, and gendered understandings of emotions may prevail (McAdam 1988).

Finally, a positivist epistemology of dispassionate investigation that views emotions as distorting observation and impeding knowledge (Jaggar 1989) has produced a devaluation of those methods that can provide access to the emotional lives of activists and emotional climates and dimensions of their movements. A small number of studies based on ethnographies and in-depth interviews have provided important insights into the emotional dimensions of contentious politics. But, with some notable exceptions (Hart 1996; Laslett and Thorne 1997; Passerini 1996), the life history methods that historians have identified as central to uncovering emotional experiences, climates, and dynamics have not yet figured prominently in social science research on movements and revolution nor have the findings of those using life history methods been incorporated into theoretical work on contentious politics.

What Can Scholars of Contentious Politics Learn from the Study of Emotions: Promises and Pitfalls

The study of emotions, write Katherine Lutz and Geoffrey White (1986:431) can "reanimate the sometimes robotic image of humans which social science has purveyed" and enable us to present "a fuller view of what is at stake for people in everyday life." The sociology of emotions offers students of contentious politics powerful conceptual tools, such as emotion labor and feeling rules, that can be the source of valuable insights about the origins and trajectory of social movements and revolutions. Hochchild's (1979; 1983) pioneering research on emotion work ("the act of trying to change in degree or quality an emotion or feeling") and its gendered and class character suggests numerous questions for future research. These questions concern how movement leaders and staff perceive, assess, evoke, and suppress their own and other peoples' emotions while pursuing movement goals. For example, do movement leaders routinely appeal to different emotions when engaging in the different tasks required of them, attempting to mobilize hope, shame, or anger to recruit members, pride or guilt to maintain commitments, and sympathy or empathy to attract bystander publics? The emotion work required for fundraising or bargaining with authorities differs from that demanded by the need to mobilize activists' time and energy. Just as different types of jobs, like service sector employment, produce workers who specialize in emotion labor (Hochschild 1983), different leadership and staff positions within movements entail a (typically gendered) emotional division of labor that has not yet received adequate attention. Emotion labor requires certain knowledge and movement leadership requires emotion management skills for which, according to Hochschild (1979), middle-class families invest more time preparing their children. What sort of emotional intelligence does efficient and successful work within social movement organizations require? How gendered and class and race-based are emotion-management skills within movements? How do activists respond to leader and staff efforts to secure their emotional labor?

The concept of feeling rules, defined by Hochschild (1979:566) as "guidelines for the assessment of fits and misfits between feeling and situation," has generated debate among scholars of emotions, some of whom challenge the culturalist approach in which this concept is embedded. Critics point out that norms are not guides for action but outcomes of practices, hence subject to revision and instability, and that some emotions, such as implicit trust or bypassed shame, are often experienced below the threshold of awareness, thus not subject to social representation in the prevailing culture (Barbelet 1998:24). Nevertheless, this orienting concept suggests the need to explore shifting and often-contested beliefs within movements about the appropriate range, intensity, duration, and targets of various emotions and the process by which movement participants learn such guidelines. When do movements foster unconventional emotions or alternative emotion rules and when do they encourage conformity to the dominant emotion rules of the wider society? Oppositional movements of protest may adopt quite conventional emotion rules in order to appear "respectable" to bystander publics or they may adopt tactics or develop rituals that challenge existing feeling rules and foster what Jaggar (1989:161) labels "outlaw emotions." The validation and public expression of such emotions, which challenge dominant conventions, typically depends on movement organizations and subcultures. Social movements enable oppressed groups who experience unconventional emotions, for example, angry housewives or proud gays and lesbians, to seek out those who share their situation and collectively target their anger or pride at public institutions rather than individually seek professional counseling or psychiatric treatment. They often challenge those rules of politeness and rationality that "make it impossible to say what needs to be said by making certain topics impolite, certain tones of voice or emotions irrational, or simply defining topics as psychological and not political" (Lyman 1981:59).

25

Although we have much to learn from sociologists of emotions, there are a number of pitfalls within this literature. The sociology of emotions has been dominated by a symbolic interactionist perspective that focuses on microlevel analysis rather than "big structures" and "large processes" and by ahistorical case studies of workplaces in the United States. This contrasts with the work of historical sociologists like Norbert Elias, whose (1982) study of the "civilizing process" highlighted the long-term processual dynamics of emotion complexes, micro-macro linkages, political institutions, and cultural variation. In Elias's account, changing manners concerning disgust, shame, and embarrassment about bodily functions, such as nose-blowing, spitting, and defecating, were connected to large-scale structural change, especially the centralization of power in modern states.[4]

Most of the recent innovative work on emotions and contentious politics has focused on feminist movement organizations, but this research has not yet been systematically incorporated into theory nor has it informed the study of other movements. A number of studies have explored the internal dynamics of feminist movement organizations. Morgen (1995) analyzes emotional discourses in the work cultures of feminist health clinics while Simonds (1995) documents how abortion clinic workers' emotional experiences and discourses shaped and were shaped by power relations. Other studies have examined the relationship between the feminist movement and the emotion culture of the wider society. Verta Taylor's (1997) research on self-help movements documents movement emotion cultures that resist codes of femininity by challenging or redefining the dominant emotion norms of motherhood, "persuading women to trade their guilt, shame and depression for anger and pride over the injustices of motherhood and having survived. . . ." Her research also makes a persuasive case for the centrality of feelings in motivating womens' organized resistance to male domination (1995) and in the ability of feminist activists to maintain their convictions when the movement was "in abeyance" (1989).

---

[4] Social historians have also explored the connection between large-scale structural change and the dynamics of emotion cultures. Stearns (1993), for example, traces changing rules about female expressions of anger to the impact of industrialization, which separated home and work roles and reenvisioned family life as an emotional haven for males from the competitive marketplace. For a review of the social history literature on changes in emotional standards and experiences, see Stearns 1993. The focus has been on families, with some research on workplaces, leisure, and the law, but the emotional dimensions of political conflict have not yet received attention.

Despite recent advances, much remains to be done, including systematically tracing changes in emotional labor, feeling rules, and emotional landscapes over the course of different movement's histories. We need to extend existing work to explore the diversity of emotional rules and climates across movements and cultures and the play of different emotional processes and dynamics during the emergence, development, and decline of collective action. But before we take up these phases of contention, permit us a very important caveat. In speculating about the "typical" emotional dynamics that characterize this or that stage of a movement, we are mindful that we are talking about crude aggregate tendencies that are played out against a backdrop of great individual and small group variation. Thus, before turning, in a stylized way, to a discussion of these "typical" patterns, we want to give equal time to the sources of emotional variation within movements and revolutions.

Emotional Variability within Movements

This variation derives from at least three sources. First, individual adherents vary greatly in the extent of their participation and related *emotional investment* in a movement. Indeed, in sheer numeric terms, it may well be that, for many movements – especially broad and successful reform movements – the single largest group of participants are emotionally only superficially and sporadically engaged by the struggle. Consider the contemporary environmental movement. Taking a broadly inclusive view of movement participation, it seems clear that the modal pattern of environmental "activism" is defined more by certain characteristic behaviors (for example, recycling) and attitudinal patterns than by any deep and sustained emotional engagement with the issue.

The second source of variation stems from the coexistence of different *emotional universes* within the same movement. By emotional universes we mean different subgroups or wings within a movement defined, in part, by their adherence to different feeling rules and characteristic emotional profiles. The sudden shifts in the perceived emotional "tone" or character of a movement derives, in large measure, not from some universal affective transformation of all movement adherents, but rather the replacement of one emotionally distinct wing of the movement by another as the dominant force within the movement. Movement analysts have long recognized the analytic significance of intramovement competition, but without attending to the critically important affective dimensions of the phenomenon. The widely perceived shift, in the mid-1960s, from "civil rights" to "Black Power" as the dominant focus of the black struggle was as much a shift of emotional tone as ideological orientation. Notwithstanding the very real diversity which continued to characterize the struggle, the movement qua movement came to be seen by most whites as angry and threatening rather than determined and prideful. The increasing ambivalence and fear with which white America regarded the struggle was, in part, a reaction to this perceived shift in the *emotional* orientation of the movement.

The third, and final, source of emotional variation within a movement stems from the overlapping, but temporally disjoint, processes by which individuals and whole cohorts of activists enter and exit movements. That is, at any given moment, some participants will be entering the movement for the first time, newly imbued with the particular mix of emotions characteristic of their temporal and social organizational location within the struggle. These new recruits will be "emotionally fresh." Simultaneously, others will be exiting the movement, emotionally spent by the physical and affective demands of the struggle. A variety of other subgroups will be arrayed in between, influencing the movement with their own distinctive behavioral and emotional trajectories. Most of the time, this mix of trajectories is largely invisible to analyst and public alike. But, at crucial moments, the normally latent emotional/ideological contradictions inherent in these trajectories may become manifest, altering the course of the movement in the process.

The 1964 Freedom Summer Project would seem to afford an interesting instance of this dynamic. That summer some 1,000 primarily white, northern college students came to Mississippi to help register black voters and teach in Freedom Schools, among a host of other activities (McAdam 1988). They were recruited in this effort by 100 or so veteran Student Nonviolent Coordinating Committee (SNCC) field workers, many of whom had been engaged more or less continuously in the struggle since the heady days of the initial sit-ins in the spring of 1960. To say that the two groups were on different emotional/behavioral trajectories would be a serious understatement. While many of the volunteers had been politically engaged before, few had experienced this level of intense and sustained activism. And for the most part, they responded to the experience very positively and emotionally. The modal volunteer left Mississippi at the close of the summer with a deep affective commitment to the interracial movement and an abiding sense of optimism about its future prospects. They were "emotionally fresh" and ready to engage the same struggle in their home institutions or communities.

Collectively, the SNCC veterans were in a very different place ideologically and emotionally. In his capacity as staff psychologist for the Freedom Summer Project, Robert Coles had occasion to observe and interview a good many of the SNCC veterans. Among the symptoms he ascribed to the workers were those of "exhaustion, weariness, despair, frustration and rage" (1964:308). The marked difference in the emotional profiles of the two groups is, of course, attributable not only to their different racial, class, and gender characteristics, but to their very different entry points and experiences in the movement.

What had happened [to the SNCC veterans] was Mississippi. The experience of confronting American racism in all its savagery for nearly three years had made SNCC's Mississippi troops immeasurably more radical. As a result of their "education" in Mississippi, many of the SNCC veterans had come to question the central tenets on which the movement and their organization had been founded; and on which the white volunteers were now being recruited to come South. Perhaps the major casualty of this process of disillusionment within SNCC concerned the doctrine of interracialism itself. Finally, the logic of the project may itself have fueled the growing hostility toward whites in the movement. For the success of Freedom Summer was premised on the recognition and conscious exploitation of America's racism. The logic ran as follows: if the murders, beatings, and jailings SNCC workers had endured in Mississippi had not been enough to stir public attention, perhaps America – and, in turn, the federal government – would take notice if those being beaten and shot were the sons and daughters of privileged white America. But to even conceive, let alone act on, this plan required that Mississippi's SNCC staff acknowledge a kind of strategic dependence on the white volunteers that could only have exacerbated the normal racial tensions to be expected on such a project. Imagine the volatile emotional cross-currents the plan must have aroused among the veteran Mississippi staffers (McAdam 1988:31–33).

In short, the black separatist turn in SNCC and the movement more generally has typically been explained in ideological terms on the basis of the need to build black leadership and pride and so on, but without discounting these clear ideological motivations, we also need to acknowledge the decisive emotional processes that fueled the shift. In turn, these dynamics were themselves largely a product of highly variable and ultimately irreconcilable emotional and cognitive trajectories on the part of the white volunteers and black SNCC staffers.

Having acknowledged the very real emotional diversity within movements, we now want to take up the opposite topic: the typical patterning of emotions that we think can be discerned over the course of most sustained episodes of contention.

The Mobilization of Emotion Over the Life of a Movement

In the chapter on temporality in this volume, McAdam and Sewell differentiate between four distinct "temporal rhythms" that are evident in the study of social movements and revolutions. Two of these temporalities have dominated the study of political contention. The first of these is the long-term change processes that have been widely credited with shaping the prospects for insurgency both by strengthening or weakening regimes and by changing the social organizational bases of mobilization.

The second and even more dominant temporality in the study of contention has been the active phase of a movement or broader protest cycle. Rupp and Taylor (1987) have alerted us to the importance of the "doldrums" or less active phase of a movement, but in our provisional effort to better understand the role of emotions in contention, we will limit ourselves to the more active temporal rhythm. For heuristic purposes, we will divide the active period of a movement or revolution into three admittedly reified phases: emergence, development, and decline.

The Emergence of Contention

Little of a systematic sort has been written on the initial mobilization of emotions in contention, but there is no shortage of suggestive ideas in the literature. Here we want to take up five provisional leads.

Cognitive Liberation

In an earlier work, McAdam (1982) argued that "cognitive liberation" was a necessary adjunct to the initial mobilization of a social movement or revolution. "Movement emergence," he wrote (1982:51), "implies a transformation of consciousness within a significant segment of the aggrieved population. Before collective protest can get under way, people must collectively define their situations as unjust and subject to change through group action." But these two perceptions imply something more than dispassionate cognitions. Each of these beliefs would seem to have a critically important emotional referent: anger in the case of perceived injustice and hope regarding the prospects for change. When joined together, these two emotions would appear to serve as the necessary affective bedrock on which many movements are built. In the case of such movements, the key question then becomes, what processes or conditions are productive of anger and hope. We turn next to some partial answers to this question.

Injustice Frames and Injustice Framing

William Gamson's (1992a; 1992b) stress on the importance of emotion in the fashioning of "injustice frames" may provide one piece of an overall answer to the above question. Gamson insists that, absent a "hot button" component, collective action framing is not likely to motivate people to act. The emotion he clearly has in mind here is anger at perceived injustice.[5] And while we think there is a class of movements for which fear, rather than anger, tends to motivate action, we nonetheless think Gamson is right to assert the critical importance of strong and sustained emotion in the emergence of contention. In the case of the kind of movements Gamson has in mind, the necessary emotional component comes courtesy of a highly charged "injustice frame" that not only seeks to dramatize the illegitimacy of social conditions, but to blame particular others for the injustice. This "personalizing" of injustice, Gamson suggests, would appear to be one of the keys to mobilizing anger at the outset of a struggle. While Gamson underscores the general role of anger across movements, the specific *form* the anger takes would appear to be variable. Consider the contrast between the visceral expressions of rage that helped to fuel the "urban disorders" of the mid to late 1960s versus the indignation, rooted in a sense of entitlement betrayed, that tends to characterize many middle-class movements.

The Mobilization of Hope

But, in and of itself, anger is not likely to produce organized collective action, but rather other (usually individual) forms of resistance and/or

---

[5] Working within the sociology of emotions, Barbelet (1998: ch. 6) reaches a conclusion very similar to Gamson, arguing that rights seeking movements are generally fueled by shared emotions of "resentment and vengefulness."

expressions of discontent. It is only when anger gets joined with hope that the forms of action we normally associate with social movements and revolutions are apt to take place. So how is hope mobilized? We offer several possibilities, while inviting the reader to expand the list.

Facilitative Cultural Shifts   Among the many suggestive topics that the "cultural turn" in movement studies has brought to the fore is an interest in the long-term cultural impact of social movements (Jasper 1997; McAdam 1988; 1994; Melucci 1985; 1995; Sewell 1990). We share the interest in this topic, but think it may well be worth considering whether the relationship between cultural change and movement activity might be reciprocal. Perhaps certain broad cultural shifts have the potential to facilitate movement emergence even as movements often act to reshape the cultural terrain within which they develop. We offer but a single example in support of this possibility.

Numerous commentators have noted the very real cultural shift that accompanied the rise of the Old Left, the related ascendance of the Labor Movement, and the forms of inclusion associated with the New Deal, especially in matters of race. So while African-Americans remained starkly disenfranchised in political terms, the 1930s were witness to various forms of *cultural* inclusion, which were accorded enormous significance within the black community. Among these instances of "cultural inclusion" were Joe Louis' successful quest for boxing's heavyweight crown, Jessie Owen's three gold medals at the 1936 Berlin Olympics, and Marion Anderson's widely publicized concert at the Lincoln Memorial in 1939. The latter event was made all the more dramatic and culturally significant by Eleanor Roosevelt's efforts to secure the Lincoln Memorial as a venue for the concert following the Daughter's of the American Revolution's decision to bar Anderson from using their hall in Washington, D.C.

Expanding Political Opportunities and the Impact of Institutionalized Contention   McAdam, Tarrow, and Tilly (2001) argue that many of what we would call social movements and revolutions actually develop out of less visible instances of "institutionalized contention." Generally triggered by "exogenous changes" which render existing power relations more vulnerable to challenge, these periods of "institutionalized contention" have the potential to set in motion broader and more visible episodes of popular mobilization. But the significance of these instances of institutionalized contention is affective as much as it is structural/political. Such episodes tend to yield policy shifts that, even if modest in themselves, can cue popular mobilization when they give rise to widespread feelings of hope regarding the prospects for future change. At one level, this is what would appear to have happened in the case of the revolutions in Eastern Europe in the late 1980s as Gorbachev's reforms and articulation of the "Sinatra doctrine" occasioned a dramatic shift in felt efficacy among dissidents and ordinary citizens alike.

Transforming Events William Sewell (1996a) has pointed out the significance of key events in helping to birth revolutions or social movements. (Indeed, in this volume, the aforementioned chapter on temporality and contention takes up this issue anew.) Such events serve many functions, but among the most important would seem to be the significant transformative potential they may have regarding the "emotional landscape" of the challenging group. Take the two events used as illustrative examples in the chapter on temporality in this volume. Both the march on the Bastille and the initial week of the Montgomery Bus Boycott transformed both the cognitive and, more importantly, affective understandings of the respective challenging groups. In both cases, the events served as important generators of hope, while simultaneously undermining the fear that ordinary citizens had understandably felt in the face of what seemed to be arbitrary and all-powerful regimes. Thus, these events not only mobilized emotions crucial to collective action (for example, hope and anger), but also damped down another emotion – fear – that can shortcircuit protest, even under otherwise emotionally promising circumstances.

The transformative character of highly emotional movement events is captured in Susan Harding's account of her participation in an antiwar teach-in of the late 1960s: "It was outside of ordinary time and ordinary structures. . . . Some of the excitement of it was the emotional quality of the event; it wasn't just dry, academic, neutral discussion; it was charged with meaning and emotion, and political implications. I walked away from the event transformed" (quoted in Gamson 1991:35).

Small Victories Some of the same emotional payoffs that result from transforming events can be manufactured, on a much smaller scale, through judicious organizing practices. Or at least that is the popular wisdom among organizers who subscribe to some version of the Saul Alinsky model of organizing. That model holds that hope can be manufactured and fear overcome through small, but tangible, victories that gradually demonstrate the power of collective action at the local level.[6] In its focus on organizers, this final topic raises the more general issue of the role of leaders, not only in the mobilization of hope, but in the overall emotional dynamics of movements. This topic lies at the intersection of two important silences – emotions and leadership – addressed in this volume. In a later chapter, Aminzade, Goldstone, and Perry, take up the surprisingly neglected topic of leadership. Here we focus specifically on the important role that leaders play in the emotional life of a movement or revolution.

Leadership and the Mobilization of Emotions

To motivate people to act collectively against injustice, notes William Gamson (1995:104–105), movement leaders need to connect abstract cognitions of unfairness to the emotion of moral indignation and to sustain emotions that will dissipate in the absence of a clear target. This requires complex cultural knowledge, that is emotional intelligence, in order to mobilize emotional energies and effectively frame grievances in a way that resonates not only with the lived experiences of followers and potential recruits but also with their emotional lives and understandings. Many analysts contend that the distribution of this emotional intelligence is highly gendered. "Womens' work of emotional nurturance," argues Jaggar (1989:165), "has required them to develop a special acuity in recognizing hidden emotions and in understanding the genesis of these emotions. This emotional acumen can now be recognized as a skill in political analysis. . . ."

Although charismatic leaders often act in noninstrumental ways, the power and status enjoyed by leaders within movements is often connected

---

[6] Ironically, one of the things that make possible the victories that may generate hope within a movement is *fear* among authorities. This fear may create a "radical flank effect" (Haines 1988), which can also significantly alter the threats and opportunities available to activists. Fear of "extremists" can lead authorities to openly tolerate, actively sponsor, or provide concessions to what they perceive to be the more moderate wing of a movement. The fear that extremists may take control of a movement can trigger a reevaluation of certain movement groups or leaders, who were previously perceived by authorities as dangerous threats to social and political order. This was the case for the nationalist movement in Tanganyika, where fear generated by the rise of a radical racial nationalist party, the Tanganyikan African National Congress, after 1958 prompted British authorities to dramatically revise their view of the Tanganyikan African National Union (TANU) and its leader, Julius Nyerere.

to their ability to deploy emotional knowledge and define or manipulate emotion rules. The skills of effective leaders include an ability to assess emotional climates, induce mobilizing emotions that motivate followers by altering definitions of the situation, create/reconfigure emotion vocabularies, and transform emotion beliefs and feeling rules into moral obligations. Such leaders can accurately appraise the mood of bystander publics and authorities, seizing the appropriate time to act. Leaders ability to foster "role taking emotions" (Shott 1979), such as sympathy, empathy, guilt, or pity, may elicit altruist behavior and encourage bystanders to contribute time or money to the cause. During periods of negotiation, leaders may utilize, or even encourage, emotional outbursts on the part of more confrontational factions within their ranks to signal authorities about the unacceptability of concessions and the danger that less respectable elements may seize control of the movement.

Gendered understandings of emotion can protect grassroots leaders in situations of high-risk activism by offering women different opportunities for collective political action. For example, the mothers of the disappeared in Argentina were able to engage in public protest against the military regime without inviting harsh repression, in large part because socially defined expectations about the gendered expression of grief for deceased children generated sympathy among bystander publics. Harsh repressive action against grieving mothers would have generated widespread public resentment against the government, given maternalist values and public sympathy for their plight.

Leaders' tactical choices require eliciting and inhibiting certain emotions. Debbie Gould's (2000) analysis of the lesbian/gay community's ambivalent response to the AIDS crisis documents how feelings of fear (of repression and backlash) and shame (at being seen as disreputable) had the effect of initially repressing or containing anger thereby promoting reform-minded activities, such as lobbying and negotiation. After 1984, she argues, movement emotion dynamics – in part fostered by leaders – resulted in internally oriented pride in the community and in oneself rather than expressions of anger. After 1987, however, when conventional political tactics appeared ineffective in altering the government's response to the AIDS crisis, community leaders came to embrace public expressions of anger and the more confrontational tactics and rhetoric of ACT UP as the appropriate response to the crisis.

Fear as a Mobilizing Emotion

In another chapter for this volume, Goldstone and Tilly have sought to redress the longstanding neglect of "threat" – as opposed to "opportunity" – as a stimulant of collective action. We mention the chapter here because the focus on threat has implications for a full accounting of the emotional dynamics involved in the emergence of contention. To wit: If opportunity implies hope as a necessary affective component of mobilization, a similar relationship would seem to exist between threat and fear. That is, certain kinds of threats to either group or individual interest would seem to have the power to motivate collective action, with fear typically serving as the principal affective mediator of the relationship. In the remainder of this section, we offer two examples of the way in which threat may encourage mobilization through the intervening emotion of fear.

Threats to the Quotidian In a recent article, Snow, Cress, Downey, and Jones (1998) have argued that social movement scholars have been too quick to dismiss "strain" as a precipitant of collective action. We concur in this judgement. This is not to revive the widely – and in our view, rightly – discredited classic psychological versions of "strain theory" (Kornhauser 1959; Lang and Lang 1961; Le Bon 1960). Rather the conception of strain that Snow, Cress, Downey, and Jones seek to articulate has to do with what they call, "threats to the quotidian." More specifically, they argue that the sudden disruption of taken-for-granted life routines or the perceived threat of such disruption is often enough to precipitate collective action. What these authors do not discuss is the emotional dynamics underlying this phenomenon. But from the examples they draw upon and others we might offer, it seems clear that the dominant emotion animating the threat/action link is fear. One example should help to underscore the affective salience of fear as a motivator of collective action.

In an important 1983 article, Edward Walsh and Rex Warland documented both a general rise in antinuclear protest around Harrisburg, Pennsylvania in the wake of the accident at Three Mile Island and a strong relationship between extent of mobilization and proximity to the plant itself. The perspective sketched by Snow, Cress, Downey, and Jones would seem to help make sense of the Walsh and Warland findings. While the accident occasioned some level of disruption for virtually all of the residents of south central Pennsylvania, the extent of that disruption and the salience of the attendant fears (for example, of long-term health effects,

36

of a decline in property values, of forced and sustained eviction from their homes, and so on) was obviously much greater for those closest to the Three Mile Island plant. Jasper (1998) also cites Three Mile Island as an example of what he calls a "moral shock," but criticizes the overly cognitive nature of the concept of "suddenly imposed grievances" which Walsh uses to explain the rapid mobilization that took place. As Jasper (1998:409) writes: "the term 'grievance' has primarily cognitive connotations, whereas 'shock' at least hints at the emotional power of these experiences. . . . it implies a visceral, bodily, feeling on a par with vertigo or nausea."

Threats to "Meaning and Membership" The other way in which fear would appear to play a role in the initial mobilization of contention is through the threatened loss of member status in connection with the process of "social appropriation" that almost always accompanies movement emergence (McAdam 1999:xxiii–xxvi). By "social appropriation" we refer to the critically important cultural process by which existing (and generally apolitical) groups or associational networks come to be redefined as appropriate sites for collective action. So certain black congregations came, through a process of social appropriation, to redefine themselves, in the early days of the U.S. Civil Rights Movement, as vehicles of collective action (McAdam 1999; Morris 1984; Oberschall 1973). In the late 1970s and early 1980s, rural church and farmers associations in the Philippines were transformed, under the skillful influence of communist organizers, into associational nodes of the broader insurgent movement (Rutten 1996).

The key point here is that most social movements and revolutions develop within established social groups. And all such groups – informal no less than formal – provide bedrock identity and other ontological benefits to their members. The fact that they do affords these groups considerable leverage with which to shape the actions of those individuals who hope to retain the various solidary benefits that come with group membership. In other words, once the process of "social appropriation" has taken place and the group has committed itself to collective action, anyone resisting the new definition runs the risk of losing the mix of member benefits associated with participation in the group. To the extent that the group, and its associated collective identity, has become an integral part of the individual's life and self-identity, the kind of enduring "affective emotions" mentioned by Jasper (1998), such as fear of rejection

37

and ostracism, can be a powerful force for conformity to the new behavioral and attitudinal requirements of group membership. It is this fear of the threatened loss of member status that, we believe, helps to account for the kind of rapid "bloc recruitment" (Oberschall 1973) that typically characterizes the very beginnings of a broad-based social movement or revolution.

Once a movement is underway, the same fear can be used to prod traditional community "leaders" to endorse a popular struggle. While it has been part of the received wisdom of the historiography of the Civil Rights Movement to credit black ministers with providing much of the leadership of the burgeoning struggle, the fact is many ministers, especially those in rural areas in the Deep South, were latecomers to the struggle. And many times their entrance into the movement resulted from public criticism that impugned their leadership and threatened their stature in the community. Consider the following example taken from Charles Payne's (1996) extraordinary book on the movement in Mississippi. From a taped transcript of a mass meeting held in Greenwood, Mississippi during the first week of April 1963, Payne (1995:198) quotes Dick Gregory as saying that in the local struggle:

... the Negro religious leaders haven't played their part. [*Loud applause*]. I'm a Baptist by choice, but if I had to spend much time in this area, they'd have to force me to be a Baptist because even little kids are in the struggle and not one Baptist church has opened its doors in this area. [*Loud and sustained applause.*] ... Any good Baptists in the house? [*People murmur assent.*] When you go to church Sunday [*pause*], look him in the face [*pause*], then pray for him [*long pause*], then walk out!! [*The house comes down with applause and laughter.*] If you won't even try to get some dignity, God can't use you. They so worried about their church, give 'em their church! Give it to 'em empty! If you have to pray in the street, it's better than worshipping with a man who is less than a man! [*The clapping, laughing and foot-stomping continue for a long time.*]

Payne (p. 198) goes on to note that "pillars of the community were being denounced by name, ridiculed as cowards and hypocrites before God, and audiences of four or five hundred people were cheering and stomping." The outcome: "not long after Gregory's speech, thirty-one local ministers affixed their signatures" to a public statement endorsing "the Freedom Movement one-hundred percent and urg[ing] our members and friends of Leflore County and the state of Mississippi to register and become first class citizens."

The Development and Sustenance of Contention

As we noted at the outset, distinguishing between the emergence, development/sustenance, and decline of contention is a highly arbitrary analytic exercise. The fact of the matter is, at the group or individual level, episodes of contention can be simultaneously experienced as emergent, fully developed, or in decline. That is, some groups or individuals will be exiting the movement at the very moment others are entering. The important implication of this for our purposes is that much of what we said in the previous section regarding the emotional dynamics of movement emergence applies equally well to movements that are well established. It would, however, seem as if there are some affective states and processes that are more relevant to the sustenance of contention than its initial mobilization.

Emotional Socialization

Movements can be understood in terms of what might be called an "emotional socialization" process. Given the emotional learning processes that occur within movement organizations, the emotions that may lead people to join a movement may not be the same emotions that keep them within the movement. Organizations within the feminist movement, which challenges culturally defined gender appropriate expressions of emotions, teach new feeling rules which make the expression of certain "deviant" emotions, such as anger, acceptable for women. The socialization process within feminist organizations, notes Taylor (1995:230–31) "encourages women to trade fear and shame for anger" and promotes an "ethic of care" that legitimizes the expression of emotions of love and affection. Feminist health clinics, observes Morgen (1995:245), encourage and create institutional forms for the public expression of feelings, socializing staff into an emotion culture emphasizing self-disclosure and the public discussion of feelings. Smith and Erickson's (1997) study of paid phone canvassing workers in an environmental movement organization identified emotional socialization strategies designed to deal with workplace tensions arising from a contradiction between the need to maintain workplace productivity and the necessity to foster commitment to an activist identity that will ensure the kind of emotional labor necessary for the organization's success.

Organizers often play an active role in socializing recent members to the movement culture and emotion rules and rewards. For example, Julian McAllister Groves' (1995) study of the animal rights movement notes the importance of empathy and affection for animals at the point at which people initially join the movement. Movement leaders utilize rational arguments in pursuit of movement goals, encouraging members to become angry at causes of cruelty toward animals, an emotion more likely to sustain commitment and evoke a sense of injustice. The movement's emotional socialization process, in other words, stresses the use of rational arguments about the causes of animal cruelty – including road construction, exploiting industries, and the theft of animals for research – to replace empathy and affection for animals with anger at injustice. Ironically, the movement has adopted the larger culture's high valuation of rationality in its effort to socialize members to display emotions that can be mobilized for confrontational tactics.

The emotional socialization process within a movement entails learning appropriate "feeling rules" that guide social interaction within the movement. Such rules include the use of the proper vocabulary. Movements socialize members to use an empowering vocabulary and to avoid certain terms, such as *cripples* or *AIDS victims*, which elicit pity rather than pride and question the agency of the oppressed. Emotion rules, however, are often contested, especially when the movement is heterogeneous in terms of race, gender, and class. Thomas Kochman (1981) contends that black culture in the United States differs from white middle-class culture in terms of conventions governing emotional expressiveness and styles of engaging in public debate. Whites typically regard emotional expressiveness as "feminine," have a negative attitude toward confrontation as divisive, and adopt dispassionate, impersonal, and nonchallenging styles in public debate. Blacks, he argues, tend to view emotional expressiveness as common to both sexes, regard confrontation as signifying caring about something enough to want to struggle for it, and adopt an argumentative mode that is more animated, interpersonal, and confrontational. Blacks are much less likely than whites to believe that emotions interfere with their capacity to reason and more likely to view expressions of anger and hostility as appropriate during negotiating sessions. In multiracial movements, these cultural differences in emotional rules and styles may become a source of serious conflict, especially when some participants treat emotion norms as moral obligations while others see them as social conventions constraining the expression of opinions and identities or when blacks interpret the dispassionate and detached style of white discourse as evidence of a lack of sincerity.

Ritual, Emotions, and Mobilization

The emotional power of rituals helps to account for their widespread use in protest movements. As Verta Taylor (1995) argues, rituals can serve as a means of dramatizing injustice, discharging distressing emotions, generating emotional energy, building solidarity, and affirming identity. Rituals, note Taylor and Whittier (1995:177–78), help challenging groups "express and transform the emotions that arise from insubordination, redefine dominant feeling and expression rules to reflect more desirable identities or self-conceptions, and express group solidarity." Thus, for example, the antirape movement uses rituals to create empowering emotions, channeling womens' fear, guilt, and depression into pride in surviving the ordeal (Taylor and Whittier 1995:178). More generally, rituals of the feminist movement have served as a cultural mechanism for challenging dominant gender norms (Taylor and Whittier 1995:177).

Rituals play a central role in maintaining the emotionally charged boundaries that define movement identities. Within revolutionary movements, ritual forms of address, such as comrade or citoyen, can invoke feelings of pride and belonging as well as hostility toward outsiders. During the French Revolution, a wide variety of rituals, ranging from liberty trees dangling with effigies to red cockades, aroused intense emotions of hatred, of royalty and aristocracy, and love, of the nation (Hunt 1984). Rituals can also help to sustain certain emotions, such as anger at injustice or shame about prior inaction, and to meet the emotional needs of participants. In nineteenth-century France, republicans used funeral processions of prominent leaders or those killed in confrontations with the authorities to arouse anger at the injustice of the regime (Tamason 1980). Some ritualized protest performances, such as self-immolation or a hunger strike, may evoke anger at injustice, provided that the ritual performance resonates with cultural codes concerning self-sacrifice, honor, and martyrdom. Hyojoung Kim's (2000) study of suicides by self-burnings in South Korea, for example, suggests that these rituals induce anger, shame, and guilt among bystander publics, which fosters "cognitive liberation" and collective action.

Scholars of African nationalism have documented the role of emotionally laden rituals, including music, dance, and theater, in anticolonial movements and independence struggles. In South Africa, popular theater was a cultural counterpart of the movement toward political liberation, with performers using chanted responses, emotive music, and unison speaking as well as images of anger and resistance to arouse their audiences (Steadman 1994). Geiger (1997) documents the role that dance societies and their social networks played in recruiting women to the early Tanganyikan nationalist movement and securing their commitments, at a time when repression and high risk made many hesitant to join. Rituals can also serve to reduce anger and desire for revenge. In contemporary Mozambique, for example, traditional African cultural rituals of cleansing and forgiveness performed by local healers have played an important role in the reintegration of former Resistência Nacional Moçambicana (RENAMO) soldiers into their communities after they committed atrocities against fellow villagers during the South African apartheid-state sponsored civil war.

Historians have pointed out the bodily dimensions of rituals, which help give them their emotional power. William McNeill (1995) notes how prolonged movement in unison in military marches and drills arouses intense emotions that build solidarity and esprit de corps prior to combat. The rituals of popular protest, and the use of drilling and dancing prior to confrontations with the forces of order, can mobilize these physiological effects for collective political action, such as clashes in the streets or mounting the barricades.

In predominantly rural societies, the success of mobilizing strategies is often linked to the ability of traditional forms of communication, including poetry, music, and dance, to mobilize emotions among predominantly nonliterate populations. Urban-based movements attempting to mobilize a nonliterate rural population need resonant rituals and symbols capable of evoking powerful emotions if they are to succeed. The student activists who led the protonationalist language movement of East Pakistan (Bangladesh), realized, after failing to rally mass support via pamphlets, newspapers, and speeches, that songs, plays, artwork, and poetry were much more effective vehicles to arouse popular emotions against the government (Anwary 1997:20).

Movement rituals often include the defilement of highly emotional symbols, such as the burning of flags, to highlight group boundaries, legitimate expressions of anger, reinforce group solidarity, or attract media or government attention. Revolutions frequently involve emotionally significant events, such as the ritual desecration of the sacred objects of one's enemies. Such actions draw sharp boundaries between those on different sides of the barricades by defiling objects and places to which ones' adversaries have strong affective attachments. At the outset of the Spanish Civil War, for example, republican forces committed "rituals of collective obscenity" against the churches and convents they attacked, decapitating and disfiguring religious statutes and exhuming and publicly displaying the long-buried skeletons and mummies of priests, nuns, and saints. "In the presence of such iconoclastic acts," writes Bruce Lincoln (1989:126), "the whole of Loyalist Spain was divided into two radically separate groups, in which all prior and potential sentiments of affinity one for the other were eradicated. . . ." The acts of violence directed against the graves of one's ethnic rivals in Bosnia-Herzegovina provide a more recent example of this phenomenon.

Boundary Work

Sociologists have long stressed the role of social conflict in highlighting group boundaries and reinforcing group solidarity, with all its attendant affective payoffs (Coser 1956; Simmel 1955). Indeed, the palpable sense of "weness" that defines peak moments of collective action is among the most emotionally intoxicating and socially connective experiences one can have. Consider the following description by a Freedom Summer volunteer of a moment she shared with other workers on the eve of the group's departure for Mississippi shortly after learning that three volunteers already in the state were missing and presumed dead.

Friday evening the conference met for one last time as a whole. After discussing security regulations, Bob Moses . . . got up and spoke to us. He spoke of his fears and his weariness, of the burden he carries because of the workers who have been killed in Mississippi and because he knows that the probability is great that more will be killed. . . . He shared with us his burden of having to send us in knowing that he was sending some of us to our death. The group was very still as each person watched his leader bare his soul to the group. When Bob finished, a girl's voice rose up singing. . . . "They say that Freedom is a long, long struggle." Slowly the voices in the room joined in. We stood with our arms around each other and we sang for each other. . . . The group sang in one voice, each individual singing not for himself but for the group. Tears ran down many faces. . . . As I sang . . . I knew better than ever before why I was going to Mississippi and what I am fighting for. (quoted in McAdam 1988:72)

The point is, any action or process that serves to deepen conflict and sharpen group boundaries – as the disappearance of the three workers most

43

certainly did – tends to produce and sustain high levels of organizational and affective mobilization. Savvy organizers know this and will seek to realize the myriad benefits of this dynamic by consciously deploying tactics that serve to escalate group tensions and heighten movement participants' stark "us/them" experience of the world. Only when we take account of this central affective dynamic, can we make sense of recurring movement practices that might otherwise seem strange or even counterproductive.

One such practice, discussed above, is the time-honored tradition of defiling or desecrating sites, objects, or persons sacred to movement opponents. The staging of a march in "enemy territory" is another common movement practice that tends to produce the kind of affective payoff and solidary benefits discussed above. So when Ku Klux Klan organizers plan a march, especially in the North, they can count on confronting a hostile crowd, whose actions (for example, jeers, rock throwing, and so on) are very likely to reinforce member solidarity and their sense of themselves as an embattled and courageous band. Protestant marches through Catholic sections of Ulster function in much the same way, undermining other identities and underscoring the central us/them division of the world into Catholic and Protestant.

Finally, there is the baiting of authorities into acts of official violence which tends, unless the repression is extreme, to reinforce group solidarity and the shared resolve to "fight again another day." These exercises in strategic provocation may have an additional emotional payoff for the movement. Violence by the authorities that is widely perceived to be illegitimate may, as in the case of the U.S. Civil Rights Movement, anger an otherwise disinterested newsmedia and general public, who, in turn, respond with the kind of pressure that proves decisive in producing important movement gains (McAdam 1982; 1983).

Decline and Demobilization

Just as various emotions may mobilize people during the early days of an emerging movement, a range of emotions can contribute to movement decline. For example, in rare instances, feelings of pride and satisfaction in the attainment of movement goals can encourage demobilization. However, insofar as most movements fail to achieve their aims, we are inclined here to highlight the role of more "negative" emotions in movement decline. For example, feelings of despair may lead people to abandon their early idealism, become cynical or apathetic about prospects for an alternative future, and focus their energies on individualist pursuits and the demands of daily life. Movement leaders and staff may experience emotional exhaustion and burnout, as the demands for their emotional labor increase. Leaders and staff often make mistakes and learn from them, but during a period of movement decline, activists may see mistakes as more costly and consequential. Mistakes then generate an increased emotional burden. In the face of movement decline, members may experience feelings of anger, insecurity, and fear while leaders and staff who blame themselves for defeats may experience shame or guilt. The intensification of repression that often accompanies the declining phase of a movement may lead to demobilization through the intervening emotional state of fear. As the emotional climate shifts, the demobilizing emotions of fear, resignation, and cynicism come into play. Movement leaders may respond by using the emotional sanctions of guilt and shame against members in an attempt to prevent their exit from the movement.

Another shift in emotional dynamics during the declining phase of a movement centers on the routinization of movement activities. Participation in a march or demonstration may once have been an exhilarating and risky new experience, fraught with danger. During the declining phase of a movement, however, it may turn into yet another time-consuming commitment that reaffirms solidarities in a routine and codified manner and is unlikely to produce change or enthusiasm. But the routinization of day-to-day activities within movement organizations may have a very different impact on emotional intensities and conflicts. Studies have found that when people are seeking to create solutions to new tasks, their behavior will be cognitively driven, whereas when applying previously learned solutions, behavior is more affectively driven (Millar and Tessar 1986). The implication for movement decline is that routinization will mean lesser reliance on cognitive appraisals of situations and the potential for heightened emotional tensions and conflicts.

As the movement declines or becomes institutionalized, weariness sets in, changing the emotional labor required of movement leaders and staff. The task becomes rekindling anger and hope in order to retain and reinforce commitments and recharge worn-down emotional batteries. The popularization of movement identities may also play a role in altering the emotional landscape of the movement. As large numbers of people with minimal commitments to the movement and its organizations adopt the movement collective identity (for example, environmentalist), hard core activists may seek to differentiate themselves, thus creating feelings of superiority, resentment, and schisms within the movement during its decline. Key events, such as the imprisonment or death of a prominent leader, may create despair and thereby alter the emotional landscape of a movement in decline.

Intensified internal divisions, along the lines of race, gender, class, age, or ideology, provide yet another source of the shifting emotional climate. Factional divisions may become exacerbated during a period of movement decline. The highly committed who remain active have a much greater emotional investment than those who are at the margins of the movement. This can lead to conflicts over emotion rules concerning the appropriate range, intensity, duration, and targets of emotions or to status distinctions and conflicts based on members' different levels of emotional investment, leading members with waning commitments to perceive leaders as haughty or "holier than thou." During periods of decline, contestation over emotion rules may intensify, bringing to the fore differences that prior successes may have concealed or encouraged activists to put aside.

Class, racial, and gender divisions within a movement may also surface during periods of defeat and decline, when declining resources can make people more tense, create emotional distress, and generate feelings of anger directed against those held responsible for the decline. These divisions may prompt leaders and staff to circumvent emotionally charged participatory democratic forms of decision making in favor of less emotionally draining exercises of authority. They may also lead to conflicts over norms of formality and informality and over who should do the emotional labor and when it is necessary and appropriate.

The schisms and polarization that typically accompany movement decline are often connected to differences among activists in temporal expectations concerning commitments and goal achievements. Those with shorter time horizons become disappointed at how long it has taken to gain so little. They experience despair and, unable to sustain hope, exit the movement. In response to these defections, leaders may attempt to attract more participants by moderating their demands in order to win more concessions from the authorities. Some participants may then become angry, direct their anger at moderate leaders, and either displace those leaders or join militant factions advocating more confrontational tactics.

Revolutionary movements, like military units, often rely on the emotional dependency of their members to sustain commitments. The inability of such movements to maintain boundaries separating members from competing sources of emotional attachment may lead to a spiral of decline, as members defect to alternative sources of emotional attachment, such as family or kin. In his study of the communist-led Huk Rebellion in the Philippines, Goodwin (1997) found that sexual relations and the strong kinship ties characteristic of Philippine rural society eroded the solidarity of predominantly male guerrillas and fostered emotional withdrawal from, and weakened identification with, the insurgency.

Lessons Learned and Directions for Future Research

Emotions provide an important source of energy for activists throughout all phases of a social movement, but as the importance of different organizing tasks shifts during different phases of a movement, leaders are likely to appeal to different emotions. Pride and hope may be central to the initial recruitment of members, who are attracted by messages of collective pride and hopeful that things can be different. During the subsequent period of movement growth, the sympathy or empathy of bystander publics may be crucial. During movement decline and especially the onset of the "doldrums," the focus appears to shift to maintaining affective solidarity among a small number of career activists intent on sustaining the struggle through the lean years (Rupp and Taylor 1987).

Further research should shed light on whether movements with different emphases (for example, identity building or policy change) have different emotional climates and whether there is a relationship between appeals to particular emotions and particular movements, movement cultures, or collective action repertoires. Corwin Kruse (1995) hypothesizes that emotional appeals play a more important role in sustaining commitments within movements of conscience, which recruit members to causes beyond their own self-interest, but the comparative research needed to confirm or discount this proposition remains to be done.

The preceding discussion also suggests the need for further research to address a number of questions concerning macro-micro linkages. The shifting temporal horizons accompanying industrialization may alter conceptions of hope while the growing salience of emotional attachments to loved ones attendant to declining mortality rates or altered kinship structures may impact feeling rules about death and grieving. The latter, in turn, influence the emotional practices and dynamics of revolution and collective political violence. Cultures vary, for instance, in whether feeling rules about grieving over a friend's or relative's death at the hands of the authorities may foster collective expressions of anger and revenge or efforts at reconciliation.

Other macrolevel changes, such as the separation of home and work, may have implications for rules governing the expression of emotions in political as well as nonpolitical settings. How did this separation affect feeling rules concerning anger control for women, who have typically played a central but little acknowledged role in contentious politics? Shifts in kinship connections and obligations may affect whether, in the face of political repression, people respond to the incarceration or execution of their relatives with fear or anger. We also need to know more about how nation-state formation and long-term transformations in the character of politics have transformed the emotional dimensions of protest. For example, how did the shift in claims making into parliamentary institutions and national-level politics (Tilly 1995a) alter the emotional character of popular protest? In order to validate claims to represent the interests of a group and avoid repression, movements in "democratic" polities have traditionally tried to engage in public performances that project respectability and orderliness rather than collective anger. Did the requirement of deploying disciplined numbers and displaying unity mean greater valuation of self-control and orderliness rather than impulsiveness, a consequent identification of emotions as irrational, and a framing of enemies as irrational but the movement as rational? Scholars of nationalism have recently begun to creatively explore the process of the creation of feelings of political belonging. By viewing citizenship as an emotive as well as legal mode of incorporation, they have raised important new questions about the nature of challenges to the nation-state and the usurpation of emotional space by nondemocratic groups (Berezin 1999).

Another question meriting further research is whether globalization and the worldwide spread of mass communication technologies that do not rely on face-to-face relations has changed emotional norms in political cultures around the world. Do frequent media images of death and destruction dull the emotions and make people less capable of collectively expressing grief and anger in response to treats from the powerful? Does the presentation of economic news in the same format as weather forecasts, as natural and inevitable, inhibit expressions of the counterfactual emotions of hope or regret? Media icons, which reduce a message to a dramatic visual image and accompanying sound bite, have been effectively used as claims-making rhetoric by the environmental movement to evoke powerful emotional responses and alter peoples' attitudes about an issue

(Szasz 1994:62–64). But the emotional energy generated by face-to-face interaction may be critical to movement survival in the face of tactical and strategic failures. Global social movements linked by the internet raise the question of whether relations of trust involving deep rather than shallow commitments can be sustained in cyberspace, in the absence of face-to-face communication and the emotional bonding it can generate.

Emotional rules may vary across cultures in ways that help to systematically pattern the dynamics of contentious politics. If, as we have argued above, anger, hope, and shame play an important role in the trajectories of social movements, then norms governing how and when such emotions are appropriately expressed in public rather than private should have important political consequences. Crossnational studies should enable us to better understand the impact of different cultural patterns on movement recruiting strategies and on the extent of free-riding by potential beneficiaries. Can we identify distinctive features of a culture (for example, individualism, fatalism, and so on) that foster or legitimize certain emotions, like cynicism, resignation, or despair, which hasten the downward spiral of a cycle of protest?

In closing, we would be remiss if we did not at least touch on the daunting methodological challenges posed by the need to make the systematic study of emotions and emotional processes a more central feature of research on social movements and revolutions. An example of the difficult tasks that await those who would heed this call centers on the development of rigorous measures of emotional climates, norms, and interactions that would allow scholars to systematically compare movements and movement organizations across time and space. Measurement will not be easy, however, given what Katherine Lutz and Geoffrey White (1986:427) accurately describe as the "ambivalence, ambiguity and complexity of much emotional experience and interaction." Historical records provide traces of past action, but since feeling rules "do not apply to action but to what is often taken as a precursor to action" (Hochschild 1979:566), their latent, taken-for-granted, and uncodified character makes them very difficult to study. Retrospective accounts of activists often privilege cognitive dimensions of decision making and suppress emotional dynamics regarded as less politically legitimating. Such accounts often tell us more about emotional performances than experiences and the "backstage" information needed to access the latter is often difficult to obtain. Reading historical documents for their emotional tone requires careful self-monitoring of one's own emotions as well as an awareness of how others may have responded to given events or conflicts. It also requires knowledge of the multiple emotion cultures in which individual activists participated, the consequential ambivalence of their emotions, and the resulting instability and malleability of emotion norms.

Our effort to address the questions raised above will require a much more diverse methodological toolkit, that includes ethnographies, interviews, personal narratives, survey research, experiments, and historical analysis. A methodologically pluralist approach will allow us to take advantage of the wide range of sources that express a movement's emotion culture, from institutionalized practices such as rituals to gender ideology, emotion language, and cultural aesthetics. Organizers' manuals constitute an invaluable but rarely used source for the study of feeling rules and emotional labor in different movement settings. Some methods, which can provide access to the emotional lives of movement activists, such as biographical and autobiographical materials or life histories based on in-depth interviews, have been marginalized within the social science literature, yet they can provide access to the subjective dimensions of movement activities and insights into the process of identity formation (Laslett and Thorne 1997; Maynes 1995). Ethnographies can also provide such access, allowing us to study nonverbal as well as verbal expressions of emotion, but they typically do so at only one point in time, thus making it difficult, in a single ethnography, to capture the dynamics of change in emotional work, rules, and climates. Given that all methods entail problems of reliability and validity, a self-reflexive strategy of methodological triangulation is clearly recommended for the study of emotions in social movements and revolutions.

3

Space in Contentious Politics
William H. Sewell, Jr.

To claim that the literature on contentious politics ignores questions of space would be inaccurate.[1] Studies of contentious politics often provide descriptive narratives of protest actions and such accounts frequently include a description of the places where the action occurs. It is not unusual for analysts to highlight, at least in passing, spatial considerations that affect the strategies of actors or the dynamic or impact of protest events. Accounts of the 1963 Civil Rights March on Washington are likely to say something about the layout of the Mall or evoke the symbolic significance of addressing a crowd from the foot of the Lincoln Memorial (Fairclough 1995; Miller 1968; Oates 1982). Accounts of the Amritsar Massacre of 1919 will mention that the Jallianwala Bagh, where General Dyer's machine guns mowed down hundreds of Indian demonstrators, was surrounded by walls and was accessible only by very narrow gates so that protesters were trapped once the shooting began (Draper 1981). But most studies bring in spatial considerations only episodically, when they seem important either for adequate description of contentious political events or for explaining why particular events occurred or unfolded as they did. With rare exceptions, the literature has treated space as an assumed

---

[1] Charles Tilly and I originally intended to produce a collaborative chapter on this question. It is significant, given the topic of the chapter, that our collaboration proved impossible for basically spatial reasons: Our expectation of spending a few weeks in the same place to work out a joint conception of the chapter was frustrated by events beyond our control. Nevertheless, I have drawn shamelessly on Tilly's conversation and preliminary drafts in writing this chapter. I would also like to thank Neil Brenner, Debbie Gould, Lynn Hunt, Howard Kimeldorf, David Laitin, Mark Traugott, Lisa Wedeen, members of the Wilder House Faculty Seminar, and members of the Mellon Seminar on Contentious Politics for their useful (although not always heeded) comments.

and unproblematized background, not as a constituent aspect of contentious politics that must be conceptualized explicitly and probed
systematically.[2]

Over the past few years, there has been a spate of journal articles, mostly
written by either geographers or historians, that take on spatial issues
directly.[3] Many of these contributions are quite impressive. However,
nearly all of them are resolutely in the genre of case studies; each
examines the importance of some particular aspect of space in the context
of a given empirical instance. My ambition in this chapter is to attempt a
more systematically theoretical account of the role of space in political
contention. I believe that questions of space cannot move into the fore-
ground in studies of contentious politics as long as the concept remains
insufficiently theorized. I attempt therefore to provide a rudimentary
theoretical vocabulary for thinking about space in contentious politics
and to begin putting such a vocabulary to work. The chapter has two
parts. The first specifies concepts of spatial analysis and illustrates them
briefly with examples from the study of political contention. The second
attempts to put the theoretical vocabulary to work in two more extended
examples of spatial analysis, one dealing with the Beijing student
movement of 1989 and the other with the role of Paris in the French
Revolution.

What is Space? And How Does It Matter for Contentious Politics?

Space is a semantically complex concept; it has multiple meanings both in
ordinary language and as used by professional geographers and other social
scientists. For this reason, the seemingly simple admonition to "take space
seriously" is quite unclear in practice. I will therefore begin by attempting to sort out some of the ambiguities of the concept.

---

[2] Two early exceptions to this backgrounding of spatial factors in contentious politics are
Tilly (1964) and Bezucha (1974). I discuss both of them briefly later in this chapter.
[3] Two journals have been particularly prominent in these discussions of space and political
contention. *Political Geography* published a special issue in 1994 on the topic "Empowering Political Struggle" that included articles about space and contention (especially, Miller
1994; Staeheli 1994; Staeheli and Cope 1994; Steinberg 1994). Since that time, the same
journal has published several additional relevant articles (for example, Adams 1996; Herbert
1996; Herod 1997; Miller 1997; Routledge 1996). In 2000, the journal *Social Science History*
published a special issue on "The Working Classes and Urban Public Space," which also
included several interesting works on spatial aspects of political contention (Hurd 2000;
Pagan 2000, Porter 2000; Reiff 2000; Rosenthal 2000; Witwer 2000).

Abstract and Concrete Conceptions of Space

A measure of the semantic complexity of the term *space* in ordinary language is that entries under this word occupy more than two full pages in the *Oxford English Dictionary*. The meanings of the term most relevant for the study of social life tend to cluster around two poles – what might be called abstract and concrete conceptions of space. Abstract space is based above all on Cartesian and post-Cartesian metaphysics, according to which space is "continuous, unbounded, unlimited extension in every direction, regarded as void of matter or without reference to this" (*Oxford English Dictionary* 1971). Space in this sense may be thought of as a pure, abstract, three-dimensional mathematical grid. The application of this abstract metaphysical concept of space to the material world results in a metrical approach to space. As the *Oxford English Dictionary* puts it, space in this sense signifies "linear distance; interval between two or more points or objects" or "superficial extent or area; also extent in three dimensions." Here, space is conceptualized as a quantifiable characteristic of the real world. It is a matter of distance, area, and volume; of vastness, narrowness, nearness, or remoteness – which can always, at least since Descartes, be expressed in a universal, strictly comparable, quantitative form.

But in ordinary language, we also speak of space in a more concrete sense. To quote the *OED* again, space may refer to "a certain stretch, extent, or area of ground, surface, sky, etc.; an expanse." Space in this sense is a definite location of a particular size and shape. Used in this way, space is defined not by objective quantifiable characteristics, although, of course, it might well be measurable. Rather, concrete space is defined in relation to human occupation, use, or gaze. Concrete space is a space for some person or collection of persons. It is a space that is used, seen, and experienced.

Both abstract and concrete conceptions of space also appear in the language of the social sciences, although at any given time one may be emphasized more than the other. In the immediate post-World War II decades, the avant garde of professional geography was dominated by a metrical conception of space, one that rested on an essentially abstract spatial metaphysics. This movement within geography was a part of the general positivist wave that washed over the social sciences in these years. Positivist geographers were searching for universal geographical laws – laws that operated across time and space and that could be specified quantitatively. The spatial metrics developed by geographers then and since may be highly sophisticated and are by no means limited to measurements of absolute linear spatial distance. One can, for example, produce maps of space based on time and/or cost of travel rather than on kilometers, maps that show how spatial technologies "distort" simple physical distance.

Beginning in the 1960s, a number of geographers began to fault the positivists for their lack of interest in concrete space, which, by the 1980s, they increasingly designated by the term *place* (Massey 1994). These insurgents insisted on a more historical approach to space, a stronger focus on the significance of the built environment, and a greater understanding of the cultural meaning of specific spaces. This trend swelled in the 1970s and became a serious rival to positivist approaches within the geographical profession by the 1980s. Moreover, during the 1980s and 1990s, spatial approaches, primarily in the "concrete" mode, have become increasingly prominent outside the academic discipline of geography – for example in cultural studies (for example, Sorkin 1993; Zukin 1992) and in social theory (for example, Giddens 1984). According to Edward Soja we are now experiencing a wide-ranging "reassertion of space in critical social theory" (Soja 1989). But it is important to recognize that both concrete and abstract/metrical conceptions of space remain alive and well in the contemporary geography profession and in the work of other social scientists. Indeed, given that mapping remains a central technique of geography, and that modern mapping depends crucially on mathematical operations, it is hard to imagine a geography entirely shorn of abstract and metrical conceptions of space.

Spatial Structure and Spatial Agency

Social scientists tend to think of space as objective or given, as constituting a kind of container within which social processes are constrained to take place. For this reason, space seems a prime example of what social scientists call *structures* or (alternatively) *social structures*. Spatial or geographical structures might be regarded as parallel to economic structures, occupational structures, political structures, or demographic structures – that is, as entrenched facts of social life that have their own autonomous (or at least relatively autonomous) logics and that determine or at least tightly constrain social action. I think it is entirely appropriate to think of space as a structure or an aspect of structure – but only if structure is properly understood. As Anthony Giddens has pointed out repeatedly, the objective or given character of structure, while real, is only one of structure's faces. Structure must be conceptualized as *dual*: as simultaneously the *medium* and the *outcome* of social action (Giddens 1976, 1979, 1984; see also Bhaskar 1998 [1979]; Sewell 1992). Structures shape people's actions, but it is also people's actions that constitute and reproduce structures. Moreover, as Giddens insists, "structures must not be conceptualized as simply placing constraints on human agency, but as enabling" (Giddens 1976:161). Structure forms the capacities and provides the resources necessary for human agency, enabling humans to reproduce themselves and their social world, but also enabling them to act in innovative ways and therefore occasionally to modify the very structures that shaped them. Spatial structures, like other sorts of structures, are durable and constraining, but they also are subject to transformation as a consequence of the very social action that they shape.

Such spatial structures as the built environment, transportation and communications infrastructures, the distribution of pilgrimage sites, or the conformation of mountain ranges, coastlines, and river valleys pose very real constraints on social actions of all kinds. But even the seemingly most solid and durable of these constraints are also enabling. For example, river valleys divided by steep mountain ranges constrain communication between adjacent valleys. But this very spatial constraint gives certain advantages to those who are positioned – for example, by their occupation or geographical location – to serve as agents of communication between adjacent valleys. Moreover, the relative isolation of mountain valleys, combined with superior local knowledge of the arduous terrain, enhances the likelihood that mountain dwellers will be able to engage successfully in illegal or subversive activities like smuggling and guerilla warfare.

Contentious politics might almost be defined as concerted social action that has the goal of overcoming deeply rooted structural disadvantage. It follows therefore that in studying the role of space in contentious politics we should be especially attentive to what might be called spatial agency – the ways that spatial constraints are turned to advantage in political and social struggles and the ways that such struggles can restructure the meanings, uses, and strategic valence of space. Social movements and revolutions not only are shaped and constrained by the spatial environments in which they take place, but are significant agents in the production of new spatial structures and relations. (On the idea of the production of space, see Lefebvre 1991 [1974].) Insurgents are normally resource-poor – at least by comparison with the states, established churches, local oligarchies, corporate capitalists, and other entrenched interests against whom they are contending. This limits the forms of spatial agency that are available to them. Whereas business corporations or states can engineer massive changes in the physical environment – by building factories, roads, canals, ports, new urban neighborhoods, and the like – insurgents involved in contentious politics must generally accept the physical environment as a given. Insurgents produce space above all by changing the meanings and strategic uses of their environments. The second part of this chapter, and most particularly the discussion of space in the French Revolution, attempts to demonstrate that insurgents' spatial agency can have far-reaching political consequences.

Location and Spatial Differentiation

All social life is located. The fundamental fact on which all theories of space are built is that a thing cannot be in two places at the same time. Obvious as this statement may seem, it has profound consequences for thinking about social life. Social life is located in the double sense that it takes place in specific locales – neighborhoods, factories, forests, fields, streets, bedrooms, bars – and that these locales stand in specific relation to other locales and to social, economic, and political processes that operate at wider scales – for example, flows of investment, modes of political representation, or international migration regimes.[4]

Because varying activities are carried out in different locations, social life is spatially differentiated. This is true on a micro level, in that a person's daily succession of tasks will be performed in different places – kitchens, bathrooms, parks, offices, fields, public squares, shops, back yards. It is also true on a more macro level. Cities are divided into distinct areas – business, shopping, residential, industrial, entertainment, warehouse, or gallery districts; gold coasts, slums, and bungalow belts; Italian, Jewish, African-American, Polish, and Chinese neighborhoods. Rural areas are also highly differentiated, ranging from swamps to cultivated fields, to woodlands, to sand dunes, to range lands. Agricultural regions specialize – for example, in livestock, wheat, fruits, dairying, soybeans, vegetables, sugar cane, cotton, or vines – and these different crops entail different modes of cultivation, settlement patterns, densities of settlement, relations of production, and class structures. At an even more macro level, the world

---

[4] John Agnew calls these two aspects of the locational dimension of social life "locale" and "location" (Agnew 1987).

is divided into politically and culturally distinct nation states, and into different global regions – into tropical, subtropical, and temperate zones; into zones of savannas, rain forests, deciduous forests, deserts, and tundra; into core, semiperipheral, and peripheral zones of the world economy. Different spaces vary not only in function and in their natural and built environment, but also have different cultural meanings, both to those who live and work in them and to outsiders. City neighborhoods may be coded as chic, dangerous, sedate, or youthful; rural areas as sleepy, industrious, scenic, hardscrabble, or pious; nations as rich, poor, warlike, peaceful, internationalist, or xenophobic.[5]

Like any other aspect of spatial structure, location and spatial differentiation are changed over time by concerted human action. Forests may be cut down by lumber companies or settlers – or may be spared the ax as a consequence of social movements. Poor countries may become rich; farmland may be turned into suburban subdivisions and shopping malls; neighborhoods previously regarded as dangerous may become chic. The meanings, demographic characteristics, economic values, and landscapes of different locations are always potentially subject to change. The initiation, management, and content of such changes may be targets or occasions of contentious politics.

Space and Copresence

Spatial location enables and constrains *copresence*. In order for persons to interact with one another, they must be brought into each other's presence, either personally and bodily or in some mediated fashion (for example, by writing or electronic media). (On the general significance of copresence in social life, see Giddens 1984.) Where people and things are located in space powerfully constrains or enables copresence, especially bodily copresence. The question of copresence is relevant to many aspects

---

[5] Because persons and activities are so differentially located in space, analysts of revolutions and social movements have often used the location of contentious episodes or the residences or workplaces of insurgents as clues to the etiology of events. When George Rudé remarks that the insurrection that overthrew the French monarchy in 1792 drew disproportionately from inhabitants of the faubourg Saint-Antoine and the faubourg Saint-Marcel, he means to imply among other things that this was above all a revolt of the *menu peuple* – both neighborhoods were populated above all by skilled artisans (Rudé 1959). Space, in the sense of location, can thus serve as a proxy for explanations that are not exclusively spatial in nature. This is a point I owe to Charles Tilly.

of contentious politics. Here I will merely mention some of the ways it matters.

The physical assembling of large numbers of people into limited spaces is an important feature of nearly all forms of contentious politics. Insurgent movements generally pit groups with relatively little by way of financial, coercive, and organizational resources against resource-rich organizations – most commonly states. One means by which insurgent groups overcome their general inferiority in resources is to take advantage of one resource they have – the force of numbers. Movements attempt to mass large numbers of people into public spaces where they can rally, march, and demonstrate as a means of pressing their claims. Such massing of insurgents can have a number of positive effects for movements. It gives an insurgent group publicity, both in person, by its ostentatious occupation of public spaces, and indirectly, through mediated accounts of the gathering – whether by word of mouth, by newspapers, or by modern electronic media. Secondly, it also serves to enhance the group's solidarity. Big demonstrations or mass meetings not only persuade the political authorities that the insurgents are, in Charles Tilly's words, "Worthy, United, Numerous, and Committed," but also help to persuade the insurgents of the same things (Tilly 1998). Mass demonstrations give participants the sense of being engaged in a common cause with a vast number of like-thinking persons. The collective experience of the demonstration – the chants, the cheering, the exhilaration – results in the kind of contagious excitement that Durkheim called "collective effervescence," and which, as he pointed out, enhances the participants' sense of efficacy and feeling of solidarity with other participants (Durkheim 1995 [1912]). Finally, mass demonstrations also serve (in the military sense) as a kind of "concentration of forces" that will enable the crowd to stand up to the repressive forces assembled to control and intimidate it.

The strategies of movements and of those attempting to suppress or dampen movements very frequently revolve around the question of enhancing or preventing the physical and/or mediated copresence of insurgents. Authorities may concentrate overwhelming coercive forces at the place where demonstrations are expected, refuse permits to demonstrators, or negotiate restricted itineraries for their marches. When demonstrations cannot be physically prevented, regimes with tight control over the electronic or print media may suppress news coverage of marches or even of street battles. During "The Events of May" in 1968, when the

French state had a monopoly on television, the evening newscasts for several days made only the briefest mention of the street battles that were occurring every evening in the Latin Quarter and showed no images of the fighting whatsoever – in what turned out to be a futile attempt to keep the French in cities outside Paris from taking advantage of the chaos in the capital to mount strikes and demonstrations of their own.

A perennially important task facing movement organizers is to establish mediated forms of communication between units of the movement organization or between the organization's militants and its supporters. States normally have impressive space-bridging technologies at their disposal: networks of scribes; centralized bureaucracies; mobile agents (whether judges riding the circuit or automobile state troopers); secret police; dedicated telegraph, telephone, or computer links; and so on. Modern states are, from a certain perspective, organizations that specialize in information gathering and in the control, policing, and coordination of activities over wide-flung territorially defined jurisdictions. In order to challenge states, insurgent organizations must build their own rival communication networks. The nature of the insurgent networks, of course, varies with the available communication technology and with the degree of repressiveness of the regime.

During the late eighteenth and early nineteenth centuries, movement organizations took advantage of the regular mail services that were an important aspect of the emerging public sphere. The Committees of Correspondence during the American Revolution, the French Jacobin Clubs during the French Revolution, and the network of British radical clubs pioneered in the 1790s by the London Corresponding Society: All of these early insurgent political societies were linked by an incessant flow of letters that assured coordination of initiatives and rapid flow of information between organizations distant in space. Among the most treasured resources of organizations working in oppressive conditions has been the clandestine printing press or mimeograph machine, which assured the organization would be able to get its broadsheets, posters, pamphlets, or announcements out to a wide public. One of the first acts of social movements in the United States in the 1960s or 1970s was to form a "telephone tree" to make it possible to get decisions about meetings, protest demonstrations, and the like to a spatially scattered membership in a hurry. By the 1990s this problem was solved largely by email list servers.

Time-Distance

As some of the above examples illustrate, copresence is enabled and constrained by sheer physical distance, but more importantly by time-distance, the length of time required for persons, objects, or mediated messages to get from one place to another. Time-distance is determined both by natural conditions (for example, topography and climate) and by the existing modes of communication and transportation and by their cost and availability. Different classes and organizations usually face different effective time-distance conditions, as do different types of goods. A wealthy person in late eighteenth century France could travel by coach from Paris to the German border in a couple of days, but a poor person who could not afford the fare might require a few weeks to cover the distance on foot. In the contemporary world, oil crosses oceans relatively slowly in tankers but oil price quotations from New York can be posted in Singapore in a few milliseconds. The technological advances of the past two hundred years or so have resulted in dramatic general declines in time-distance, what David Harvey dubs "time-space compression" (Harvey 1989). Hence the space-time constraints facing contemporary movements are very different from those operating in earlier periods. One general effect on social movements is that it is now much easier than it was in the past to organize movements on a national – or even international – scale. For example, the antivice societies that were formed in a number of American cities in the late nineteenth century operated primarily on a strictly local scale (Beisel 1997), whereas comparable movements in the present, for example Mothers Against Drunk Driving or the antiabortion movements, are national in organizational scope.

Time-distance is such a common strategic preoccupation in contentious politics that it is hard to think of any contentious action in which it is not an issue. The local or grass-roots organization of most movements of poor people is largely a consequence of their concentration in certain neighborhoods (which makes them easy to reach by door-to-door organizing) but also of their relatively restricted mobility and limited access to communications technology (it's not easy for them to fly to Washington to lobby Congress and they don't have email networks because they don't have computers.) Strategies based on calculations of time-distance are also important in revolutions. The Chinese Communists were more difficult to put down when they switched to a strategy of organizing peasants (because it was very difficult for the government to get sufficient concentrations of troops to widely dispersed locations in the countryside) than when they attempted the Bolshevik strategy of urban insurrection. Guerrilla movements, which became the dominant type of revolutionary movement in the third world in the era following World War II, are always based on a strategy of minimizing the length of guerrilla supply lines (guerrillas live off the local peasants) and stretching government supply lines to the breaking point.

Built Environment

Copresence is also enabled and constrained by the built environment. Space is, in a very literal sense, culturally and historically constructed. Because it is largely the networks of roads, city streets, canals, ports, railways, and airports that govern movement through space, the built environment is a major determinant of the time-distance constraints under which social movements operate. But the built environment has effects beyond mere time-distance constraints. By shaping social interaction, the built environment also shapes the nature and possibility of social protest. For example, a densely built pedestrian city with urban squares or a college campus with quadrangles, plazas, and other clearly marked public gathering places provides ready-made spaces for political demonstrations and assures that an appropriate audience will witness them. In suburbs predicated on the automobile, the only well-populated public spaces may be privately owned shopping malls, where dissidents have no legal right of assembly or free speech.

The rural built environment is no less important in determining the shape of political contention than the urban. Charles Tilly showed that the counterrevolutionary Vendée Revolt of 1793 was limited precisely to the areas of Western France known as the *bocage*, which had scattered settlements and enclosures, and entirely spared the *plaine*, adjacent areas that had nucleated villages and open fields. Among the crucial differences between these regions is that the clergy played a particularly pivotal role in the social lives of inhabitants of the bocage, acting as the primary intermediary between the dispersed households and the outside world, whereas inhabitants of the plaine had a much wider range of intermediaries to choose from in the more diverse populations of their nucleated villages. When the revolutionary state began to persecute the clergy, it was in the bocage, where such persecution appeared as an attack on the rural community itself, that a popular movement formed in defense of the Church.

Peculiarities of the rural built environment thus did much to determine the extent and the character of the deadliest civil war of the revolutionary era (Tilly 1964).

In the eighteenth and nineteenth centuries, European capital cities were the classic locus of urban insurrections. Old cities such as Paris, Berlin, Vienna, and Rome had a particularly flammable combination. Not only did they have densely built poor neighborhoods whose labyrinthine streets were susceptible to barricades, but these working-class quarters were within easy striking distance of the neighborhoods of the rich and of the grand public squares of the ceremonial city. (For a similar argument, see Traugott 1995a.) Contemporaries were, in fact, quite aware that the built form of the old capital city posed a danger to public order. It is well known that one motive for Haussman's rebuilding of Paris during the Second Empire was to make it harder for insurgents to defend against cavalry and artillery in case of insurrection (Jordan 1996:188–92; Pinkney 1958:36).

Spatial Routines

Social life is organized into spatial routines. In addition to the unavoidable constraints imposed by time-distance and the nature of the built environment, copresence is determined by spatially located, socially constructed routines. Categories of social actors perform particular kinds of social actions in particular places (and at particular times). The commute to work, the funeral procession, summer vacations at the seashore, the Sunday afternoon stroll after church, the backyard barbecue with family and friends, the weekly meeting of the sewing club in members' living rooms, the drink with coworkers at closing time, the shopping trip to the mall: People's lives are marked by a succession of spatially sited routines and specific places or locations are marked by particular kinds of activities.

The sites and the strategies of contentious political movements are shaped in various ways by the spatial routines of daily life. Contentious events often arise out of spatial routines that bring large numbers of people together in particular places. Food riots commonly began at weekly or daily markets where women gathered to buy provisions and where grievances about high prices could build into very public disputes (Tilly 1972). Funeral processions for men or women who have come to symbolize political causes often become political demonstrations and sometimes result in riots or insurrections. Spatial routines also shape the strategy of movements: Labor organizers will haunt the pubs and wineshops where workers go for a drink after work; antiabortion activists are thick at Southern Baptist conventions. But spatial routines can also affect movement strategies in more surprising ways. Jessica Sewell (forthcoming) shows that suffragists in San Francisco in 1911 used women's financial potential as shoppers to persuade downtown storeowners to fill their windows with displays of yellow-colored goods (yellow was the official color of the suffrage campaign), and sometimes to display prosuffrage posters and banners as well. The shop-window displays enabled the suffragists to reach not only the thousands of middle-class shoppers (mostly female) who patronized the downtown stores, but also the equally numerous but enfranchised male lawyers, insurance salesmen, brokers, bankers, accountants, and businessmen who worked in the nearby business district and walked the same streets as the shoppers. This case nicely illustrates the duality of spatial structure and the nature of spatial agency in contentious politics. From the standpoint of a historian of consumer capitalism, the shopping landscape was an entrenched structure with a specific purpose and effect: The shops with their large display windows lured women into downtown San Francisco and defined them as gendered subjects of a particular kind – passive middle-class shoppers. But the suffragists saw this structured space with its well-established window-shopping routine as an opportunity and appropriated the conventional visual language of shop-window display for unconventional political purposes. By doing so they effectively demonstrated that female consumers were also active and ingenious citizens, fully capable of participation in the public sphere of politics.

Contentious politics, then, is shaped by and responds to the spatial routines of everyday life. But it is also true that contentious politics develops its own specific spatial routines with their own histories and trajectories. Charles Tilly coined the phrase *repertoires of contention* to refer to the historically changing array of means available to a given population for making contentious political claims (Tilly 1977, 1983, 1995; see also Tarrow 1994:2). A moment's reflection makes it clear that the routines composing these repertoires – whether the charivari, field invasion, grain seizure, and forced illumination of buildings common in the eighteenth century; or the strike, election rally, public meeting, and demonstration that became prominent in the nineteenth and twentieth; or the sit-in made famous by the American Civil Rights movement; or the barricade whose longue durée history has been sketched out by Mark Traugott (1995b); or the use of shop windows to publicize a political cause – are themselves *spatial* routines. They are, that is, known and transposable formulae for particular kinds of occupation and use of space. The question of how the spatial routines of contentious politics and the spatial routines of daily life are related – for example, how changes in spatial relations of work, leisure, or public ceremony affect and are affected by changing modes of protest – seems a particularly promising avenue of research.

Space and Meaning

Spaces are culturally marked as particular kinds of places. Places may be designated as private or public; they have different symbolic values as sacred, festive, banal, trendy, sedate, politically charged, dangerous, and so on. Spaces are gendered, raced, and classed. In San Francisco in 1911, downtown shops were regarded as feminine spaces and offices as masculine; when the term *South-Side man* is used in the Chicago press (as in "South-Side Man Slain in Shoot-Out"), the clear implication is that the man is black; in New York in the 1950s *Fifth Avenue* meant rich while *Bowery* meant destitute. In part, these differences in meaning correspond to real differences in the places' built environments, inhabitants, and activities. The South Side is in fact home to a disproportionate number of Chicago's African-Americans; most shoppers in downtown San Francisco were women. But the meanings of spaces are by no means simple reflections of the facts on the ground. In San Francisco in 1911, downtown shops were largely owned and staffed by men. Many North-Side Chicagoans are afraid to visit South-Side neighborhoods like Hyde Park or Beverly that are actually more middle-class and safer than their own, and trendy shops open in refurbished workers' cottages that line many North-Side streets while magnificent Victorian mansions are boarded-up ruins on the South Side. The meanings of place are socially constructed and therefore open to change; they are, in the words of Molotch, Freudenburg, and Paulsen, "accomplishments" (Molotch, Freudenburg, and Paulsen 1998). Real estate developers, who have seen artist colonies turn run-down neighborhoods like New York's SoHo, Chicago's River North, or San Francisco's South of Market into desirable gentrified loft districts, are only too aware of this fact.

The meanings of places are crucially important to contentious politics both as contexts and as stakes. Sometimes the normative meanings and uses of places are themselves a significant focus of social movement activity. One of the most important and most universally achieved goals of the

American Civil Rights movement was the desegregation of public accommodations – lunch counters, busses, beaches, drinking fountains, theaters, public washrooms, and the like. It was the sit-ins, swim-ins, bus boycotts, and freedom rides that challenged and eventually overturned the previously authoritative marking of certain spaces as white only. Similarly, the Take Back the Night marches by feminists and kiss-ins by Gay Rights activists also challenge the standard cultural marking of permissible or hegemonic uses of public spaces.

Protesters typically attempt to mount demonstrations or rallies in places with politically salient meanings. By occupying such locations as Tiananmen Square in Bejing or the Mall in Washington, D.C., protest marches and demonstrations not only gain the public limelight but make a particular sort of statement – that the cause they represent belongs at the top of the national agenda. But while insurgent movements make use of the preexisting meanings of places, they can also – either intentionally or unintentionally – transform the significance of protest locations. Sometimes places with no particular political associations gain such significance in the course of contentious actions. During the Free Speech Movement at Berkeley in the 1960s, Sproul Hall Plaza became a highly politicized gathering place where students could catch up on the latest turns of campus politics by listening to the harangues of student orators from the Sproul Hall steps. This meaning became so entrenched, that the University recently renamed these the "Mario Savio Steps" in honor of the most famous of those orators. Protest actions can also transform the significance of spaces that already have political meaning. The 1963 March on Washington gathered on the Mall in front of the Lincoln Memorial for the obvious symbolic reason that Lincoln had been the author of the Emancipation Proclamation. But the success of the March had the unintended consequence of changing the meaning of the Mall, of making it henceforth the preeminent site for national protest marches, beginning a long series of gigantic demonstrations ranging from marches against nuclear energy, to gay rights marches, to the Million Man March.

This example points out one of the most remarkable effects that protest activities can have on the meanings of places – their sacralization as sites of transcendent significance. In sacred spaces, actions take on an enhanced significance, in the eyes of the participants and witnesses alike. In these sacred places, participants' emotions are heightened, orators' tongues are loosened, and citizens dream impossible dreams. Sometimes, as in the case of the various demonstrations on the Mall, the sacred quality of the site seems to carry over from one event to the next. But in other cases, the site becomes highly contested – sometimes being desecrated or desacralized before it can be resacralized with a new significance. The hunger strikes and endless political discussion carried on by Chinese democracy activists in 1989 effectively de- and resacralized Tienanmen Square. Tienanmen was already a politically potent sacred place. During the Maoist period, it was a key point of contact between the Chinese "masses" and the Communist Party leadership, but the contact always took the form of carefully staged ceremonial acclamations of Party leaders by an anonymous crowd. By staging public fasts in this spot, the demonstrators were proclaiming that this supposed site of inspiring regeneration, of unity between the Party and the masses, was in fact a site of continuing fraud and, symbolically, a place of death. But while the hunger strikers were engaging in an act of desacralization, they were also resacralizing Tienanmen by staging their own public martyrdom. At the same time, the resacralization was given a positive content through the students' incessant and frenetic exercise of democratic freedoms, which were eventually symbolized by the famous statue of the Godess of Democracy. The square became a microcosm of the new order projected by the students, an inspiring site of political discussion, debate, and self-government, where the protesters acted out and lived with maximum intensity the form of democracy they envisaged for China as a whole (Calhoun 1994:188–89, 195–96). It was partly their astonishing success at changing the political meaning of Tienanmen that made the Chinese leaders willing to use deadly force against the demonstrators – effectively desacralizing it yet again. In the ten years since, the government has been wary of the square's sacred powers, making little use of the square for ceremonial purposes and turning it into an increasingly commercialized tourist destination.

Spatial Scale

Spatial processes are organized simultaneously at multiple scales, ranging from households and neighborhoods to states and the capitalist world system. Until fairly recently, geographers tended to think of scale as a matter of the level at which the analysis of spatial phenomena is carried out, much as scale on maps in an atlas may vary from $1:25,000,000$ for a map of the Eurasian landmass to $1:100,000$ for a map of Quebec City. But more recently, analysts have begun to insist that scale is also a produced quality of social relations itself (Brenner 1997; Lefebvre 1991 [1974];

Marston 2000; Smith 1992, 1993). Different social relations are carried on and constructed at different spatial scales. A business corporation controls the labor process within the bounds of a particular factory, recruits labor from an urban region, and may advertise and sell its products and obtain capital in national or global markets. But these scales are not fixed for all time. The business corporation may produce different scales by shifting the geographical range at which a given activity is carried out – by, for example, using a national-scale headhunter to recruit labor or tailor its advertising to particular local markets. Or a labor union may produce a new scale of industrial decision making by coordinating its collective bargaining campaigns over a larger and larger region – as the International Association of Longshoremen did on the Atlantic and Gulf coasts from the 1950s to the 1980s (Herod 1997).

Questions of scale figure prominently in social movements and revolutions. Local labor struggles in the contemporary United States must simultaneously engage the local scale where scabs must be prevented from strikebreaking, the national scale on which the National Labor Relations Board (NLRB) rules on the legitimacy of tactics, and the scale of international capitalism on which the company weighs the option of moving its production facilities to lower-cost labor markets in other countries. One of the means available to insurgents for transforming the spatial structures that face them is to engage in what Neil Smith calls jumping scales (Smith 1993; see also Adams 1996). Labor organizers operating at a power disadvantage in a particular workplace may get assistance from the national union or appeal to the NLRB to enjoin employers from using intimidating tactics. Of course, analogous moves may be made by the other side: Employers who are unable to change work-rules because of the power of a local union will use the threat of shifting production to nonunion locations in other states or countries as a means of gaining local leverage. Indigenous communities in Brazil, hopelessly overpowered by the superior power of settlers, the national army, international corporations, and a state apparatus controlled by urban interests may be able to call in international nongovernmental organizations, North American and European rock and film stars, and world media to block projects that would be detrimental to their way of life (Turner 1991). The Civil Rights Movement in the American South overcame its crushing local disadvantages partly by using media coverage to mobilize northern liberals who then pressured the federal government to intervene on behalf of southern Negroes (McAdam 1982). Although scale jumping is usually a matter of calling broader-scale forces into a local struggle, it can also work in the opposite direction, with national-scale forces seeking refuge from unequal struggles by retreating to a more local scale where their chances are much better. This is, for example, the classic strategy of guerrilla warfare.

The Spatiality of Power

Space is an object and a matrix of power. All power is, ultimately, power over people. One way of exercising control over people is by controlling the spaces where people live and work. The organization of power in the modern nation state is particularly space-based, or territorial, in character. The laws and administrative apparatus of the modern state are at least supposed to extend equally over the whole of the national territory; the territorial boundaries of the state are carefully mapped and marked; people or goods passing across the boundary must pass through immigration and customs checks; and the internal territory of the state is meticulously divided up into districts, provinces, states, or counties that have their own boundaries and jurisdictions. This is in marked contrast to a feudal polity, in which territorial boundaries were relatively fluid and power was exercised primarily through control over chains of vassalage, and in which jurisdictions were often based more on the status of the person than on territory – so that free men were judged by different courts than serfs and clergy by different courts than laymen. It was only in the aftermath of the democratic revolutions of the late eighteenth century that purely territorial jurisdiction became the universal rule even in such Western European countries as France, Britain, and the Netherlands.

Crucial to states' control over territory is policing – the surveillance of the activities of citizens and the use of coercion to enforce laws and maintain order. Not all state policing is carried out by police forces. The military, the tax authorities, and various branches of the bureaucracy also engage in policing in this sense. To be fully effective, the state's policing must cover the entire space of the territory. But there are also limits on the police powers of the state, limits both intrinsic and legal. Policing is intrinsically limited because the police are vastly outnumbered by the people whose activities they are supposed to monitor and control. Policing is legally limited by restrictions on access to certain spaces. Police can exercise their functions only within their territorial jurisdictions and entry to certain kinds of spaces is restricted or forbidden. For example, in many countries police officers must have a valid search warrant in order to enter a private dwelling. But it is not only states that engage in the policing of space – that is, in activities of surveillance and coercion. Both private firms and labor unions police the factory floor, youth gangs cruise their neighborhoods protecting their boundaries against incursions by gang members from other neighborhoods, and eighteenth century neighborhoods were kept under informal surveillance by gossiping shopkeepers and market women. This private policing ranges from highly formal to extremely informal in both its procedures and its punishments. Large corporations employ armies of supervisors who enforce an elaborate code, while neighborhood gossip networks depend on volunteered time and punish by means of slander and ostracism.

Safe spaces of one kind or another are a sine qua non of social movements.[6] Oppositional movements need to control spaces in order to organize their activities and to recruit activists without being subject to crippling surveillance and repression by the state (or by landlords, employers, or other dominating groups or agencies). In the case of legally tolerated social movements in liberal states (for example, Mothers Against Drunk Driving, the Sierra Club, or the United Auto Workers) most of an organization's business can be conducted in public – even state-policed space is safe for them. Nevertheless, when the UAW attempts to organize a new workplace it needs significant sheltering against management surveillance and coercion – although the state may be liberal, workers still check many of their civil liberties at the factory gate. And when the state is repressive and hostile – as in the American South during the Civil Rights Movement, in Korea during the students' prodemocracy movement of 1987, in silk-weaving neighborhoods of Lyon during the revolt of the canuts in the 1830s – the very survival of the movement depends on the creation or appropriation of safe spaces.

The nature of the safe spaces varies enormously from case to case. The reasons why they are safe often involve either intrinsic limits of police power (the impenetrability of insurgent networks) and/or legal or customary limits on repression. The segregated character of religious institutions and America's strong tradition of noninterference in religious affairs made Black churches effective sanctuaries for Civil Rights activities that eventually overthrew the segregationist order in the American South (McAdam 1982; Morris 1984). Radical republicans in rural Provence during the Second Republic were able to operate beyond the reach of the

---

[6] Again, I owe this point to Charles Tilly.

state authorities partly by penetrating the traditionally private social clubs or *chambrées* that met in the back rooms of cafes, thereby taking advantage of socially enforced conventions about privacy (Agulhon 1970). The age-segregated character of university life and the partial autonomy of universities from state surveillance and repression made it possible for Korean students to sustain a radical movement under a harsh dictatorship and to provide the crucial leadership for an urban uprising that led to democratic reform in 1987. The extraordinary concentration of silk weavers in the Croix-Rousse quarter of Lyon and the weavers' strong tradition of tolerating quasicorporate organization enabled the canuts to launch an epoch-making workers revolt in 1831 and to rise again in response to repressive legislation in 1834 (Bezucha 1974). These examples all involve insurgent control over particular localities within the formal jurisdiction of state authorities. But it is also sometimes possible for insurgents to make use of spaces on scales wider than those controlled by the authorities they are opposing. Thus the Freedom Summer civil rights campaign of 1964 was organized largely at universities outside the South and the prodemocracy demonstrators in Tiananmen Square in the spring of 1989 made use of a safe hyperspace of fax and email networks to get out news and coordinate international support (Adams 1996; Calhoun 1994:204; McAdam 1988).

Once an insurgent movement is up and running, authorities are likely to respond by attempting to gain or regain control of the insurgents' safe spaces by such means as increasing police presence, attempting to change or bend legal rules that impede the police, using paid informers, reorganizing jurisdictions, making use of private antiinsurgent citizen's groups to gather information or intimidate rebels, or declaring martial law. Meanwhile, the insurgents will attempt both to defend spaces they already control and to extend their control to additional spaces. The struggles between challengers and authorities that are so ubiquitous a feature of contentious politics are to a very considerable degree struggles over the control of space, and they frequently have the effect of transforming spatial structures.

Contentious Politics and the Spatialities of Power: Two Examples

In the previous section, I have used a number of examples in an attempt to demonstrate that a self-conscious theoretical vocabulary might illuminate the role of space in contentious politics. But thus far the examples have been very brief and no more than suggestive. In this concluding section of the chapter, I shall attempt to demonstrate the value of spatial analysis by looking more systematically and in somewhat greater detail at the spatial dimensions of two important moments of contentious politics: the Beijing students' prodemocracy movement in 1989 and the French Revolution of 1789–94. One value of these two extended examples is that they illustrate with some clarity both the importance of spatial structure in shaping protest and the significance of spatial agency in reshaping structure.

The Spatial Ecology of Student Insurgency in Beijing: April 27, 1989

The Beijing students' prodemocracy movement in the spring of 1989 was one of the most astonishing developments of that astonishing year – although the denouement of the movement, the army's assault on the demonstrators massed in Tiananmen Square, had more in common with the Soviet troops' tragic suppression of the Prague Spring of 1968 than with Prague's "Velvet Revolution" of 1989. Dingxin Zhao has recently published an analysis of one of the most important episodes of the student democracy movement, the demonstration of April 27, 1989 (Zhao 1998). Zhao argues that questions of space were of crucial importance in this event, which was unquestionably a turning point in the student movement (see, for example, Calhoun 1994:49–54).

The student movement arose in a time of widespread prodemocracy dissent among Chinese intellectuals, but it was the death of Hu Yaobang on April 15 that launched collective protests. Hu was a former head of the Communist Party who had been demoted in 1987 when he failed to suppress by force a previous student movement. He was regarded by dissidents as the most sympathetic to democracy and western ideas of the current Chinese leadership. In the days following April 15, students marched in mourning for Hu and made speeches and put up posters contrasting Hu's integrity with the hypocrisy of the remaining leadership. The protests mounted daily and met little government opposition until April 26, when a harsh editorial in the *People's Daily* denounced the students as attempting to undermine the government and forbade further demonstrations. The students responded by staging a gigantic march on April 27 that swept through several police lines and continued on to Tiananmen Square. The April 27 demonstration was a huge victory for the students. In the words of Craig Calhoun, it was "a transformative experience for those who participated," one that reshaped "people's ideas about themselves and about what was possible" (Calhoun 1994:52). Without the victory on April 27, the better-known events at Tiananmen a few weeks later would have been unthinkable.

Zhao closely examines the "ecology" of the student movement that made the victory of April 27 possible, particularly emphasizing the importance of the built environment. Nearly all of Bejing's sixty-seven universities, he points out, are clustered in the Haidan district, about eight miles to the northwest of Tiananmen. The campuses are generally separated from the surrounding neighborhoods by brick walls, and contain not only dormitories, classrooms, libraries, laboratories, and faculty offices, but also dining halls, a cinema, barber shops, a hospital, grocery stores, and recreational facilities. They are "so self-contained that hard-working students can live on campus for a whole semester without going outside once" (Zhao 1998:1502). Undergraduate students live six to eight in a dormitory room and dormitory social life is very intense. The institutional autonomy of the universities, combined with their physical separation from surrounding neighborhoods, made it possible – given the right political circumstances – for them to be made into safe spaces for the development of dissident ideas and the organization of contentious political action. The densely networked and self-contained character of campus social life also made for quick communication of ideas and for very strong pressures to conform with majority sentiments. This ecological condition may have fostered political conformity during the Maoist period, when it made surveillance by informers particularly easy, but it enhanced dissidence in 1989. During the student movement, waverers tended either to fall in line with the majority or were ostracized (Zhao 1998:1506–07). At the same time, the close proximity between campuses meant that ideas and information could pass quickly from one university to another.

The built environment of Beijing universities affected student mobilization partly by shaping what sociologists would call social networks. The layout of the campus and the structure of dormitories was a crucial condition for the establishment of dense social ties within each university's student body – ties that could then be mobilized in the prodemocracy movement. But, as Zhao points out (1998:1508–12), the spatial ecology of the universities also influenced the student democracy movement in ways that escape the conceptual equipment of social network analysis, which assumes that actors are linked by relatively enduring and stable social relations that serve as conduits for the exchange of privileged information and resources (Laumann and Pappi 1976). Much of the communication that

72

was crucial to the success of the student democracy movement was based more on copresence in public spaces than on diffusion through pre-established social networks. For example, activists at Beijing University capitalized on students' ordinary spatial routines – and developed new politicized spatial routines that constructed an activist student spatial culture. They would recruit participants for demonstrations by putting up posters at "the Triangle," a centrally located area through which nearly all students on that particular campus would pass in the course of a day. The posters would announce a time and an on-campus meeting place. Once a group of students had assembled at the announced place, the demon-strators would march back and forth through the dormitory area chanting slogans. This would attract more students from the dormitories, eventu-ally swelling the crowd to the point that the leaders felt ready to go out onto the streets (Zhao 1998:1508–09). This common scenario for recruit-ing demonstrators can be described better by a vocabulary of spatial analy-sis than by a network vocabulary. The organizers of the demonstrations took advantage of students' ordinary spatial routines by placing posters in the Triangle. They recruited more students by taking advantage of the tightly clustered built environment of the dormitory area, using the fact of spatial copresence to lure students into the demonstration. And the massing of bodies into a marching column that loudly chanted slogans created a collective effervescence – a nearly irresistible sense of excitement that attracted waverers into the march. It was the physical proximities of the campus and the powerful emotional effects of public spatial massing, not just the operation of space-based social networks, that swelled the demonstrations to their enormous size.

Zhao's analysis of the April 27 demonstrations has equally interesting things to say about the spatial relations between universities within the Haidan district. The demonstration of April 27 was potentially an excep-tionally dangerous affair. The *People's Daily* editorial had declared that the student dissidents were unpatriotic and had forbidden further demonstra-tions – with the clear implication that demonstrators would be dealt with very harshly. The editorial was greeted with outrage on the campuses and the autonomous student unions decided to stage a protest on April 27. But students who decided to participate did so in spite of palpable fear. A number of them went so far as to write wills in anticipation of their deaths (Calhoun 1994:50–51). The problem facing the students on April 27 was how to make a public demonstration of their outrage without precipitat-ing a bloodbath. This was a strategic conundrum at two levels. First, within each university, the crucial task was to get very widespread participation – in a dangerous situation like this, there was considerable comfort in numbers. Second, once a given university had achieved a high level of mobilization, the key problem was to assure that students on other campuses were equally willing to put their bodies on the line.

Within universities, the mobilization took place according to the means discussed above – wall posters, speeches in the "Triangle" (or in the comparable public meeting ground on other campuses), intense discussions and the exertion of social pressure in the dormitory rooms, and marches within the confines of the campus until a sufficiently large contingent had joined. On the campus of People's University, a sizable group of students gathered but hesitated to march outside the campus and began by filing around the campus itself. After five or six tours of the campus, the demonstration grew large and excited and finally broke out onto the streets. Although the presumed destination of the march was Tiananmen Square, the People's University students headed off in the opposite direction, avoiding a police line, hoping to meet up with students from Beijing University and Qinghua University who would swell the demonstration's numbers. They were preceded by "liaison men" – who constitute a fascinating case of spatial agency specific to the Bejing student movement of 1989. The liaison men were students on bicycles who, over the course of the crisis, had become unofficial interuniversity political couriers. On April 27, the liaison men at People's University rushed to adjacent universities and announced that People's University had come out (Zhao 1998: 1514–15). Analogous scenarios were played out on other campuses, with excited but anxious demonstrators from each hesitating to come out of the campus gates and to face the police lines that barred the way to Tiananmen; hoping, once they took the plunge, to join forces with demonstrators from other universities; and with liaison men rushing back and forth providing informal coordination. Before long there were thousands of students in the streets, pressing on police lines all over the district, sometimes from both sides simultaneously. The police, who turned out to be unarmed, could offer only token resistance and were repeatedly swept aside. Contingents from all over the Haidan district gradually merged into one vast column at least a hundred thousand strong and marched triumphantly to Tiananmen Square. They had achieved the first great victory of the democracy movement (Calhoun 1994:51–52; Zhao 1998:1515–18).

The key to the success of the April 27 demonstration was the complex and fluid interaction of groups of demonstrators from different universities. Once the students on a given campus had amassed sufficient numbers and worked up enough courage to go out into the streets, they still faced a serious collective action problem. By itself, the contingent of any single university was extremely vulnerable to repression – and was keenly aware of this vulnerability. But every university's contingent was also aware that it was in close proximity to dozens of other universities. Each of these constituted a safe space in which the students of other universities knew that a parallel process of mobilization might well be going on. But none knew for sure exactly which universities would turn out, or in what numbers, or how they would act when they confronted police lines. It was once again a feature of the built environment – the close physical clustering of universities in a single district – that made it possible for the disparate groups of students to sound out each others' intentions. But this, of course, was only a condition of possibility for coordination. It was the spatial practices developed over the past weeks of intense political activity that rendered coordination practicable in this moment of crisis. Thus the contingents of students marched off in search of one another once they entered the streets – guided by the information provided by the liaison men and buoyed by the knowledge gained over the previous weeks of struggle that students from other universities must be engaged in a similar search. The initial fear turned to confidence and then to exhilaration as contingents of different universities met up, swept past police lines, merged with yet more contingents of demonstrators, and surged on to Tiananmen. Any adequate understanding of the particular course and the ultimate success of the April 27 demonstration requires a spatial analysis. The immense massing of bodies and the tremendous collective effervescence that ensued was dependent on the particular built environment of the Haidan district and on the innovative practices of spatial agency, both preexisting and improvised in the heat of the moment, that made coordination of distinct university groupings possible.

Paris and the Politics of Space in the French Revolution

Zhao's spatial analysis of the Beijing student's demonstration concentrates on a relatively restricted scale – the ecology of a particular urban district, of campuses within that district, and of particular spaces such as "the Triangle" or dormitories within the campuses. It also treats a brief period of time, the few days leading up to and including April 27. Finally, it deals mainly with strategic questions – about how the built environment and specific spatial practices both enabled and constrained student mobilization in April 1989. Finally, these practices were components of a movement that ultimately was unsuccessful – although it grew to immense proportions and effectively challenged existing forms of politics in China by late May, it was brutally crushed in early June. For this reason, the structural transformations of spatiality effectuated by the student movement, however significant in their context, proved ephemeral. The second example of spatial analysis I shall present in this chapter differs in a number of respects. First, it is concerned with a much wider scale: The key question it attempts to answer is why French national politics were so dominated by the local politics of Paris during the heroic years of the French Revolution, 1789 to 1794. Second, although questions of strategy certainly figure significantly in the analysis, the central issues concern the meanings or imagination of space no less than its strategic uses. Finally it treats a much more enduring set of spatial transformations. The analysis covers a period of five years, and the phenomenon of Parisian revolutionary primacy remained an issue for nearly two centuries, at least through the Parisian "events of May and June" in 1968.

Although France was formally governed during the 1789–1794 period by a nationwide representative democracy, its fate was repeatedly decided not by majority votes of the legislature, but by violent action in the streets of Paris. Pick up virtually any history of the French Revolution and you will find that much of the narrative hinges on a series of Parisian revolutionary "journées" (days) that drove the revolution farther and farther to the left – the taking of the Bastille on July 14 and the October Days in 1789, the Champs de Mars Massacre in July 1791; the Revolution of August 10 and the September Massacres in 1792; and the insurrections of May 31–June 2 and September 4–5, 1793 that purged the Girondins from the National Convention and led to the so-called "economic terror."[7] It was only after the execution of Robespierre in Thermidor of the Year III (July 1794), that the opinions of the great majority of Frenchmen who lived outside Paris – or at least of their elected representatives – began to predominate definitively over the actions of the Parisian crowd in decid-

[7] The best general account of these journées remains Rudé (1959). Even if one agrees with François Furet (1981 [1978]) and like-minded "revisionists" that the movement from a liberal revolution in 1789 to the Terror in 1793–1794 was semiotically inscribed in revolutionary ideology from the beginning, it must be admitted that it was the political striking power of the Parisian crowd that made possible the realization of this semiotic potential.

ing the affairs of the state. Historians have come to take this sustained domination of political life by the populace of the capital for granted. Yet this experience was uncharacteristic of the history of revolutions elsewhere in the world, and it was even uncharacteristic of subsequent French history. In 1830, 1848, and 1870, the people of the French capital once again took center stage and overthrew the existing regime. But in all three of these later revolutions, it took only a few weeks or months, not five years, for the Parisian populace to lose its predominant influence in the state. There clearly was a powerful and very specific spatial chemistry at work in the French Revolution.

At the time of the French Revolution, Paris was a very large city of about a half million inhabitants. Among European cities, only London was more populous. It was the nation's center for finance, law, intellectual life, the arts, publishing, fashion, and luxury industries. It had always been the political capital as well, until Louis XIV moved the court to the distant Parisian suburb of Versailles in the late seventeenth century – in part to sequester the royal government from the rebellious potential of the Parisian crowd, whose activities had terrified the young king during the Fronde uprising in the 1650s. But Paris still functioned as a kind of co-capital in the eighteenth century and its crowds remained riotous. In short, the city had the necessary ingredients for a radical and dynamic politics once the revolution got under way: a very high population density; a large number of skilled artisans who combined class-based economic and social grievances with strong organizational resources; hundreds of writers and publicists capable of becoming political journalists and orators; and a long-standing tradition of popular political unrest. It is therefore hardly surprising that Paris developed a vigorous revolutionary movement in the years following 1789.[8] What is surprising is that Parisian politics so dominated the policies of the national government in these years.

Paris's dominance of the national agenda was especially puzzling because in many respects it ran counter to the revolution's dominant ideological thrust. In their new "regenerated" political order, the revolutionaries wished to overcome the twin afflictions of despotism and aristocracy and to replace them with the countervailing principles of popular sovereignty and equality. Because this regeneration was intended as a transformation of the French state and society as a whole, it should not be surprising that it had important spatial dimensions. Under the old regime,

---

[8] For an overlapping argument see Traugott (1995a).

places, no less than people, were profoundly unequal. Different provinces or cities had different laws, fiscal obligations, forms of government, and relations to the monarch. The revolutionaries attempted to annihilate this spatial inequality by abolishing the provinces, canceling the particular privileges of cities, and elaborating a new spatial partitioning of the national territory. The old royal provinces were replaced by new "departments," which were made as equal to each other as possible in area and population. To mark the departure from the old system, the names assigned to these departments were without historical reference and were instead referenced features of the natural landscape – the High Alps, the Mouths of the Rhone, the Lower Loire, or Land's End. Each of these departments was to constitute a political and administrative unit of the nation. Under the constitution of 1791, they were endowed with legislative bodies and broad authority over local affairs – as were the "cantons" and "communes" into which they were subdivided (Ozouf-Marignier 1989). The goal of this legislation was what one might call isotopic – an attempt to make every place in France politically and morally equivalent to every other place (Sewell forthcoming).[9] That Paris became a kind of privileged political space, with powers and responsibilities effectively denied to other places, was not foreseen or intended by the revolutionary legislatures. If Paris came to dominate French political affairs, this was in spite of, not because of, the ideological intentions of the revolutionary leaders. Parisian political privilege in the revolutionary era must be understood as a specific product of popular revolutionary agency.

That such agency was possible at all depended on certain preexisting structures of copresence and time-distance. Parisians had one huge advantage over French people living elsewhere: They enjoyed physical

---

[9] I owe the term and concept of *isotopism* to Mona Ozouf (1988 [1976]), who uses it in the very different context of revolutionary festivals. She notes that officials preferred to hold their public celebrations in vast open spaces that lacked or had been stripped of previous historical meanings. Even sites where notable revolutionary triumphs had taken place were generally avoided – except the place de la Bastille, which, once it the Bastille fortress was demolished, was itself a vast and featureless open space. The urban places in which festivals were staged were invariably bedecked with foliage, in an attempt to restore them to a sort of state of nature. The ritual activities at the center of the festivals were performed in the open air under the natural canopy of the sky, and the spectators, who were arranged so as to be able to see one another at a glance, were to experience a sense of perfect equality with their fellow citizens. That a parallel urge to isotopia was manifested in activities so different as the redrawing of internal boundaries of the state and the planning of festivals makes one suspect that both were manifestations of a deep structure of revolutionary ideology.

proximity to the institutions and personnel of government – to the king and his court, the legislatures, and the ministries. This meant that it was possible for crowds of common people to exercise intimidation, subtle and overt, over governmental agents. Crowds could cheer their champions, mill about menacingly, or, on extreme occasions, use armed force against the king, the army, the police, or the legislature. In addition to acts of intimidation, the Parisians did much to set the tone and the issues of political debate. Legislators and government officials lived in Paris and were necessarily influenced by the intense political life of a city awash in clubs, newspapers, pamphlets, and oratory. This spatial proximity of Parisians to their governors was far more important under the technological conditions of the late eighteenth century than it was in the later nineteenth century or would be today, when modern means of communication and transportation, starting with the railway and the telegraph, made legislators and government officials less dependent on strictly local sources of information and more able to call on either opinion or armed force from the provinces to counter the local Parisian balance of political forces.

But if the physical proximity of the Parisians to their governors was a necessary condition for their exercise of extraordinary power over the state, it was far from a sufficient condition. Political leaders before and after the French Revolution, both in France and elsewhere, found means of overcoming the spatial advantage enjoyed by citizens of the capital – means that included and often combined bread and circuses, state co-optation of crucial urban classes, and the threat of deadly force. The political preeminence of the Parisian people during the revolution required both a forbearance on the part of the state about using deadly force and a certain complicity between the people and at least a portion of the governmental authorities. It was, in fact, only because the governing authorities and the dominant political culture recognized insurrectionary actions of the Parisian people as having a certain ambiguous legitimacy that the Parisians were able to maintain their domination of national politics.

The Parisian people's claim to legitimacy had its origins in the taking of the Bastille, on July 14, 1789. The taking of the Bastille was an important political turning point because it gave popular forces control of Paris and assured the victory of the National Assembly in its ongoing struggle with the king. But the successful assault on the ancient fortress also had truly epochal effects on the fundamental assumptions that underlay French politics. It gave rise to the modern conception of revolution – as a legitimate rising of the sovereign people that transforms the constitutional basis of the state. The Assembly in effect sanctioned the legitimacy of its own triumph over the king in July 1789 by recognizing the crowd violence at the Bastille as a sovereign act of "the people," whose will, according to the Assembly's own political doctrines, was supposed to be the foundation of all legal authority.[10] By doing so, the Assembly effectively sacralized the people of Paris as capable of representing and enacting, in cases of extreme crisis, the will of the nation as a whole. In short, the new revolutionary regime was founded upon an implicit bargain between the Parisian crowd, which was effectively recognized as the emergency arm of the sovereign nation, and the elected representatives of the people in the National Assembly, which gained political supremacy thanks to the Parisian insurrection. This implicit bargain, which singled out the Parisian people and gave them a special role in the nation's politics, was ambiguous, dangerous, and unstable; although the doctrine of legitimate revolution was the foundation of the National Assembly's ascendancy, it also had the potential to nullify, by means of future insurrections, the power of an elected representative body.

This ambiguous bargain was renewed and revised periodically by further Parisian insurrections. The first, and one of the most significant from the point of view of the spatial story I am recounting here, was the "October Days" of 1789 (Lefebvre 1947 [1939]). On this occasion a column of National Guardsmen from Paris, accompanied by a crowd of common people among whom market women were particularly prominent, marched from Paris to Versailles. They were protesting a rumored royal desecration of the tricolor cocarde, which had become a key symbol of the revolution, and demanding an increase in supplies of grain to Paris. While they were in Versailles, skirmishes broke out between the crowd and the royal guards, and in the aftermath the crowd and the National Guard forced the Royal Family to return with them to Paris. The National Assembly acquiesced in the transfer and followed a few days later. This event had the effect of moving the seat of government from Versailles back to Paris, where, of course, it would be under the close daily scrutiny of the Parisian people. By means of this crucial act of spatial politics, the Parisians assured their continuing influence over the state and fortified their effective power-sharing bargain with the National Assembly.

[10] See the McAdam and Sewell chapter in this volume for a fuller exposition of this process. A more extended discussion is in Sewell (1996a).

Over the next several years, the Parisian people renewed their claim to emergency sovereignty in countless demonstrations and three successful insurrections. The most significant of these was the Revolution of August 10, 1792. This insurrection overthrew both the king and the Legislative Assembly, which had been elected under the limited monarchical constitution ratified by the National Assembly in 1791. This led to the declaration of a republic, the trial and execution of the king and queen, and the election of a new National Convention charged with writing a republican constitution and serving as interim legislature. The period from August 1792 to July 1994, when Robespierre and his closest collaborators were overthrown and executed, was the most turbulent of the Revolution and was the heyday of the Parisian popular movement. During this period there were numerous acts of popular violence, countless demonstrations, and two events that were regarded by contemporaries as insurrections – one that took place from May 31 through June 2, 1793, and resulted in the purging of the moderate Girondin faction from the Convention, and another that took place on September 4–5 of the same year and led to the imposition of price controls on basic necessities.

During the two years following the Revolution of August 10, 1792, Paris was subjected to a very particular spatialization of power. By means of what has since become known as the sans-culotte movement, the "Parisian people" increasingly became an organized and quasiinstitutionalized political force capable of exerting control over the entire space of the city. There were, of course political clubs and newspapers, of which the Cordelliers Club and *Le Père Duchesne* were the most celebrated. But the crucial institution was the "sections" – the forty-eight wards into which the city was divided. Each section was governed by an assembly of all adult male citizens that was charged with overseeing the application of revolutionary legislation in its neighborhood. The sectional assemblies maintained political surveillance over residents and issued or denied certificates of civic virtue, oversaw the operation of wartime requisitions, and examined the conduct of state employees. Originally constituted as electoral assemblies, they had by 1792 become de facto administrative and political bodies, jealous of their autonomy and engaged in a direct application of popular sovereignty to local affairs (Soboul 1964:106–27). During this period, the policing of space in Paris was in large part ceded to the popularly controlled sections. The sections also discussed and made declarations on national issues of all sorts, constantly sending petitions, statements, and delegations to the municipality and the Convention. Although open to all citizens, they were in fact dominated by a minority of leftist political militants, who alone found time to attend them on a daily basis. The sectional assemblies coordinated their initiatives and their policing efforts with other sections, constantly sending each other correspondence and delegations. A fascinating spatial strategy of the sectional movement was what was known as "fraternization." If a section deemed its neighboring section to be falling into the hands of "moderates," it would engage in the ritual of "fraternization" – visiting the offending section's meeting hall en masse, expelling the moderates, embracing and exchanging fraternal kisses with the remaining sectionnaires, and then holding deliberations in common. By this means the leftist sectional militants effectively managed to extend their political control even to relatively conservative areas of the city (Slavin 1986:23–46; Soboul 1964:153–95).

Virtually all of the mass demonstrations of this period emerged from the sections, and it was the sections that mobilized the mass of insurrectionaries who imposed their will on the Convention in May–June and September. The insurrection was a highly elaborated spatial routine. One after another, the sections would declare themselves "in insurrection," sending delegations carrying this declaration to other sections. They would then march into the street carrying pikes and muskets, often to the sound of the tocsin – the great bell of the local church, which was rung repeatedly whenever a general alarm was necessary. Ringing the tocsin was a specific spatial strategy that immediately communicated the imminence of insurrection to all within earshot and called the would-be insurrectionaries, as well as the merely curious, into the streets. The insurrectionaries would then converge on the Place de Grève in front of the city hall – a destination consecrated by its key role in the taking of the Bastille in 1789. By 1793 it was routine to gather there, obtain the support of the generally compliant Paris Commune (the municipal government), and only then march on the Convention. In this period of sans-culotte dominance of Parisian political life, to engage in insurrection did not necessarily mean using violence against existing authorities. To enter into a state of insurrection was to make it manifest that "the people" (represented synechdochically by the people of Paris) was resuming its sovereign power. The armed Parisians would march into the Convention, declare "the people's will," and fill the galleries and the streets outside while the members of the Convention debated the measures the people had proposed. In September 1793 the Convention complied without any insurrectionary violence, and in May–June 1793 the violence was very limited. In neither case was there anything like the bloodshed that had accompanied the taking of the Bastille or the Revolution of August 10 (Rudé 1959; Soboul 1962:165–75; Soboul 1964:129–34). By this time both the Parisian militants and their radical Jacobin allies in the Convention knew the routine well enough to make it work without significant loss of life.

As the preceding paragraphs make clear, Parisian political dominance was based on a number of Paris-specific conditions – the copresence of Parisians and legislators in the city, the marking of Paris as a whole and of particular locations within Paris as politically sacred spaces, the ceding of significant police power to the sections (which made their meeting halls the ultimate safe spaces), the evolution of specific insurrectionary spatial routines, and an effective alliance between the popular militants – who could control the local Parisian political scale – and radical Jacobin deputies who aimed to control the national political scale. But the dominance of Parisian political initiatives over the rest of the country was also constructed outside of Paris, or in the relations between Paris and the provinces.

One of the most significant accomplishments of the French Revolution was the construction of a new *national* political scale – a set of institutions and a political culture that would give substance to the statement that "the principle of all sovereignty rests essentially in the nation," to quote article three of the Declaration of the Rights of Man and Citizen. The Declaration and the various revolutionary constitutions that followed it meant to establish the sovereignty of the nation by election of representatives to a national legislative body, which would, of course, meet in the capital. But the making of national politics also meant the elaboration of uniform national administrative and political institutions; the development of a sphere of public debate and opinion in which persons from all areas of France might be heard; and the development of a sense of loyalty to the *nation* of France as what Benedict Anderson (1991) calls an "imagined community" – that is, a sense that citizens of France everywhere shared a common destiny and a felt powerful bond of loyalty. In a country of great geographical scope and regional diversity that had long been used to passive, if sometimes grudging, obedience to an absolute monarch, the construction of a national scale of political action and imagination was a major achievement.

But if the new national scale of politics was built on a presumption of equality, it is also true that the sudden and revolutionary character of the break with the old regime and the concentration of the most dramatic actions in Paris tended to reinscribe within the structure of politics a certain hierarchy – with the people of the capital generally taking the initiative and the people of the provinces responding. The pattern of Parisian initiative began with the taking of the Bastille, which sparked off a wave of local uprisings, some peaceful and some violent, in cities all over France. This widespread movement, which Lefebvre dubbed "the municipal revolution," put new "patriot" municipalities in place virtually everywhere and helped to guarantee the success of the Parisian insurrection of July 1789 (Lefebvre 1947 [1939]). In the days following July 14, these new municipalities flooded the National Assembly with declarations praising the heroism of the Parisian people and pledging adherence to the cause of the National Assembly. By means of the municipal revolutions, provincial cities at once demonstrated their solidarity with Paris and recognized Paris's revolutionary primacy in the creation of the French nation.

This primacy was extended and elaborated in part by contentious political movements. One of the prime agents was the Jacobin club. (See Furet 1989; Gueniffey and Halévy 1989; Kennedy 1982.) Originally formed in Versailles by the "patriotic" Bretton delegation to the National Assembly in the summer of 1789 as a forum for discussing issues facing the Assembly, it was soon joined by patriot deputies from other provinces. After the October days, it took over the abandoned Jacobin monastery in Paris as its meeting place (whence its name), accepted nondeputies as members, and became the most prestigious and influential of the many political clubs that formed in the capital. The Parisian Jacobins soon began to accept provincial clubs as affiliates. The provincial clubs adopted constitutions modeled on that of the Parisian society and were integrated into a Paris-centered network. In addition to an endless flow of correspondence and circulars, the deliberations of the Paris Jacobins were printed and distributed to the provinces both by the private press and by the Jacobins' own journal. The provincial clubs took an active role in local politics, where they exerted continuing pressure on municipal and departmental officials, and they supported the Paris Jacobins' efforts on the national level. The local Jacobin societies systematically employed strategies of scale-jumping. If they were relatively weak in the purely local balance of forces, they could call on the extra-local Jacobin network for support – for moral encouragement, for effective revolutionary rhetoric, for strategic advice, and in some cases for coercion from the National Guard units of a nearby Jacobin-controlled town. By this means local rivalries of all sorts were overlain – and frequently restructured – by being recast in terms of national political issues. In this way and in many others, the country-wide network of concerted opinion and civic activism constituted by the Jacobin societies was probably as central to the creation of a national scale of politics as was the organization of national elections.

In the wake of the taking of the Bastille and the victory of the National Assembly, provincial civic enthusiasm was spontaneous – and was spontaneously pro-Parisian. What the Parisian Jacobin Club did was to harness these spontaneous tendencies and fashion them into a durable Paris-centered political machine. Although a huge volume of petitions and declarations converged on Paris from the provinces in response to the circulars sent out by the Parisian society, the provincial societies in fact had little influence on the positions taken in Paris. The Correspondence Committee, always the most important of the Parisian society's committees, would write circulars calculated to generate support for their chosen positions and then used the "fabricated" support of the affiliates to impose their views on the "sometimes reluctant" general assembly of the Parisian club (Gueniffey and Halévy 1989:465). It was largely by means of its assiduous cultivation of relations with the affiliate societies that the militant minority of the Paris club survived a walkout and the formation of a rival "Feuillant" society by the majority in 1791 and went on to orchestrate the insurrection that deposed the king and established a republic in the following year.

In 1792 and 1793, the Paris Jacobin Club became the node of an alliance between the Parisian sectional movement and the leftist Montagnard faction of the Convention. It was deeply involved in the insurrection of May 31–June 2 and instrumental in the establishment of the Terror. Robespierre dominated politics from the Jacobin Club as much as from the Convention and the Committee of Public Safety. The relationship between the Parisian society and the affiliates remained strong during this period, but it changed fundamentally in character. Increasingly, the provincial societies became instruments of the Paris-organized "emergency government." The emergency government, which was run by a dictatorship of the Committee of Public Safety, dispatched trusted members of the Convention – the so-called "representatives on mission" – to the provinces and granted them extraordinary powers. These representatives on mission used the local Jacobin Clubs – appropriately purged, if necessary – as their local cadres in carrying out the Committee's orders. This improvised dictatorship succeeded against extraordinary odds. The French government was involved in desperate warfare against the leagued monarchies, compounded by bloody civil war in the Vendée and massive popular revolts in Marseille, Lyon, and Bordeaux, the three largest cities outside Paris. And while the survival of the revolution owed a great deal to the cooperation of the local Jacobins, their claim to independence and their standing in their own communities was in fact fatally compromised in this period. The Jacobins' ability to dominate the political scene both in Paris and in the provinces could not survive the downfall of Robespierre, although the national scale of political action and debate that the Jacobins helped create remained a permanent feature of French political life.

The Terror broke the spell of Parisian domination of French politics in three distinct ways. First, the general revulsion against the indiscriminate slaughter caused by the Terror undermined the overall legitimacy of the Parisian popular movement, which had been the most ardent advocate of a policy of terror in 1792 and 1793. Second, the symbiotic relationship between the Jacobins and the sans-culottes soured in the course of 1794 – a victim of the inevitable relaxation that followed the revolution's decisive victories over its foreign and domestic enemies and, according to Soboul, of the suffocation of sectional autonomy and initiative that resulted from Jacobin centralization (Soboul 1964). And third, the clear subordination of the provincial Jacobin Clubs to the Robespierrist representatives on mission not only destroyed the clubs' popularity but also had the effect of making provincials far more wary than before of Parisian domination. Complaints about Parisian dictation to provincial centers were actually a central issue in the so-called "Federalist" urban rebellions in the late spring and summer of 1793 – in Caen, Marseille, Toulon, Lyon, and Bordeaux. Although the central authorities eventually put down all these uprisings, the very fact of widespread resentment of Parisian supremacy indicates that the spell created by the taking of the Bastille and reproduced by a string of insurrections had at last broken. From the Spring of 1793 on, Parisian dominance was more a matter of military coercion than of legitimacy, and once the coercive apparatus had been disassembled, automatic provincial deference to the capital disappeared.

Yet if the myth of the Parisian people's special mission was in eclipse after 1794, it had not altogether perished. There were two unsuccessful attempts at Parisian insurrections in the next few years – the Prairial rising in 1795 and Babeuf's "Conspiracy of the Equals" in 1796. The more efficient and cold-blooded repressive apparatus assembled by Napoleon and copied by the Restoration rulers managed to hold off further insurrectionary attempts until the late 1820s, although such apostles of revolution as the Carbonari kept the tradition alive. Over the next few decades, attempted insurrections in the capital came thick and fast: 1827, 1830, 1832, 1834, 1839, three in 1848, and one each in 1849, 1851, 1870, and 1871 (Traugott 1995a). Only three of these – the insurrections of 1830, of February 1848, and of 1870 – actually toppled regimes and even in these cases the dominance of the national agenda by the Parisian popular movement was only fleeting. Yet the continuing series of attempts to recreate the heroic era of 1789 to 1794 indicates how deeply French political culture was imprinted by the spatial politics of the revolutionary era. For several decades – indeed, arguably as recently as the events of May and June of 1968 – the myth of Paris's sovereign destiny lingered on long after the specific spatial chemistry of the Revolutionary political conjuncture had disappeared. I would argue that that myth and the spatial imagination it embodies have been constitutive of the distinctive French sense of national identity.

This is only a rapid and incomplete sketch of what might be called the spatial dynamics of the French Revolution. But I think it is enough to suggest that questions of space – and spatial questions at many different levels – are crucial in making sense not only of relatively limited social movements but also of the vast social and political transformations we call revolutions. Indeed, the question of revolutionary spatial dynamics seems to me a major, fascinating, and virtually unexplored question for the comparative study of revolutions. That revolutions vary enormously in their spatial dynamics can be seen by even the most cursory glance at the Mexican Revolution, which seems in this respect to be the French Revolution's opposite. In Mexico the capital remained stolidly unrevolutionary, revolutionary dynamism was located mainly on the periphery, and the spatial politics of the revolution were based more on control of land by rival armies than on control of political institutions by rival ideological factions (Katz 1998; Knight 1986; Womack 1969). How such striking differences in spatial dynamics might be accounted for and what effects they had on revolutionary outcomes are questions that should interest all students of contentious politics.

Finally, I hope that the analyses of both my examples – the Bejing student's prodemocracy movement and the French Revolution – will indicate something of the value of a more systematic and theoretically informed treatment of space in the study of contentious politics. Contentious politics is a complex phenomenon: at once an exercise of political strategy, a mobilization of resources, an overcoming of collective action problems, a seizing of political opportunities, and an enactment of collective action frames. But it is also an exercise of spatial agency, an ensemble of work within and upon spatial structures that produces new spatial structures, meanings, and routines. I believe that giving voice to this spatial dimension of contentious politics will significantly enrich our understanding.

4

It's About Time: Temporality in the Study of Social Movements and Revolutions

Doug McAdam and William H. Sewell, Jr.

The title of this volume is *Silence and Voice in the Study of Contentious Politics*. This title is meant to signify that we are not simply interested in noting and articulating that which has been left out of the study of social movements, revolutions, and the like, but in relating these "silences" to the dominant "voices"; those topics, concepts, and theories that have set the intellectual agenda in recent years in the various fields that comprise the study of political contention. Necessarily, however, most of the chapters are focused on a topical silence, with the relationship between the topic and the dominant lines of theory and research addressed only briefly, if at all, in the chapter.

The case of temporality is a bit different, however, from most of the other topics addressed in the individual chapters. It is not that the general topic has been ignored, but that specific temporal rhythms have been emphasized at the expense of others. In this chapter, then, we will devote nearly as much space to a discussion of the dominant conceptions of temporality as to the temporal rhythms that have gone largely unexamined in the study of contention. In this chapter we hope to do four things in particular. First, we will briefly highlight the two temporal rhythms that have dominated the study of social movements and revolutions. Second, we will take up two other rarely studied temporalities that strike us as highly relevant to an understanding of the emergence, development, and decline of political contention. Having sketched these four different temporal rhythms, we will then speculate a bit concerning the relationships among these temporalities. Throughout the paper, we use two familiar but very different cases – the French Revolution and the American Civil Rights Movement – to illustrate the relevance of these intersecting, but distinct, temporal rhythms to the study of popular contention.

Temporality in the Study of Political Contention

In discussing dominant temporalities in the study of social movements and revolutions, we would be remiss if we failed to point out that much, if not most, scholarship in the field – especially in social movement studies – betrays no temporality whatsoever. So most survey research on movement activists (Oliver 1984; Walsh and Warland 1983; Wiltfang and McAdam 1991) or qualitative work on "framing strategies" (Benford and Hunt 1992; Noonan 1995), to cite only two research genres, is informed by no particular conception of time. But where temporal logics or images have been invoked in the study of political contention, they have tended to conform to one of two analytic templates: *long-term change processes or protest cycles*.

Long-Term Change Processes

The attempt to link broad change processes with the development of political and cultural insurgency has a long and proud history in the social sciences. Most sociological theory from the early nineteenth century to the 1930s – for example, Comte, Marx, Spencer, Tonnies, Durkheim, Weber, Giddings, Ross, Ward, Sorokin – was, in fact, concerned with the largely invisible social trends that resulted, over the long run, in what were viewed as profound and generally progressive transformations in the nature of societies. Marx was certainly the pioneer in applying this gradualist and progressive conception of temporality to contentious politics. Marx saw the rise of the labor movement and its inevitable culmination in a proletarian revolution as tied irrevocably to the historic unfolding and deepening contradictions inherent in industrial capitalism.

Notwithstanding these pioneering luminaries, no one has done more to insinuate this particular temporality into the contemporary study of social movements and revolutions than Charles Tilly. The contrast between the explicit historicity of Tilly's early work (Snyder and Tilly 1972; Tilly 1964; Tilly, Tilly, and Tilly 1975) and the generally ahistorical character of social science theory in the 1950s and 1960s concerning the origins and development of collective action (Gurr 1971; Lang and Lang 1961; Smelser 1962; Turner and Killian 1972) is especially striking. If there was a temporal logic to the classical collective behavior or other "strain" models it was a sketchy and very limited one. Movements were generally thought to be responsive to sudden, dramatic disruptions in people's lives which motivated them to restore social and psychological order through collective action. Tilly (and his colleagues) asserted a very different causal logic and temporality for the origins of contention. Writing in 1975, the Tillys (p. 254) noted that the kinds of strains identified by classical theorists ". . . are by no means irrelevant to collective [action]. It is just that their effects do not work as . . . [classical] theories say they should. Instead of a short-run generation of strain, followed by protest, we find a long-run transformation of the structures of power and of collective action."

The roots of political contention, then, were to be found in long-term change processes (for example, industrialization, urbanization, state formation) that simultaneously destabilized existing power relations and afforded groups new organizational/associational bases for mobilization (for example, the industrial work place, the urban neighborhood). This temporal logic was soon incorporated into what was termed the *political process* model of social movements (McAdam 1999). As this perspective has grown in influence, so too has the temporal orientation that informs it. And there is no reason to doubt the relevance of such long-term change processes in the emergence of many movements and revolutions. The American Civil Rights Movement and the French Revolution would appear to be two cases in point.

Long-Term Change Processes in the Origins of the Civil Rights Movement Scholars have long linked the rise of the U.S. Civil Rights Movement to long-term change processes that strengthened the organizational capacity of the African-American population while simultaneously undermining the calculations on which America's racial political economy was structured. Initially these shifts were keyed by domestic change processes. Chief among these was the gradual collapse of the southern cotton economy in the early decades of the twentieth century. Among the factors that weakened "King Cotton" were increased competition from foreign cotton producers, the development of synthetic fibers, a series of devastating boll weevil epidemics, and the collapse of the domestic cotton market at the outset of the Depression.

More important than the causes of the collapse were the consequences that followed from it. Two in particular are worth noting. The first was the massive migration of blacks (and poor whites) out of the South between 1910 and 1960. In these fifty years, the South lost five million blacks to out-migration. Moreover, neither the points of origin or destinations of the migrants were random. Rather the migrants were drawn disproportionately from states that had both the highest percentages of black residents *and* lowest percentages of African-American voters (McAdam 1982:77–81). These migrants wound up moving overwhelmingly to seven states in the North (and West) that have long held the key to success in presidential politics. These states – New York, California, New Jersey, Pennsylvania, Ohio, Illinois, and Michigan – absorbed fully 87 percent of the total number of southern black out-migrants between 1910–60. "The electoral significance of this selective migration was evident in both the 1944 and 1948 presidential contests. In both instances, had blacks reversed the proportion of votes they gave the two major candidates, the Republican challenger, Thomas Dewey would have defeated his Democratic opponents, Franklin Roosevelt and Harry Truman" (McAdam 1999:81). By the 1940s, then, the "Black Vote" was firmly established as an electoral resource of national significance.

But the demographic/political impact of the decline of the cotton economy was felt regionally as well as nationally. While the lure of northern industrial jobs and the collapse of the cotton economy prompted many blacks to flee the South, many more stayed behind and took part in a massive rural to urban redistribution within the region. In 1930 nearly 70 percent of all black southerners still lived in rural areas. A scant thirty years later the percentage was down to 42 percent. By 1950, this demographic transformation and the general postwar economic boom had created a sizeable black middle-class in most southern cities. Writing in 1954, Burgess (1965:344) discussed this trend and linked it to organizational developments within the African-American community.

It is in the city that the greatest educational opportunities have become available to the Negro. It is here that expanding occupational opportunities have been possible, and that a rise in income and standard of living have gradually been realized. In the urban black belts, Negro institutions . . . have flourished. These social institutions provide the breeding ground for a new kind of leadership trained in the values and skills of the middle class.

It was not only the personal resources of this emerging black urban middle class, however, that encouraged the institutional development noted by Burgess. The physical proximity and improved communications characteristic of urban life were crucial factors as well. So, too, was the increase in the sheer size of the black community in urban areas, and the greater protection from racist violence the urban setting afforded. In the middle decades of the century this mix of factors combined to produce an era of rapid institutional expansion in the black communities of the urban South. In the forefront of this process was the burgeoning black middle class and the three institutions – the black church, black colleges, and local NAACP chapters – within which the movement developed in the 1950s and early 1960s (McAdam 1999:94–106).

But if the first domestic challenges to the racial status quo had begun to appear as early as the 1920s, widening perceptibly in the 1930s, it was World War II and the *international* realignments that followed the war that doomed Jim Crow and the broader system of racial politics that had allowed it to flourish. Consider the seemingly puzzling contrast between the political circumstances of Presidents Roosevelt and Truman and their civil rights policy initiatives (or lack thereof). In 1936 Franklin Roosevelt was elected to serve his second term as president of the United States. Indeed, his margin of victory – popular as well as electoral – was one of the largest in the history of presidential politics. The election also marked a significant shift in racial politics in the United States. For the first time since African Americans were granted the franchise, black voters deserted the Republican party – the party of Lincoln – to cast the majority of their votes for the Democratic presidential candidate. The New Deal reforms had been accompanied by a general leftward swing in political attitudes and had conditioned the general public to countenance assertive government action on behalf of the "less fortunate" segments of American society. Finally, Roosevelt was himself a liberal – socially no less than politically – as was his outspoken and influential wife, Eleanor. Yet, in spite of all of these factors, Roosevelt never willingly proposed civil rights legislation throughout his four-term presidency, refusing even to support anti-lynching bills on the numerous occasions such bills were brought before Congress.

Just ten years later, Roosevelt's successor, Harry Truman, inaugurated a period of active executive advocacy of civil rights when he appointed and charged his national Committee on Civil Rights with investigating the "current state of civil rights in the country and recommending appropriate legislative remedies for deficiencies uncovered" (quoted in McAdam 1999:84). Two years later, in 1948, Truman issued two landmark executive orders, the first establishing a fair employment board within the Civil Service Commission, and the second calling for the gradual desegregation of the armed forces. Why did Truman act when Roosevelt had not? Recent scholarship (Dudziak 2000; Layton 2000; McAdam 1998; Plummer 1996;

Skrentny 1998) has shed new light on the international developments that account for the seeming mystery. The key lies not in any significant differences in the domestic contexts in which Roosevelt and Truman were embedded, but in the new international pressures and considerations thrust upon the United States and the executive branch, in particular, in the postwar period. World War II and the onset of the Cold War effectively terminated "the isolationist foreign policy that had long defined America's relationship to the rest of the world. As a result, national political leaders found themselves exposed, in the postwar era, to international pressures and considerations that their predecessors had been spared. Locked in an intense ideological struggle with the USSR for influence among the emerging Third World nations, American racism suddenly took on international significance as an effective propaganda weapon of the Communists" (McAdam 1999:83). Writing in 1944, Gunnar Myrdal showed great prescience in anticipating the significance of this postwar shift. "The Negro problem," wrote Myrdal (1970:35):

has also acquired tremendous international implications, and this is another and decisive reason why the white North is prevented from compromising with the white South regarding the Negro.... Statesmen will have to take the changed geopolitical situation of the nation and carry out important adaptations of the American way of life to new necessities. A main adaptation is bound to be a redefinition of the Negro's status in American democracy.

Long-Term Change Processes in the Origins of the French Revolution

The question of what long-term processes made the French Revolution possible has been asked continuously since the time of the revolution itself, but there is still no consensus as to its answer. One cannot say, in other words, that we now know with any certainty what long-term processes underlay the revolution, but one can say with perfect confidence that disputes over the issue have remained central to scholarly (and not merely scholarly) discussions of the revolution.

The current state of doubt has not always prevailed. During the two decades following World War II, there was a widespread consensus that the underlying cause of the French Revolution was socioeconomic: the rise of capitalism and the consequent economic ascendance of the bourgeoisie. Albert Soboul, writing in 1956, began his pathbreaking book on the Parisian sans-culottes with the following statement, which he himself characterized as a commonplace: "The French Revolution, together with the English revolutions of the seventeenth century, marks the culmination of a long economic and social evolution which brought the bourgeoisie to power" (Soboul 1962:1). This claim was the keystone of the interpretive synthesis enunciated by Soboul's predecessor and mentor, Georges Lefebvre, in a series of important books (1971[1949]; 1973[1932]) and substantially accepted by a wide range of historians, both Marxist and non-Marxist (Godechot 1965; Hampson 1963; Rude 1959). In Lefebvre's hands, the argument was far from simplistic: The economic dominance of the bourgeois class was increasingly incompatible in the long run with a monarchical and aristocratic mode of government, but for this general incompatibility to eventuate in a revolution required a number of other sociopolitical processes, including chronic fiscal difficulties that led to a state of bankruptcy in 1786, and a series of economic downturns, intensified by crop failures, in the three years before 1789.

Over the course of the 1960s and 1970s, this consensus about the long-term causes of the revolution was challenged and eventually dismantled. The challengers, for example Alfred Cobban (1964), Elizabeth Eisenstain (1965), and Francois Furet (1971), attacked Lefebvre's central argument, claiming that the revolution was not launched or led by actors identifiable as representatives of the bourgeoisie and that in any case the French "bourgeoisie" was virtually indistinguishable in its economic interests, values, and behavior from the aristocracy. These "revisionist" scholars, as they were termed, insisted that the French Revolution was above all a political rather than a social revolution. The net result of their intervention has been double: to redirect efforts toward understanding the immediate, short-term political dynamics of the revolution; but also to direct the search for long-term processes toward politics and the state, rather than economics and class. One major line of attack on the question of long-term processes has focused on political culture, arguing that the moral stock of the French monarchy was gradually undermined by the writings of scurrilous journalists and publicity-seeking lawyers that circulated in the burgeoning print media of the capital (Darnton 1982). Another line of argument has focused on the long-term structural and administrative problems of the state, which was weakened by a mounting debt that was impossible to overcome without a wholesale attack on privilege, but whose short-term management consistently reinforced privilege (Bien 1987; Bossinga 1991). Social and economic interpretations of long-term changes are currently out of style, although there are signs of a revival (Jones 1991). At the moment, there is no counter synthesis with anything approaching the authority of Lefebvre's in the 1950s. But specifying the long-term processes that made the revolution possible remains a central topic of research and discussion.

Protest Cycles

The term *protest cycle* was introduced into the conceptual vocabulary of students of movements and revolutions by Sidney Tarrow in his 1989 book, *Democracy and Disorder*. In introducing the term, Tarrow had in mind a fairly regular, sequence of stages that seemed to characterize many periods of generalized social unrest, such as those that convulsed most of the western democracies in the late 1960s and early 1970s. More generally, the term has come to demarcate a peak period of active mobilization and protest by or on behalf of various segments of society. Scholars of movements or revolutions have long evidenced the same general temporal preoccupation with the most active phase of whatever struggle they are studying.

Notwithstanding the truncated understandings that result from this privileging of active mobilization as the signature of movements/ revolutions, it should be clear that this second temporality captures an important and empirically demonstrable aspect of political contention. The notion of an active protest or revolutionary cycle can certainly be applied to both of the cases under examination here.

The Cycle of Contention in the American Civil Rights Movement The concept of the protest cycle has always been equated with that temporally narrow period which defines the most active phase of a given movement or revolution. In the case of the Civil Rights Movement, virtually all scholars mark the beginning of this period with the onset of the Montgomery Bus Boycott in December 1955. There is, however, considerably less consensus regarding the "end" of the cycle, with different analysts attributing significance to a host of different events or "moments" in the history of the struggle (for example, the assassination of Martin Luther King, Jr., the end of the "urban disorders" in 1969–70, and so on). There is little disagreement though (and ample empirical support; McAdam 1999) that the most active phase of movement lasted from the mid-1950s until at least the late 1960s, with its heyday coming in the first half of the 1960s. As with the French Revolution or any other broad episode of contention, however, one can discern various phases or distinct temporal rhythms within the civil rights protest cycle.

The first phase corresponds to the flurry of activity set in motion by the Montgomery Bus Boycott. Inspired by the campaign there, similar boycotts were organized in at least six southern cities (Atlanta, New Orleans, Birmingham, Tallahassee, Chattanooga, and Rock Hill, South Carolina) during the years 1955–1957. The second phase, coming in 1958–59, marked a temporary lull in direct action campaigns as southern civil rights forces coped with a series of repressive legislative measures and other manifestations of the southern resistance movement of the late 1950s. Phase three, corresponding to the movement's integrationist heyday, spanned a five-year period, beginning with the initial Greensboro sit-in on February 1, 1960 and running through the Selma campaign in early 1965. These years were characterized, not only by a large volume of protest activity, but by a strong consensus among movement adherents regarding the fundamental goal of the struggle – integration – and the central means – nonviolent direct action – that was to be used to achieve this goal.

Several events and/or processes conspired to bring phase three to a close and to usher in phase four. Among the events were the Watts Riot in 1965 and Stokely Carmichael's call for "black power" amidst the tumult of the Meredith March in the spring of the following year. The larger dynamics shaping the transition from phase three to four was the movement's own success in dismantling Jim Crow segregation and effectively restoring black voting rights in the South. All of these factors inspired the movement's "turn to the North" after 1965. Phase four lasted roughly until the King assassination in April 1968, or perhaps, the election of Richard Nixon as president seven months later. This phase was marked by the largest "urban disorders" of the period and by the partially effective rhetorical exploitation of the riots by movement leaders and liberal reformers alike. Phase five corresponds to the movement's gradual decline in the late 1960s and early 1970s. Confronting a general "law and order" backlash, an administration with no electoral allegiance to African-Americans, and a radical black power wing decimated by repression and internal dissent, the movement – as an organized force capable of mounting sustained protest activity – gradually ceased to exist.

The fact that the movement grew generally more, rather than less, radical over time contradicts one of the longstanding "truths" about social movements; that, as Weber and Michels argued, progressive change efforts typically grow more conservative and oligarchic as they age. Clearly, not all movements or movement organizations conform to this pattern.

Indeed, in its embrace of increasingly class-oriented issues, and the temporal succession of ever more radical groups – from the NAACP to the Black Panthers by way of the Southern Christian Leadership Conference (SCLC), the Congress of Racial Equality (CORE), and SNCC – the black struggle bears more than a passing resemblance to the escalating rhythm of the French Revolution. This resemblance underscores one of the central themes of the volume; that the neat typological distinctions we have drawn between nominally different forms of contention (for example, social movements, revolutions, ethnic conflict, and so on) often obscure more than they reveal. In the unfolding of its active "protest cycle" the civil rights/black power struggle comes to simultaneously embody elements of revolution, ethnic conflict, regional democratization, as well as the social movement.

The Cycle of Contention in the French Revolution The French Revolution has long been understood as forming a cycle of contention; indeed French revolutionary terms such as *Terror* and *Thermidor* are often used to signify phases in the cycles of other revolutions. It is true of both revolutions and social movements that an initial rupture often leads to a major expansion of the number and variety of organizations seeking change, of the programs for change they offer, and of public demonstrations, meetings, and incidents of disorder. George Lefebvre gave what remains one of the most lucid accounts of the broadening of the forms and constituencies of protest in the early phases of revolution in *The Coming of the French Revolution* (1971[1949]). Lefebvre observed that the event we call the French Revolution was in reality composed of four overlapping but largely autonomous revolutions made by four different classes or social categories. When financial collapse weakened the French state, the initial effect was to enable the aristocracy to reclaim the preponderant role in the state that it had lost to the long offensive of the absolute monarchy over the past two centuries. It was thus, ironically, the aristocracy that began the revolution. But once the aristocracy showed the way, other classes followed. If the offensive of the aristocrats occurred in 1787–88, the bourgeoisie seized the initiative in 1789, finally managing to transform the Estates General into a revolutionary National Assembly in June 1789. But when the monarchy threatened to roll back the gains of the aristocracy and bourgeoisie, the urban common people intervened violently by taking the Bastille and pushing the revolution in a more sharply democratic direction. Finally, in the aftermath of the Bastille, a rising of the peasants destroyed what remained of the feudal regime and secured the primacy of the National Assembly.

The general pattern of this progressive opening of the revolution to additional classes has often been repeated in revolutions and in other episodes of contention. The revolution began with action by the group that possessed the best organization and the most institutional leverage within the state. This was followed by actions taken by classes increasingly distant from the state and increasingly less endowed with organizational or other resources. Groups with few organizational and other resources became active only after better endowed groups had weakened the state and provided new opportunities for redress of grievances.

But the dynamics of the revolution were hardly played out by August 1789, when the peasants made their decisive entry into the struggle. The newly created revolutionary state apparatus remained relatively weak and its legitimacy was precarious. Moreover, the political factions and social groups that lost out in the first round – most obviously the aristocracy – harbored hopes of doing better in a future round. Because such groups and factions rallied around the king, who had in principle become a liberal constitutional monarch, the more radical groups became increasingly suspicious of the monarchy. The king showed his sympathy with the counterrevolution when he unsuccessfully attempted to flee the country in 1791. Thereafter factional struggles intensified, resulting in the overthrow of the monarchy and the establishment of a republic in 1792, and, the following year, the execution of the king. But factional struggles continued among the republicans, eventually resulting in civil war in the west of France, compounded by international war against the surrounding monarchical regimes, and the Terror. Finally, in the revolutionary month of Thermidor, 1794, Robespierre and the Committee of Public Safety, the authors of the Terror, were themselves overthrown and executed, restoring relative calm and a more liberal republic.

Historians have long argued about precisely what accounted for this dynamic of radicalization. Albert Marthiez (1928[1922]), writing in the wake of World War I, argued that radicalization and terror resulted from the dire threats to the republic posed by the foreign and domestic wars. Crane Brinton (1965), writing at the height of Cold War suspicion of revolution, argued that revolution followed the sequence of a disease, from initial onset (the liberal revolution) to fever and crisis (the Terror) to convalescence and recovery (Thermidor). Albert Soboul (a communist) and Daniel Guerin (an anarchist) both attributed the radicalization to pressures from the Parisian sans-culottes, disagreeing only (but violently) about whether the sans-culottes represented a nascent proletariat (Guerin 1946) or an unstable alliance between a subordinate working-class and a dominant petty bourgeoisie (Soboul 1962). Finally, Francois Furet (1981) argues that radicalization was inherent in the ideology of the revolution from the beginning, and that the factional struggles represented no social forces but simply the playing out of a pregiven script. Many plausible arguments are on offer, and an analyst might also opt for a combination of two or more of them.

Neglected Temporalities in the Study of Social Movements and Revolutions

There is nothing inherently problematic about either of the temporal perspectives reviewed previously. That is, anyone seeking to understand the emergence and development of social movements and revolutions will typically need, in our view, to pay attention to those long-term change processes that condition the prospects and social structural bases of mobilization as well as the shorter-term temporal dynamics that shape the unfolding of an active protest or revolutionary cycle. Our complaint is that by ignoring other temporal rhythms students of social movements and revolutions have painted an incomplete and overly deterministic portrait of popular contention. The portrait is incomplete because it ignores other temporalities that strike us as crucial to an understanding of contentious politics. In this chapter we will focus on two such temporalities: *transformative events* and *cultural epochs of contention*.[1] More importantly, the

---

[1] In no way do these two unconventional temporalities exhaust the range of understudied temporal frameworks that could be (or have been) applied to the study of contentious politics. Rupp and Taylor's (1987) compelling account of the period of feminist consolidation between the end of the women's suffrage movement in the United States and the rise of the modern women's movement – what they call the *doldrums* – is another temporal rhythm that could be studied profitably in other social and revolutionary movements. Moreover, the very different *subjective temporalities* that appear to characterize different episodes of contention could also profit from more study. One intriguing example is Keith Baker's analysis of the distinctive sense of temporality that pervaded the French Revolution and that contributed importantly to its radicalism. The revolutionaries, he writes, saw themselves as living in "a 'mythic present' in which eternity and contingency meet." They regarded the revolution as totally discontinuous with the past, but also regarded the victory of revolution as highly uncertain, as under constant and deadly threat from its enemies. Hence they experienced "time itself . . . as a succession of moments in which life and death hang in the balance." Every day was "the turning point that decides the fate of France and

implicit portrait of contention that emerges from an emphasis on the two dominant temporalities is deterministic in its account of the origins of movements/revolutions. Without acknowledging other temporal dynamics, one is left to conclude that long-term change processes lead inexorably to the kinds of protest cycles or peak periods of mobilization we have come to equate with popular struggles. Acknowledging these other temporalities yields a less determinist and more culturalist perspective on social movements and revolutions.

Transformative Events

No narrative account of a social movement or revolution can leave out events. The Montgomery Bus Boycott or the March on Washington, the taking of the Bastille or the revolution of August 10, the Haymarket Riots or the Flint sit-down strikes are moments of high drama in the Civil Rights Movement, the French Revolution, and the American Labor Movement. But the study of social movements and revolutions – at least as normally carried out by sociologists and political scientists – has rarely paid analytic attention to the contingent features and causal significance of particular contentious events such as these. This is in spite – or perhaps because of – the thriving methodological tradition known as "protest *event* research." (For an insightful discussion of the relationship of research on particular events to the "event research paradigm" see Tarrow 1998b.) Indeed, a host of classic works in the study of social movements (and to a lesser extent, revolutions) have made "protest events" the fundamental unit of analysis (Beissinger 1998; Kriesi et al. 1995; McAdam 1999; Olzak 1992; Tarrow 1989; Tilly 1993; Tilly, Tilly, and Tilly 1975). But work in this tradition has never focused on the unique temporality of the singular event; instead, it has used the identification and coding of events to create time-series distributions of events geared primarily to revealing the shape and dynamics of the "protest cycle" discussed previously. So, for example, McAdam (1999) used the technique to demarcate the overall duration and distinctive phases of the "protest cycle" of the Civil Rights Movement.

humanity" (Baker 1990:223). This is a very different subjective temporality than, for example, that of the German social democrats who believed that the force of history would inevitably bring about the victory of the labor movement or the Victorian temperance reformers or suffragists who felt that the general progress of civilization assured the long-term success of their campaigns. Subjective temporalities are surely an important ingredient in the rhythms and strategies of most social movements.

What we are encouraging here is an altogether different conception and analytic approach to the study of events; one most closely associated with the anthropologist Marhall Sahlins (1981; 1985). Writing about the arrival of Captain Cook in Hawaii, Sahlins treats events neither as mere incidents marking the progress of a cycle of contention, nor as random and utterly contingent ruptures in historical continuity, but as specific and systematically explicable transformations and rearticulations of the cultural and social structures that were already in operation before the event. Events thus become turning points in structural change, concentrated moments of political and cultural creativity when the logic of historical development is reconfigured by human action but by no means abolished. The event has a temporality very different from that of the long-term change process or the protest cycle. It is punctual and discontinuous rather than cyclical, linear, or continuous. The precise sequencing of actions over the course of a few hours or days and the particular contingencies faced by actors at particular times may have structuring effects over a very long run. The analytical fascination of the event is that in events very brief, spatially concentrated, and relatively chaotic sequences of action can have durable, spatially extended, and profoundly structural effects. And if the temporality of the event is important in any field of human social action, it surely must be so in revolutions and contentious social movements.

Anyone who has actively participated in a social movement has surely experienced at least one of these moments of concentrated transformation, when dramatic confrontations and feverish activity definitively change the course of the movement's history. Yet social scientists who study social movements, in spite of the fact that many of them were initially attracted to the field because of their own movement backgrounds, have suppressed this aspect of their own experience – presumably because the fleeting quality and emotional headiness of the transformative events they have lived through are hard to capture or validate within the conventional analytic language of social science. We take a contrary approach: If transformative events loom large in activists' experiences of social movements and revolutions, we should accord them the closest possible analytic attention and, if necessary, develop whatever new language and scholarly conventions may be necessary to understand them.

Transformative Events in the French Revolution   The fruitfulness of a focus on the temporality of the event can be demonstrated in practice. Sewell (1996a) has analyzed at some length the taking of the Bastille, one of the most significant events of the French Revolution. It has long been recognized by historians that the taking of the Bastille marked the definitive intervention of the common people of Paris into the revolution and that the victory at the Bastille turned back what might well have been a fatal royal offensive against the National Assembly. The Bastille was recognized at the time as a major turning point and July 14, the day the Bastille was taken, is still the French national holiday. But Sewell shows that the significance of the taking of the Bastille was even more profound than previous historians had recognized: It was in the course of this event that the very category of revolution as we now understand it was created.

As of early July 1789, the word *revolution* had a very different meaning than it now does. It could be used to refer to any sudden change in the fortunes of a state – the fall of a ministry, the death of a king, the loss of a battle. And it was a passive rather than active category. A revolution was something that happened to a state, not an act undertaken to transform it. It was only in the aftermath of the taking of the Bastille that the term *revolution* came to be associated with popular uprisings and to be understood as the self-conscious act of reconstituting a state (Baker 1990; Sewell 1996a). This was a change of epoch-making proportions. It profoundly shaped the possibilities of political action for the remainder of what was thenceforth called "the French Revolution," making it possible for actors to contemplate and carry out further revolutionary transformations – like overthrow of the monarchy on August 10, 1792 – and for political enemies to be cast as "counterrevolutionaries." It introduced, as we will argue later, a new and potent category or "template" for political action, one that governments all over the world have had to worry about ever since, and a new category of political actors – "revolutionists" or "revolutionaries" – who dedicated their lives to the making of revolutions. Part of the scholarly fascination with the taking of the Bastille is that one can show how very local dynamics and contingencies had long-term effects on the structural possibilities of politics, both in late eighteenth century France and in the modern world more generally.

It is, of course, not possible here to do more than hint at the complexities involved in the taking of the Bastille or at the theoretical and methodological problems involved in the analysis of events. The invention of the modern concept of revolution involved the coding of an episode of urban popular violence as an act of the sovereign will, and hence a legitimate basis for a new form of government. The recoding was made possible by a significant semantic ambiguity: the term *peuple* signified both the urban poor (and hence those who captured the Bastille) and *the people* who, according to the abstract social contract theory then dominant in "patriotic" circles, made up the sovereign. The modern concept of revolution was born when the uprising of the Parisians was authoritatively interpreted as an instance of the sovereign people expressing its will. Not surprisingly, this recoding was not accomplished during the four or so hours of the afternoon of July 14, 1789 during which the fortress was captured, but over the following several days. The emergence of the category of revolution was the outcome of a complex dialectic between the Parisian people, the National Assembly, and the king, one in which the National Assembly, which already had a strong claim to be the supreme representative of the people, took the lead.

The initial response of the National Assembly to the news of the fall of the Bastille was not joy but despair. The National Assembly sat in Versailles, several miles from Paris, and upon hearing of the capture of the fort, its members feared that Paris would dissolve into violence and that this would actually play into the hands of the king, whose troops alone would be able to restore order. But when it became clear that the capture of the Bastille constituted a major victory for the National Assembly in its ongoing struggle with the king, speakers in the National Assembly began to rethink the meaning of the people's violent action. Rather than speaking of what the people had done as "massacres" and "bloody executions" that had "carried the people to an excess of fury," to quote a speech given on the evening of July 14 (*Reimpresssion* 1858:155), the Parisians' actions were praised on July 16 for their "courage and energy" and characterized as a revolt of "liberty" against "despotism" (164). But it was only over the next few days that the National Assembly actually began to claim that the taking of the Bastille had been a solemn act of the sovereign people and that as such it legitimated the effective shift of power from the king to the National Assembly that had taken place between July 14 and 17. It did so without premeditation in response to the dizzying flow of events. The modern concept of revolution was, in fact, improvised by the National Assembly when it was forced to distinguish the legitimate popular violence at the Bastille from subsequent acts of popular violence that the National Assembly regarded as utterly illegitimate but that were in many respects all too similar to those of July 14.

There is no doubt that the successful seizure of the Bastille and the retreat of the royal troops created an atmosphere conducive to popular violence. And when the people of the nearby towns of Poissy and Saint-

Germain-en-Laye attempted, on July 17 and 18 to lynch millers accused of hoarding grains, a conservative member of the National Assembly responded by introducing a motion condemning all forms of violence. The "patriots," who correctly saw this blanket condemnation as a thinly veiled attack on the violence at the Bastille, succeeded in getting the motion tabled by distinguishing the legitimate violence of July 14 from the illegitimate violence of a grain riot. Robespierre claimed that the proposed motion "presents a disposition against those who have defended liberty. But is there anything more legitimate than to rise up against a horrible conspiracy formed to destroy the nation?" (181–82) Another deputy warned against "confusing popular riots with legitimate and necessary revolutions" (182).

A few days later, the patriots were faced with a much more difficult case. On July 23, a crowd of Parisians attacked two prominent royal servants who had been arrested and held at the city hall for vaguely defined conspiracies against the people. The crowd killed both men and paraded around the square in front of the city hall with their severed heads displayed on the ends of pikes. This act of "popular justice" was particularly disturbing because it mimicked almost exactly the lynching of the commander of the Bastille in the same square on July 14. The patriots were appalled by the violence of July 23, but had to choose their words carefully to distinguish what had just happened from the "necessary and legitimate revolution" of July 14. Until July 23, the speeches justifying the taking of the Bastille were abstract in character, referring only to the "energy" and "courage" of the Parisians who took up arms for "liberty" against "despotism." But in order to condemn the murders of July 23 they actually had to justify those of July 14. One deputy noted that "the first blows struck by the people are due to the effervescence necessarily inspired by the annihilation of despotism and the birth of liberty. . . . The governor of a fort taken by assault, of a fort which was the abyss of liberty, could hardly have had any other fate; fallen into the hands of the defenders of liberty, of a numerous people whom he had wished to sacrifice to despotism, he got what he deserved" (192).

But at a time when the people's generous actions had brought peace and harmony to the state, "nothing can justify the fury that has just been expressed against two individuals" (192). Such "bloody and revolting scenes" must cease, otherwise "the people could get accustomed to these bloody spectacles and make a game of spilling blood" (192). Although the bloodshed of July 23 was barbarous and unacceptable, that of July 14, however similar in appearance, had a wholly different character. The slaughter of the commander of the Bastille was, as another deputy observed, part of "a national insurrection against despotism" which had "a character superior to the power of the laws" (197). It was, in other words, a sovereign act of the nation itself, and therefore not subject to ordinary laws. But as a sovereign act that had defeated despotism and established liberty, it had reestablished the rule of law on a new and higher basis; in this context, the National Assembly argued the bloodshed of July 23 was doubly criminal.

It was, thus, the unpredictable flow of events that led the National Assembly to sanctify the taking of the Bastille as an act of sovereignty, and thereby to articulate the modern concept of revolution. It is interesting that the speeches in which the deputies fabricated this new concept were not laboriously penned by candlelight on the evening before they were given, but improvised spontaneously in the heat of debate. The new concept of revolution, this suggests, was not the inevitable or the pre-meditated outcome of the Parisian people's action. It was, rather, a con-tingent product. Had the factional debates been patterned differently, or had the mimetic slaughter of July 23 not occurred, the concept of revolu-tion as a particular category of contentious political action in which a popular uprising overthrows a government and established the legitimacy of another might never have come into existence.

We have dwelt at such lengths on the case of the Bastille because it so spectacularly illustrates the significance of events for understanding the development of political contention. Of course, most events do not estab-lish hitherto unimagined categories of political action. But it is true that the course of contention never runs smooth and that the bumps and turns in the road tend to occur in concentrated temporal bursts. If the taking of the Bastille was, arguably, the most notable event of the French Revolu-tion, there were many others that also shaped the course of political con-tention, not only over the short and medium run, but over the longer term as well. This was true, for example, of the Great Fear, the rural panic and peasant insurrection that followed on the heels of the taking of the Bastille; of the night of August 4, 1789, when the nobles and clergy renounced their privileges amidst high emotion and tears of joy; of the abortive flight of the king on June 20–25, 1791; of the republican revolution of August 10, 1792; of the ninth of Thermidor, 1794, when Robespierre was overthrown and executed; of the eighteenth Brumaire, 1799, when Napoleon Bona-parte came to power in a coup d'etat. In all of these cases, as in the days following July 14, 1789, contingent sequences of actions and purely local causes helped to produce surprising, significant, and enduring effects.

Transformative Events in the U.S. Civil Rights Movement The same could be said for the role of events in the Civil Rights Movement. But having focused on a single event in the French Revolution – the taking of the Bastille – we want to underscore, in our discussion of the Civil Rights Movement, the idea that broad episodes of contention tend to pivot on multiple turning points. To illustrate the claim, we will briefly touch on two highly consequential events in the Civil Rights Movement. The Montgomery Bus Boycott is not among the two events we have chosen to analyze. This omission is not intended to downplay the significance of the boycott. If any one event can be seen as marking the movement's "birth" it would have to be Montgomery. But all too many popular histories of the black struggle convey the impression that, following Montgomery, the movement unfolded in a determinist fashion, propelled by the momentum generated by the boycott and the charismatic brilliance of its leader, Martin Luther King, Jr. The history of the movement is far more complicated and interesting than that, as the other two events suggest.

The Greensboro Sit-in, February 1, 1960 Though the Montgomery Bus Boycott probably does merit the designation as the birth of the direct action phase of the civil rights struggle, it is not clear that there would have been any sustained movement to celebrate had the Greensboro Sit-in not taken place. What popular histories of the movement typically obscure is the fact that aside from the few boycotts it inspired elsewhere (and perhaps the desegregation of Little Rock High School in 1957), the events in Montgomery were followed by a generally fallow period in the black struggle. The late 1950s were marked, not by heightened civil rights activity, but by a resurgent Ku Klux Klan and "massive resistance" to integration by southern authorities. By all appearances, there was no organized and sustained Civil Rights Movement as the 1960s dawned.

The Greensboro Sit-in changed all this, ushering in the mass Civil Rights Movement that we celebrate today, and in so doing, highlighted the idiosyncratic and unexpected capacity for decisive human agency that inheres in events and which makes their inclusion in the study of social movements and revolutions so critical. Indeed, without diminishing the significance of the bus boycott, a case can be made for Greensboro as an even more consequential and surprising event than Montgomery. While the boycott was conceived within and sustained by an established "movement center" (Morris 1984), the Greensboro Sit-in was the brainchild of four college freshmen at North Carolina A & T. The actions of Ezell Blair, Jr., Franklin McCain, Joseph McNeil, and David Richmond also are hard to square with the determinist account of movement emergence implied by the dominant temporal preoccupation with "long-term change processes." While change processes of the sort reviewed previously may have created a generally favorable context for civil rights activity, they are powerless to help us understand why these four individuals took the actions when and where they did. Only a close, textured reading of the events themselves are apt to yield this crucial piece of the puzzle.

What is hard to deny is the extraordinary impact the sit-in itself had on the pace of civil rights activity. Franklin McCain remembers: "back at the campus, there was just a beehive of activity. Word had spread. As a matter of fact, word was back on campus before we ever got back. There were all sorts of phone calls to the administration. . . . The mayor's office was aware of it and the governor's office was aware of it. I think it was all over North Carolina within a matter of just an hour or so" (quoted in Raines 1983:79). For ten days, the burgeoning movement was confined to North Carolina. Then the dam burst. After February 10 "demonstrations spread to neighboring states, with sit-ins occurring in Hampton, Virginia on February 11; Rock Hill, South Carolina on the twelfth; and Nashville, Tennessee on the thirteenth. In succeeding weeks the movement surfaced in such traditional centers of southern black life as . . . Atlanta and Montgomery, having finally encompassed the entire south (except for Mississippi) by the middle of March" (McAdam 1999:139). In the process, the sit-ins revitalized all of the major civil rights organizations, led to the creation of SNCC, reinforced a tactic that was to dominate the movement in the next few years, and generally set the black struggle in motion once again. The impact was as dramatic as the event itself was unpredictable. As Franklin McCain put it: "What's likely to happen? Now, I think that that was the question that all of us asked ourselves. . . . What's going to happen once we sit down? Of course, nobody had the answers. Even your wildest imagination couldn't lead you to believe what would, in fact, happen" (Raines 1983:76).

The Mississippi Freedom Democratic Party (MFDP) Challenge at the 1964 Democratic Convention   Both Montgomery and Greensboro marked clear "victories" for civil rights forces. But it should be clear that major "defeats" can also serve as decisive "transformative events" in the life of a movement or revolution. Such, we argue, was the case with the credentials challenge mounted by the Mississippi Freedom Democratic Party (MFDP) at the 1964 Democratic National Convention in Atlantic City. The story has been told many times, but requires a brief retelling here.

In the summer of 1964 SNCC (as the leader of a broad coalition of civil rights organizations) brought some 1,000 primarily white, northern college students to Mississippi for what was initially conceived of as a massive voter registration campaign. Early on, however, it became clear that Mississippi's political establishment was intent on maintaining the franchise as the more-or-less exclusive prerogative of white voters. In response to this impasse, the SNCC brain trust devised an ingenious stratagem. Having documented the closure of the official political system to the state's African-American residents, project organizers set about creating a parallel political process designed to select an alternative set of delegates that would challenge the seating of the state's "lily-white" party regulars at the Democratic National Convention to be held in Atlantic City in August. Aided by an emotional appearance by Fannie Lou Hamer before the Convention's Credential's Committee, it actually appeared for a time as if the challenge would succeed. But determined to hold the "solid South" for his party, the Democratic nominee, Lyndon Johnson, played "hard-ball" politics as only he could and, in the end, beat back the threatened revolt of the Credentials Committee which, properly cowed, voted to seat the regular Mississippi delegation. The MFDP delegation was offered a "consolation prize" of sorts: two at-large convention seats and a promise that the whole matter of racial exclusion would be reviewed prior to the 1968 convention.

The delegates overwhelmingly rejected the compromise. Fannie Lou Hamer summed up the feeling of most when she said, "we didn't come all this way for no two seats!" ... That was not quite the end of it, though. Using credentials borrowed from sympathetic delegates from other states, a contingent of MFDP members gained access to the convention floor and staged a sit-in in the Mississippi section. The sight of black Mississippians being carried from the convention floor by uniformed, white security officers was but the ultimate ironic denouement to Freedom Summer. (McAdam 1988:120)

And the impact of the failed challenge? According to SNCC's Executive Director, James Forman (1972:395–96):

Atlantic City was a powerful lesson, not only for the black people of Mississippi but for all of SNCC.... No longer was there any hope ... that the federal government would change the situation in the Deep South. The fine line of contradiction between the state governments and the federal government, which we had used to build a movement, was played out. Now the kernel of opposites – the people against both the federal and state governments was apparent.

Following the convention, Forman's conclusion came to be almost universally shared within SNCC and gradually other circles within the movement. But this conclusion created a real tactical problem for the direct action wing of the movement. As tactically radical as SNCC, SCLC, and CORE could be, their general approach had still been premised on the federal government's willingness to respond to "moral suasion," albeit of a forceful sort. Events in Mississippi had undermined SNCC's confidence in this strategy. But it was the convention challenge that foreclosed this strategic option once and for all. In the eyes, first of SNCC, and then other movement activists, the northern liberal elite had decisively shown its true colors; moral force had proven no match for naked political power. Though it would be nearly a year and a half before Stokely Carmichael would utter the phrase "black power," the decisive shift toward this alternative frame of reference emerged in response to the events in Atlantic City.

Clearly the convention challenge had quite a different impact on the movement than either Montgomery or Greensboro. But as turning points in the life of the black struggle, they share the key features of all "transformative events." We close our treatment of such events by noting several of these features, using our three civil rights events – including the Montgomery Bus Boycott – as convenient points of reference. In our view, the key feature of transformative events is that they come to be interpreted as *significantly disrupting, altering, or violating the taken-for-granted assumptions governing routine political and social relations*. In so doing, they serve to dramatically ratchet up (or down in the case of demobilizing events – for example, the Tiananmen Square massacre) the shared sense of uncertainty (with its partisan variants, "threat" and "opportunity") on which all broad episodes of contention depend. By increasing this sense of uncertainty, such events also fuel a dramatic escalation in the mobilization of emotion by all parties to the conflict. The increase in perceived threat typically heightens fear and anger on the part of movement opponents, while "rising expectations" expands hope and anger among insurgents.

Illustratively, the Montgomery Bus Boycott confounded normative expectations in a host of significant ways. First, and most importantly, the black community responded quickly and aggressively to the arrest of Rosa

Parks. And it did so, not in the "approved" manner of sending an older, "trusted" representative of the community to meet privately with city officials, but publicly and collectively. The fact that something on the order of 90–95 percent of the black community honored the boycott shocked whites, contradicting the myth among whites that blacks were either impossible to organize or generally content with the status quo. The favorable attention granted the boycott by the northern media and some politicians marked another significant departure from the longstanding tradition of ceding to the South exclusive control over the "Negro question." As such, Montgomery represented an important step in the renationalization of the issue. Finally, the fact that the boycott ended in a clear victory for civil rights forces fundamentally altered the psychology of southern race relations. The massive edifice of Jim Crow had been cracked, and not by Supreme Court decree, but through concerted action by African-Americans.

The Greensboro Sit-in was similarly destructive of the cognitive and affective foundations of "the southern way of life." Like their white counterparts, black college students had long been viewed as conformist and apolitical (Frazier 1957; Searles and Williams 1962). The sit-in movement constituted a stunning refutation of this "fact." The confused and generally hapless response of southern authorities to the sit-ins likewise confounded expectations. Consider Franklin McCain's recollection of the impact this had on the initial sit-in: "the other thing that helped us psychologically quite a lot was seeing the policeman pace the aisle and not be able to do anything. I think that this probably gave us more strength, more encouragement, than anything else on that particular day . . ." (quoted in Raines 1983:77). Finally, as in Montgomery, the success of the campaign – the desegregation of lunch counters through out the South – further undermined the social, political, and economic foundations of Jim Crow.

And what of the convention challenge? Didn't Lyndon Johnson's reassertion of "business as usual" restore, rather than undermine, the normative order? It depends on who you ask. Clearly, the SNCC brain trust came to view the outcome of the challenge in this way. And, predictably, this interpretation had a demobilizing effect on the organization (McAdam 1988:118–26). But for other parties to the conflict, the events in Atlantic City only confirmed the general thrust of civil rights reform. The regular Mississippi delegation, for instance, was so incensed by the convention challenge that they packed their bags and returned to Mississippi, never occupying the seats awarded them. To them, and other traditional Dixiecrats, Atlantic City constituted the definitive betrayal of the Party's longstanding "understanding" on race. In November, Mississippi was one of only two states to return electoral majorities for Lyndon Johnson's Republican opponent, Barry Goldwater. Four years later, the previously "solid South" keyed Richard Nixon's narrow presidential victory, by deserting the Democratic Party en masse.

The very different reactions of SNCC and the Mississippi Party regulars underscores, once again, the important interpretive basis of transformative events. It is not the event itself, but the importance that comes to be assigned to it in the immediate aftermath of the event that determines its transformative potential. The culturalist nature of events affords scholars a useful way of studying them. Rather than focus only on the events themselves, analysts are encouraged to systematically study the process by which different communities make sense of them in the wake of the occurrence.

Cultural Epochs in Contention

Thus far in our exposition we have moved steadily from a long-term temporality (long-term change processes) to a medium-term temporal rhythm (cycles of contention) to a short, punctuated temporality (the event). Our fourth temporality, however, returns to the long term. It is based on the observation that certain forms of contentious politics, once invented, tend to remain available for long stretches of time – certainly across more than one Tarrowian cycle of contention – and often across considerable reaches of space. The revolution, the millennial movement, the national liberation struggle, the crusade, the civil rights movement, the labor movement, or indeed, the social movement as such, are what might be called "master templates" of contention: All have had more-or-less extended periods during which this form of contention was repeatedly activated in a wide range of places and circumstances. We suggest that the birth, spread, and decline of such templates constitutes a collection of overlapping "cultural epochs of contention" which delimit the sorts of contentious political activities actors can conceive of.

Charles Tilly has written about a related phenomenon under the label of "repertoires of collective action" (Tilly 1977; 1982; 1995; Traugott 1995). He first observed that "any given population tends to have a fairly limited and well-established set of means for action on shared interests"

(Tilly 1977:39). So over the history of political contention certain types of collective actions come into or go out of use, so that at any given time and place actors have at their disposal a fairly limited and predictable repertoire of available contentious actions – whether charivaris, invasion of enclosures, grain riots, strikes, boycotts, petition campaigns, marches, or barricades. In Tilly's usage, the items which comprise a repertoire tend to be discrete behavioral recipes for the making of claims rather than the master templates in terms of which making a given kind of claim or mounting a given type of action makes sense. The items in a repertoire might be the sit-in, the protest march, and the freedom ride rather than the category "civil rights movement" within which they were invented and deployed. Nevertheless, the concept of repertoires belongs to the same family as our concept of master template: Both are cultural recipes for the making of contentious claims and both typically have a temporality – or more accurately, a duration – that is considerably longer than a single cycle of contention.

But although the cultural epochs of contention we are attempting to delimit have a relatively long temporal rhythm, the nature of that temporality is very different from the other type of long-term temporality we have specified in this chapter – what we termed *long-term change processes*. Long-term change processes tend to be incremental and cumulative, like the decline in sharecropping, the migration of African-Americans to northern cities, the formation of an urban proletariat, the rise of the bourgeoisie, or a secular increase in the production and circulation of printed material. The opening and closing of cultural epochs of contention tends to be far more punctual, linked, in fact, to another of our temporalities: the "transformative event." We might think of the master templates as being more-or-less suspended or preserved between discontinuous events, rather than being subject to fairly continuous processes of erosion, empowerment, growth, decline, and the like as in long-term change processes.

The Revolution as Master Template Revolution, as we have argued above, was invented in 1789 (with an assist, to be sure, from 1776 and 1688). Once invented, it became available as a modular form of contentious politics for a very long time. Moreover, the French model (a popular uprising that puts into power an elected assembly charged with drafting a new constitution) could be and was taken up in many different countries: among other places, Spanish America in the 1820s; France in

113

1830, 1848, and 1870; Germany, Austria, Hungary, and Italy in 1848; Russia in 1905 and 1917; Iran in 1906; the Ottoman Empire in 1908; Mexico and China in 1911. Nader Sohrabi has dubbed revolutions of this type "constitutional revolutions" (Soharabi 1995). Although there were important changes in tactics, goals, and ideologies across these cases and across time, it is also clear that there was a definite template for making a revolution and that the template depends on a particular conception of political legitimacy: that a legitimate state must be based on popular sovereignty as expressed through an elected constituent assembly.

Although this model of revolution remains available to this day, it has undergone mutations in the course of the twentieth century, producing variant models of revolution. The first variant to emerge was the Bolshevik model. The Russian Revolution of 1917 began as a French-type revolution in Feburary but it was transformed by the Bolsheviks in October. Both in Feburary and in October, the revolutions gained power in urban popular uprisings. The Feburary uprising was understood quite conventionally as a rising of the sovereign people whose will was to be expressed through the election of a Constituent Assembly. But the October uprising brought the Bolshevik Party to power – which dismissed the Constituent Assembly and claimed for itself the right to rule, not on the grounds of popular sovereignty, but on the grounds that it represented the interests of the proletariat. The Bolshevik model, hence, operated a double shift in the older "constitutional" model of revolution. It shifted the ultimate claim to legitimacy from sovereignty of the people to sovereignty of the proletarian class and it shifted the mode of representation of the sovereign from an elected assembly to a vanguard party. The Bolshevik model was put into practice by the Chinese Communists, but with an important difference: That power was seized not in an urban insurrection but in a peasant-based civil war of a guerrilla type. This form was imitated widely in "third world" revolutions in the period since World War II, but now seems to be dying out, a casualty, in part, of the collapse of the Communist regimes of eastern and central Europe between 1989 and 1991.

Another variant appeared in Iran at the end of the 1970s: the Islamic revolution (Abrahamian 1993; Arjomand 1988). The Islamic Revolution in Iran arose out of an urban uprising much like those that characterized the older constitutional revolutions and it established an elected assembly that wrote a new constitution. But once again it differed both in its definition of the ultimate source of power – which in the case of the Iranian Revolution might be said to have begun as the Islamic people and eventually became Islamic tout court – and in the modality by which this source of power was to be represented – which was the Islamic clergy and jurists. It is too early to tell how widespread this model of revolution will prove to be, but it has clearly been influential in a number of Middle Eastern countries, especially Afghanistan, Algeria, and Egypt.

A final alternative model of revolution has come to the fore in the 1980s – most prominently in the movements that overthrew the communist regimes of eastern Europe and the Soviet Union (Stokes 1993). The revolutions in eastern Europe were distinguished (except in Romania) by relatively nonviolent demonstrations in which hundreds of thousands simply showed their disgust, lack of fear, and unwillingness to cooperate with the old regime in massive demonstrations in urban public spaces. There was already a precedent for this sort of nonviolent popular uprising in the "people power" movement that ousted Ferdinand Marcos in the Philippines, and the failed democracy movement at Tiananmen Square was similar in form to both the Philippines and the east European movements. This model of revolution is in fact very similar to the original "French" or "constitutional" revolution. It is based squarely on a conception of popular sovereignty and its aim is the establishment of an elected constitutional assembly. The sole difference – but an important one – is that the "people" seize power by means of nonviolent mass demonstration rather than uprisings.

The condition of the success of such "people power" revolution is that the regimes in power be unwilling to use their superior military force in putting the demonstrations down. These conditions held in eastern Europe because Gorbachev had declared that Soviet troops, the coercive force that had previously guaranteed the continued existence of the communist states, would no longer be used to put down opposition in the "satellites." They also held in the Philippines in part because the United States, which had previously stood behind Marcos regime, withdrew its support. But there are additional features of the contemporary world that make such peaceful revolutions far more possible than they had been before. First, the ubiquitous presence of electronic media means that any assault on crowds will appear immediately on the television screen of the entire world, and result in an outpouring of international outrage – as was the case when the Chinese army assaulted the demonstrators in Tiananmen Square. Second, now that virtually all states are enmeshed in electronically mediated capitalist markets, an episode of violent repression is likely to mean a loss in confidence in the country's markets, massive international disinvestment, a run on the currency, and devaluation. In the contemporary "globalized" world, bloody acts of mass repression are likely to be acceptable only to regimes that are not very vulnerable to pressure from the great powers or that are insulated from the world market and world media. Hence it is hardly surprising that the Marcos regime crumbled before "people power," but the Chinese and Burmese regimes did not.

The events of the past two decades seem, then, to have produced two new mutations in the template of revolution, giving rise to the Islamic and the "people power" models of revolution and to have caused the eclipse of one previous model: Bolshevik. We seem to be living in a time when the model of revolution is in a state of flux unparalleled in its two hundred year history. But revolution itself, in one or another of its variants, remains a key template for contentious political action.

The Civil Rights Movement as Master Template Like the French Revolution, the American Civil Rights Movement seems to have made available to other claimants not simply particular repertoires, ideologies, or organizational forms, but a more-or-less predictable "package" of cultural items out of which a coherent movement might be fashioned. The characteristic elements of the package include: an ideological framing of the issue that relies on appeals to the rights of some constituency; a tactical reliance on a combination of marches or other public events to demonstrate mass support for the cause and radical direct action to achieve bargaining leverage; a general adherence to nonviolence; and an organizational approach that tends to downplay bureaucracy and formal leadership. These elements diffused widely through the family of "new left" movements which the civil rights struggle helped to inspire. Native Americans, chicanos, feminists, students, gays and lesbians, farmworkers, and others patterned their struggles after the Civil Rights Movement. But the imprint of the civil rights template can be seen at considerable temporal and geographic remove from the United States of the late 1960s. The European "new social movements" bore a striking resemblance both to the Civil Rights Movement and the other "new left" movements it helped spawn. In the contemporary United States, movements as otherwise dissimilar as animal rights, prolife, and the antidrunk driving crusade nevertheless adhere to the basic elements of the civil rights template. It could even be argued that the "people power" form of revolution played out in the Philippines in 1985 and eastern Europe in 1989–91 was but a civil rights variant on the theme of revolution. The same might be said for the contemporary democracy movement in Burma. Certainly the stress on nonviolence, mass demonstrations, and the rights of the Burmese people are consistent with the basic civil rights "package."

On the Relationships Among Contentious Temporalities

In the preceding section, we sought to describe and underscore the importance of two somewhat neglected temporal rhythms in the study of social movements and revolutions. So far so good. But, to this point, we have treated all of our temporalities in singular and noticeably static terms. In this section, we want to speculate a bit about the *dynamic* relationships among some of them. We begin with the two dominant temporal rhythms and the deterministic model of emergence implied by the standard account of the relationship between them.

Long-Term Change Processes and Cycles of Contention

We think it fair to say that the dominant models of social movements and revolutions are elaborated glosses on the relationship between these two temporalities. The "political process" or "political opportunity" perspective on social movements relies heavily on the cumulative effect of long-term change processes to explain the emergence and subsequent development of peak periods of movement activity. Long-term change processes are held to condition the likelihood of protest activity in two ways. First, such processes are likely to weaken previously stable elite power relationships, thus rendering the regime more vulnerable or receptive to challenge. Second, broad economic, demographic, political, and cultural processes can also strengthen the internal organization of a given challenging group, making it a more formidable claimant vis-a-vis established interests.

In similar fashion, the dominant structural perspectives on revolution (for example, Goldstone 1991; Skocpol 1979) also rely on the presumed causal connection between a host of long- and medium-run change processes and the onset of a revolutionary crisis. In her influential book, *States and Social Revolutions* (1979), Theda Skocpol stressed the crucial role of international pressure – stemming from either military incursions from without or debilitating and expensive military commitments on the part of the regime – in weakening "old regime" states. Attempts to stabilize the weakened state led, in turn, to divisive internal conflicts between state

117

leaders and important political, economic, and/or social elites. The result was ruptured elite alliances and a drastically weakened – often inert – state, unable to resist the popular mobilization that inevitably followed from the crisis of state breakdown.

In his 1991 book, *Revolution and Rebellion in the Early Modern World,* Jack Goldstone adhered to a similar historiography of revolutionary origins, even as he criticized specific aspects of Skocpol's formulation. In particular, he criticized Skocpol for structuring her general model around certain idiosyncracies of her cases. To remedy this deficiency, Goldstone used his book to sketch what he saw as a more elaborated and generalizable model of revolutionary origins. Specifically, he:

. . . proposed that long-term economic and demographic changes should be added to international pressures as sources of state weakness and that one should look at the conjunction of (1) state fiscal weakness and debt, however it was caused; (2) competition and alienation among elites, both inside and outside of the state; and (3) the growth of popular grievances among urban, as well as rural, popular groups. When such long-term changes worked to intensify popular grievances at the same time that states were weakened and elites were in conflict, the result was massive state breakdown leading to revolutionary change. (Goldstone 1995:495)

Events as Mediating Between Long-Term Change Processes and Cycles of Contention

As compelling as the relationship between long-term change processes and the onset of popular contention might appear to be, it is, in our view, clearly incomplete as an account of the origins of movements and revolutions. Absent the collective processes of interpretation, attribution, and social construction, our current models of contention are incapable of explaining *how* various change processes conduce to popular struggle. That is, as with all of social life, it is the ongoing interpretation of events that shapes the likelihood of contentious politics. Indeed, these continuous processes of sense making and collective attribution are arguably more important in popular contention insofar as the latter requires participants to reject institutionalized routines and taken for granted assumptions about the world and to fashion new world views and lines of interaction. And yet, for all of their importance, these crucial interpretive dynamics are largely absent from our theories of social movements and revolutions.

There is virtually no mention of these processes in the dominant structural accounts of revolution.[2] There is perhaps a bit more attention to processes of this sort in the contemporary literature on social movements. Much of this attention has centered around what have come to be known as "framing process." But most of the conceptual work on framing betrays a more strategic/instrumental, and therefore later temporal, orientation to collective interpretation/construction than we have in mind here. The earliest work in this tradition by David Snow and some of his colleagues (Snow and Benford 1988; Snow et al. 1986) equated framing with the "conscious strategic efforts of groups of people to fashion shared understandings of the world and of themselves that legitimate and motivate collective action" (McAdam, McCarthy, and Zald 1996:6). In other words, framing has generally been conceived of as an activity pursued by groups that already define themselves as engaged in struggle. One part of that struggle involved the group or its agents in conscious efforts to "frame" their activities in ways that resonated with various audiences (for example potential adherents, the media, policymakers, bystander publics) whom the group hoped to influence. Our point is that, for all of their importance, these later framing efforts depend on earlier and far more contingent interpretive processes. Strategic framing implies adherence to a nonroutine and conflictual definition of the situation. But this definition is itself a product of earlier processes of collective interpretation and social construction.

What are the processes that help to produce the emergent understandings that are the beginnings of this adversarial definition of the situation? How do long-term change processes become visible to potential insurgents? How do latent challengers come to attribute significance to such processes and to adduce opportunities in otherwise opaque environments? There is no single causal pathway to these interpretive breakthroughs, but transformative events would seem to be among the most common mediators of the change/protest relationship. Events serve this function by apparently distilling and expressing the potential for insurgent action inherent in a particular environment. We say "apparently" because it is not the events themselves, but their *collective interpretation* that is so

---

[2] In recent years there has developed a more "bottom up" culturalist approach to the study of revolution that does pay serious attention to the kinds of interpretive processes under discussion here. Proponents of this perspective would include: Goodwin (1994), Hunt (1984), McDaniel (1991), and Sewell (1990; 1996) among others.

consequential. In other words, Montgomery catalyzed the Civil Rights Movement, not by exposing some objective vulnerability in American racial politics, but by serving as the vehicle through which civil rights forces came to construct a new understanding of themselves and of the potential for change in U.S. race relations.

It is important to note that events can and generally do play this role throughout the life of a movement or revolution. So, if Montgomery and the Greensboro Sit-in served, in turn, to convince black insurgents (and other parties to the conflict) that the time was rife with new promise, then the assassination of Martin Luther King had an obverse "chilling effect" on movement adherents. In this sense events serve as something equivalent to Weber's ideational "switchmen" in the history of movements and revolutions. That is, events are the central source of "evidence" out of which insurgents (and other parties to the conflict) construct their shared understandings of the system's vulnerability at every stage of the protest cycle. They thus mediate between long- and medium-term change processes and the ebb and flow of protest activity, distilling and illuminating the former and shaping the latter.

Events, Master Templates, and Cycles of Contention

We have already remarked that the temporality of master templates is punctual and that this punctual character is linked to the occurrence of historical events. Events like the Greensboro Sit-in or the taking of the Bastille not only mark, but to a significant degree constitute, the emergence of new possibilities for the conduct of contentious politics. They bring to articulation novel schemes of political action, serve as an example of how such action might proceed, and advertise widely the power of the new action template. By demonstrating the vulnerability of the regime these events also embolden other challengers to map their claims onto their own variants of the new templates. As a consequence, they typically give rise to a succession of mimetic actions that instantiate and reproduce the master template. The taking of the Bastille initiated a string of more-or-less violent assertions of political will by the people – beginning with the slaughters of July 23, but continuing through the October days of 1789, during which the king was forced to relocate his residence and the capital of the nation from Versailles to Paris; the revolution of August 10, 1792; the September massacres in that same year; the purging of the Girondins from the Convention in 1793; the supposedly counterrevolutionary "federalist" uprisings against the dictatorship of the Committee of Public Safety in Lyon and Marseille in that same year; the revolt of Prarial in 1795; or the attempted "Conspiracy of the Equals" in that same year.

Some of these revolutionary actions were successful (in that the insurgents imposed their will on the state) and others failed or were crushed. But all of them were in one way or another predicated upon the template of revolutionary insurrection; the collective and potentially violent assertion of popular will that was instituted by the taking of the Bastille and sanctioned by the subsequent actions of the National Assembly. In characterizing these direct assertions of popular will as mimetic and as resulting in the reproduction of the template, we do not mean that they were simply the automatic copies of the taking of the Bastille. Rather, each effort constituted in effect a collective interpretation of the template; an attempt to apply it or to explore its possible implications in what were necessarily novel circumstances. The "copies" produced in such actions were therefore never just copies; their success or failure resulted in delimitations, amplifications, dead ends, extensions, and reconfigurations of the template in question.

These considerations have three important implications for thinking about contentious politics. First, templates are always undergoing modification; most obviously in events themselves, but also in actors' reflections on events and in plans and strategies for future actions. As Sahlins (1981; 1985) and Sewell (1992) have pointed out, the reproduction of structures always entails some degree of modification of the structures being "reproduced." The distinction between continuity and change is one of degree, not of kind.

Second, sometimes these modifications are significant enough to constitute the birth of new templates or subtemplates, as we have argued the Bolshevik seizure of power on behalf of the proletariat did. It is the inventions or modifications that occur in events that give birth to new templates. Indeed, the taking of the Bastille itself was in some respects only a modification of a long series of urban revolts in France (see Tilly 1986).

Finally, the invention or mutation of a template frequently touches off a cycle of contention. From this perspective cycles can be seen as loosely coordinated attempts to explore and expand the boundaries of new templates of political contention introduced to the world in well-publicized events. So it was with the cycle of insurrectionary actions that followed the taking of the Bastille; or the hundreds of sit-ins (or variants thereof; for example, "wade-ins," "read-ins," and so on) inspired by the events in

Greensboro; or, for that matter, the national and international cycle of "student movements" that followed close on the heels of the 1964 "free speech" movement at Berkeley.

Long-Term Change Processes and the Birth and Death of Master Templates

Although the sorts of long-term change processes traditionally discussed in social science analyses of social movements and revolutions certainly do not, in any direct sense, "cause" the birth, diffusion, or death of master templates, they do create or limit the conditions for the templates exis-tence. Space constraints preclude a full exploration of this important, but complex, relationship. All we can do is offer a few suggestive examples of the ways in which broad-change processes might facilitate (or constrain) the creation of new master templates. So, for example, it was the gradual development of a public sphere (via printing, expansion of commercial wealth, and so on) that made the modern notion of public opinion and popular sovereignty conceivable, thus producing a situation in which the modern notion of revolution is possible. In similar fashion, industriali-zation, urbanization, and proletarianization are clear preconditions for the emergence of the labor movement. The global reach of the media, together with smaller nations' dependence on the good opinion of the rich countries, makes it possible for a "people power" movement to overthrow a government without initiating antigovernment violence.

These examples could be multiplied many times over. The important point is, in highlighting the pivotal moments of cultural creativity in which new templates of contention are fashioned, we are certainly not suggest-ing that such events or the templates they give rise to are independent of the broad-change processes that have shaped the social context in which they occur. Quite the contrary; the possibilities for cultural creativity will always be broadly constrained by the long-term change processes that precede and shape the moment.

Conclusion

So how does the addition of these two "submerged" temporalities to the dominant rhythms of long change waves and protest cycles alter our understanding of social movements and revolutions? In closing, we want to underscore what we see as two important implications of the fuller array of temporalities now before us. We begin with what our broader set of temporalities – and especially a focus on events – implies about the nature of social movements and revolutions.

First, a more event-centered approach to the study of popular contention necessarily changes our view of the long-term change processes that analysts have tended to see as critical to the origins of movements and revolutions. We are not disputing the importance of such processes, but arguing for a more "eventful" conception of the *longue duree*. From one perspective, long-term change processes are nothing but aggregations of countless events, a few with catalytic significance (for example, Brown v. Board of Education), and the great majority that reverberate only in the individual lives of those effected (that is, a depression-era move from Georgia to Illinois by a black sharecropper). But even if we want, for analytic reasons, to reserve the term *event* only for those occurrences that come to be imbued with at least some degree of public visibility and significance, we will quickly see that our long-term change processes are in fact punctuated by and, in important ways, fueled by events and the collective processes of interpretation and social construction by which meanings are assigned to those events.

The Civil Rights Movement provides a convenient illustration of the point. If the Montgomery Bus Boycott was the event that catalyzed the mass movement into action, it was preceded by a host of key events, dating from at least the mid-1930s, whose interpretation contributed to a growing sense of threat (on the part of white supremacists) and opportunity (by proponents of civil rights) regarding the structure of American racial politics. A complete listing of these events is beyond the scope of this chapter, but any such list would certainly include the following:

- the wholesale switch of black voters from the Republican to the Democratic Party in the 1936 presidential election;
- Eleanor Roosevelt's help and support in arranging for black singer Marion Anderson to perform at the Lincoln Memorial in 1939 after she was denied use of the DAR Hall in Washington, D.C.;
- A. Philip Randolph's abortive 1941 March on Washington which forced President Roosevelt to issue an Executive Order establishing a Fair Employment Practices Commission to investigate charges of discrimination in hiring by defense contractors;
- President Truman's 1946 appointment of a Committee on Civil Rights charged with investigating the "current state of civil rights in

the country and recommending appropriate legislative remedies for deficiencies uncovered";
- Jackie Robinson's entrance into major league baseball at the start of the 1947 season;
- the strong civil rights plank approved by the Democratic Party at its 1948 Convention;
- Truman's surprise victory in the 1948 presidential contest, despite the active opposition of southern Dixiecrats;
- Truman's 1948 executive order calling for the desegregation of the armed forces;
- the brief filed by the U.S. Attorney General in December 1952 supporting civil rights litigants in a public school desegregation case – *Brown v. Topeka Board of Education* – then before the Supreme Court;
- President Eisenhower's 1953 executive order desegregating the District of Columbia;
- the Supreme Court's 1954 ruling in the *Brown* case declaring education segregation unconstitutional.

We could add to this list indefinitely, but our point should by now be clear. The long-term changes that rendered American racial politics more vulnerable to change in the post-World War II era were encoded, if not produced, by a string of events that stretch back several decades prior to the onset of the mass movement. Briefly, long-term change processes do not simply lead up to catalytic events; they are informed and amplified by them at every point in time.

A similar point can be made about the "eventful" nature of those peak periods of popular contention we tend to equate with movements and revolutions. As noted above, "event research" has long been one of the empirical staples of movement scholarship. Event research has typically involved the identification and coding of newspaper accounts of protest events aimed at creating a detailed time-series representation of a movement protest cycle. In this sense, one might say that we have long conceived of the second dominant temporal rhythm in "eventful" terms. But while useful as a crude means of mapping a cycle, event research has erred in weighting all protests, demonstrations, and speeches as equally important. As a complement to this approach, we would argue for a more nuanced form of event analysis that would focus, not so much on the facts of *each* event, but the degree of public attention and significance that came to attach to *particular* events nested in the broader stream of protest. Such an approach would quickly designate a small number of events as key shapers of the escalating and deescalating conflict. More importantly, it would serve to remind students of movements and revolutions of the numerous contingent outcomes embedded in empirical phenomena we often tend to depict in somewhat determinant, aggregate terms, thereby restoring to these struggles the very real prospects for human agency that inhere in them.

5

Leadership Dynamics and Dynamics of Contention

Ron Aminzade, Jack A. Goldstone, and Elizabeth J. Perry

Leadership is one of the most extensively researched topics in psychology and organization studies (Rosenbach and Taylor 1993; Sashkin and Lassey 1983). A focus on leadership as the wellspring of political action is found in Carlyle (1849), Freud (1965), Lasswell (1948), and Weber (1954), among many others. Despite this vast outpouring of scholarship, most research has focused on explaining leadership itself, rather than on its effects. That is, the bulk of scholarship is devoted to describing what kind of person (in terms of background or personal characteristics) becomes a leader (Mazlish 1976; Rejai and Phillips 1979), the various types of leadership (Sashkin and Rosenbach 1993; Weber 1954), the situations in which leadership emerges (Burns 1978), the relations between leaders and followers (Fiedler 1967), and the detailed lives or psychohistories of individual leaders (Erikson 1962; 1969; Wolfenstein 1967). Surprisingly little scholarship, particularly in regard to social movements and revolutions, has sought to determine the effect that variation in leadership dynamics – that is, in the relationships among revolutionary leaders, or between leaders and followers – have on the course and outcomes of contentious politics.

There are three main perspectives on the effect of leadership dynamics on movement dynamics in the classic sociological literature: the circulation of elites (Pareto), the tendency to oligarchy of elites (Michels), and the need to rationalize or institutionalize charismatic leadership (Weber). All are surprisingly negative in assessing the potential for revolutionary leadership to make a significant difference. Pareto (1935) argued in effect that once in power, revolutionary leaders lose their edge, and are overtaken by a new generation of leaders who simply continue the cycle, with one elite substituting for another. Michels (1959) argued even more vehemently that movement leaders will become captured by the organizational logic of the position of leadership, by their prerogatives and power, and thus become guardians of their own power rather than their original revolutionary cause. Revolutionaries thus will inevitably turn counterrevolutionary and conservative once in power. Weber (1954), although arguing that charismatic leaders have in themselves the extraordinary power to challenge and overturn existing institutions, further suggested that unless that charisma is somehow "routinized" by becoming embedded in rational, bureaucratic institutions, the accomplishments of charismatic leaders will pass from the scene with their demise.

Those perspectives that are more optimistic about the impact of movements and revolutions to effect lasting change are, perhaps surprisingly, more diffident about the role of individuals as leaders. Instead, these perspectives follow what today is known as the "contingency" or "situational" approach to leadership (Fiedler 1967; Hersey and Blanchard 1982). In this view, leaders are essentially servants of their followers, or their historical situation. In the Marxist view of revolutions as the product of class struggles, even in the Leninist "vanguard party" form, or in the political process view of social movements as responses to the intersection of popular grievances or demands with increased political opportunities (McAdam 1982), leaders play a critical, but subordinate role, helping their followers steer through the shoals of history to reach their destined goals.

Although the social movement leader or professional revolutionary plays an essential role in framing and articulating issues (Gamson, Fireman, and Rytina 1982; Snow and Benford 1992), and in activating networks and mobilizing supporters, the emphasis in these approaches is on the movement versus the state, with leaders acting as intermediaries, facilitators, and motivators, as tacticians and foci of events, rather than as independent shapers of the course and outcomes of contention.

The tendency to relegate leadership to the status of a dependent or indirect variable, and thereby rob it of much of its agency, can be seen in all three of today's major theoretical approaches to the study of collective action and social change. Structuralists (Goldstone 1991; Skocpol 1979) explain movements and revolutions as outcomes of broad-change processes that shift resources and political opportunities; culturalists (Baker 1990; Hunt 1989) point to disembodied discourses and shared meanings; and rationalists (Chong 1991; Popkin 1979), although pointing out the role of entrepreneurs in arranging the selective incentives that

127

motivate individuals to participate, stress the configuration of individual costs and benefits as determining action and its results). In none of these approaches does variation in leadership figure as a key factor in explaining variations in the outcomes of contention. To be sure, empirical accounts of social movements by scholars in all three traditions do afford a substantial role to particular leaders. In theoretical terms, however, leaders usually are pictured as little more than instruments for enforcing structural, cultural, or rational imperatives.

In part, this is understandable given that some of the things that successful leaders do best are to take advantage of structural opportunities, to articulate cultural themes, and to manipulate incentives for action. Thus, if we examine only successful movements and revolutions, there is an inevitable confounding of the actions of individual leaders with the generalities of structural, cultural, and rationalist theories of contention, and the former tend to disappear behind the latter. Moreover, if we only give analytical attention to the origins and outcomes of contention, we will fail to see the key turning points, to note the range of plausible counterfactuals about what might have happened, and to trace the critical role of leaders in guiding the process of contention to particular outcomes. Goldstone (1991) has argued that such "process tracing" plays an important role in understanding causation in historical and comparative sociology. It is only if we examine the course of leadership actions, noting instances of success and *failure* in social movements and revolutions, and showing how *particular outcomes* arise that are often *not* achieved, such as the creation of democratic institutions, that we can hope to identify the pivotal role of leadership dynamics in contentious politics.

We can easily think of movements (China's Taiping Rebellion, India's Civil Disobedience, the Protestant Reformation) that might never have occurred – and would certainly never have taken the form they did – without the initiative and inventiveness of specific trail-blazing individuals. In such cases, leaders function not merely as dutiful stewards of social, cultural, and economic forces but also as powerful pacesetters in their own right. Suppose then that we were to put leaders at the center of our analysis, to view them as independent – rather than simply dependent or intervening – variables in the formation of social movements. Would we have anything new to say about contentious politics? Do different sorts of leaders contribute to the emergence and evolution of different types of social movements?

128

Types of Leadership: Two Dichotomies

Since Weber, the image of the "charismatic leader" has seemed an essential part of revolutionary movements. Of course, the image goes back much further; the prototypical charismatic protest leader was Jesus Christ. If we can believe the gospels, Jesus was nonviolent, an impressive orator, and inspired devout loyalty among his followers. For these skills, he was crucified as a rebel leader by the Romans. Yet there is no single "type" of charismatic leader. In the French Revolution, Danton was flamboyant, Robespierre austere; the Russian Revolution featured the dashing Trotsky and the severe Lenin. The American Revolution was led by stoic George Washington, but given its voice by the rhetorical fire of Thomas Jefferson and Thomas Paine; the Chinese Communist Revolution was stirred by the passions of Mao Zedong, but organized by the bureaucratic formality of Liu Shaoqi. The U.S. Civil Rights Movement showed the same range, with leaders varying in style from the preacherly Martin Luther King to the radical Malcolm X.

What revolutionary leaders do share is an uncommon devotion to their cause. They live for it, are willing to suffer (though they may manage to avoid dying) for it, and they inspire others to do the same. To succeed, they must convince people that they are working for a public good, rather than personal advantage. And they must manage to blend a diversity of leadership styles and attributes, including those that they themselves do not possess, but may find among other leaders, both formal and informal.

Of course, there are many more important topics in the general field of leadership and contentious politics than we can begin to address in this chapter, many of which have been the subject of excellent studies: the gendered nature of leadership (Barnett 1993; Robnett 1996), the role of intellectuals in movements (Gouldner 1979; Pinard and Hamilton 1989); the professionalization of movement leaders and the differences between formal and informal leadership (McCarthy and Zald 1973). However, our focus here will be on how, given the emergence of a certain set of movement leaders, their goals and relationships can lead to specific outcomes.

The most consistent finding of the vast literature on leadership is that there are basically two "dimensions" of leadership that appear in virtually all settings (Bales and Slater 1955; Sashkin and Lassey 1983; Sashkin and Rosenbach 1993): task oriented and people oriented. Task-oriented leaders, or leadership actions, are concerned with assembling the resources and executing the actions needed to accomplish a particular goal. Task-oriented leaders and actions are sometimes referred to in terms of "pragmatic" or (in Weber's terms) "rationalized" leadership. People-oriented leaders, or leadership actions, are concerned with evoking a particular emotional state in people, namely a state of motivation and commitment, often identification, with the leader or with a movement or goal. People-oriented leaders and actions are sometimes referred to as "visionary" or (in Weber's terms) "charismatic" leadership. Although many leaders are capable of both task-oriented and people-oriented leadership, many are not, and specialize in one or the other dimension. In such cases, various scholars have argued that cooperation between leaders of the different types is essential to the success of the group.

The people-oriented or "charismatic" type of leadership draws heavily on the emotional aspect of movement politics that we examine in more detail elsewhere in this volume. The leadership skills involved in charismatic interactions with followers, argues Patricia Wasielewski (1985) in her study of the speeches of Martin Luther King and Malcolm X, include an ability to skillfully evoke, revoke, and reframe emotions and emotion rules. Charismatic leaders evoke emotions that create a community of feeling, revoke emotions by creating affective dissidence that leads followers to rethink their worldviews, and reframe emotions by introducing new meaning structures that reshape their followers' interpretations of the world and emotional responses to it. Charismatic leaders are less likely than bureaucratic leaders to use a distancing and instrumentalist professional discourse, which translates emotional expressions of suffering into grievances that can be rationally bargained over, and more likely to express the angry voices and emotional experiences of the oppressed.

Eric Selbin's (1993) study of modern Latin American revolutions argues that only those revolutions that combined both visionary and task-oriented (which he labels *organizational*) leadership were able to succeed in both consolidating their hold on popular allegiance and in institutionalizing their revolutionary policies. Of the four cases that he examines (Nicaragua, Grenada, Cuba, Bolivia), only the first succeeded in both respects, due to effective deployment of organizational and visionary leadership. But a closer look at his cases shows that it was not elements of revolutionary leadership that were *missing* that led to failure. Grenada had both a visionary leader (Maurice Bishop) and a great organizational leader (Bernard Coard). Cuba had masterful organizational leaders (Raul Castro and Camile Cienfuegos) to complement Fidel Castro's passion and vision. And Bolivia had a great visionary ("Che" Guevarra) to complement its disciplined organization of mine workers. But in all three of the latter cases, leadership dynamics went awry: Individual actions led to the death or exile or domination of one set of leaders, so that leadership became unbalanced and ultimately unsuccessful. Bolivia's revolution failed to consolidate popular allegiance to the revolutionary cause; Cuba's revolution may not outlive its leader Fidel Castro, due to the failure of the revolution to achieve success in building viable political and economic institutions; and Grenada's revolution self-destructed in less than a decade. This suggests that leadership dynamics may have a more crucial independent effect on movement outcomes and dynamics than is generally appreciated.

We also wish to highlight a second dichotomy. Many scholars have noted a difference between "autocratic" and "democratic"-type leaders; however, this has often been taken simply as a matter of "style," either of which might, given the right circumstances, be useful for movement success. White and Lippitt (1960) even assimilated this difference to the two above-noted dimensions of leadership, arguing that autocratic leaders were just extremely task oriented, while democratic leaders were so people oriented that they sought broad participation.

However, we wish to go beyond these observations and argue that there is a crucial, independent dimension of revolutionary or movement leadership that we would define as ranging from "self-effacing" to "self-aggrandizing." Self-effacing leaders, though greatly concerned with their place in history and the success of their movement, nonetheless separate those issues from their personal power; they are thus willing to share power, and indeed to institutionalize its wide distribution, if that will help procure the success of their goals. Their careers give the impression that power came to them unsought, and that their influence depended more on personal example and virtue than on their formal authority. Examples include George Washington (who twice stepped down from positions of peak power, once as commander-in-chief of the new U.S. military and again after his second term as president), Nelson Mandela, Mahatma Ghandi, Corazon Aquino, and Vaclav Havel. Their legacies include not only success of their revolutionary movements, but the institutionalization of key elements of democracy – including separation of powers, binding consultation of government with a more-or-less extensive citizenry, and limits on the arbitrary authority of state leaders (Tilly 1998). This kind of leader, however, is fairly rare. More common are self-aggrandizing leaders, who cannot separate their personal authority from the success of their mission. Examples include Stalin, Castro, Robespierre, and Mao. For this kind of leader, a challenge to their personal leadership is tantamount to challenging the legitimacy of the movement they lead. Such leaders often are successful in leading movements or revolutions, but they do not produce democratic regimes. Often, quite the reverse; their leadership is associated with purges, terror, and cults of personality. This is not only true of revolutionary leaders, but leaders of cults (for example, Jonestown) and other movements.

We therefore wish to propose at least two ways in which dynamics of leadership influence the course and outcomes of political conflicts. First, the potential conflict or cooperation between "task oriented" or organizational and "people oriented" or visionary actions, or between different leaders who emphasize one or the other of these dimensions, is an independent shaper of the course of movement events. For example, the cultural revolution in China can be seen in part as a conflict over the priority of organizational tasks versus maintaining a certain visionary and emotional orientation. Indeed, both sides in the cultural revolution recruited supporters from the broader population that seem to divide in their own orientation along these lines.

Second, the question of whether a revolution leads to a democratic outcome does not depend simply on favorable or unfavorable social–structural conditions for the emergence of democracy, but also on the character of the chief revolutionary leaders. For example, even rather poor countries that seem unprepared for democracy (India, the Philippines, South Africa) have been able to achieve a measure of democracy under self-effacing leaders. In contrast, Cuba – which had a prior history of democracy and was the most urbanized and literate society in Latin America – failed to achieve democracy under Castro's leadership.

This chapter traces out these examples in more detail to underscore these points. We first look at how a struggle between two different "types" of leadership produced success and failure in different phases of the Chinese revolution, and particularly how this struggle gave rise to that great social movement within the revolution, the Cultural Revolution of 1965–70. Next we turn to the case of Tanganyika, where the structural realities of a colonial order promoted racial nationalism and civic exclusion based on race, but the initiatives of one forceful leader facilitated a racially inclusive vision of citizenship and a nonviolent path to independence. Finally we survey four revolutionary movements in the Americas, arguing that different types of leaders contributed to fundamentally different political outcomes.

A See-Saw Hypothesis of Revolutionary Success: The Chinese Case

Surveying the record of Chinese social movements, one can readily detect the complementary (and competitive) contributions of two quite different types of political leaders – a yin and yang of movement instigators, if you will. Political scientist Lucian Pye attributes this alternation between what he refers to as "mandarins" and "rebels" to a fundamental polarity in Chinese political culture: "at one extreme, an emphasis on conformity, repressive centralized controls, and orthodox beliefs and discipline. At the other extreme are a greater tolerance for private initiatives, a relaxation of controls, decentralization, and a liberation from orthodoxy" (Pye 1988:38–39). According to Pye this basic duality runs through the history of Chinese political culture from Confucianism to communism, helping to generate the violent policy oscillations for which the Chinese political system is famous.

Taking a page from Daoist notions of symmetry and flux, let us propose a "see-saw hypothesis of revolutionary success." In China, as elsewhere, the capacity of a social movement to attain its goals hinges in large measure upon maintaining some balance between contradictory human impulses. When leaders with opposing styles are able to work out an effective modus vivendi that affords due play to their competing approaches, the likelihood of movement success is greatly enhanced. However, if one leadership style dominates to the exclusion of all competition, the enterprise is apt to founder.

The contrast between "mandarin" and "rebel" leadership has contributed to fundamental tensions – productive as well as destructive – within Chinese social movements. A clear example can be seen in the relationship between two of the chief engineers of the communist revolution, Mao Zedong and Liu Shaoqi. Whereas "rebel" Mao was renowned for his rowdy populism, "mandarin" Liu stood as the enforcer of party discipline. To some degree, these differences reflected a natural division of labor in a complex revolutionary situation. According to an early study by John Lewis, the contrast derived in good measure from the two men's dissimilar experiences in the mobilizing enterprise. While Mao Zedong was defining his role as inspirational guerrilla leader in the revolutionary capital of Yan'an, Liu Shaoqi was serving as senior political commissar behind enemy lines – an assignment that demanded strict obedience to organizational norms. Where Mao felt free to encourage such "egalitarian" practices as the mass line and open-door rectification, Liu was drawn to a hierarchical style of command that stressed party solidarity and inner-party struggle. Lewis argues that although Mao was a consummate warrior, after the victory of the revolution and consolidation of political power, his unruly methods became an increasing liability.

Uniquely suited to the wartime environment, Mao's system was singularly inappropriate for ruling a country moving toward modernization. Even though Mao recognized that the requirements for leadership would change after the seizure of power, he rejected the notion that the essential attributes of his system would also need to change . . . It was virtually inevitable that Mao's previous charismatic role would lose its centrality . . . The problem was that Mao, the charismatic personality, was not inclined to "crystallize" and continue a new institutional structure. As the leader, Mao insisted instead that his potential heirs acquire those intangible qualities found in his revolutionary role rather than those of the political commissar. (Lewis 1968:459–60)

The full dimensions of this contradiction between rebel and mandarin, Lewis suggests, unfolded only in the turmoil of the Cultural Revolution when Mao lashed out against the commissars and the bureaucratic edifice that they had erected during the initial seventeen years of communist rule. In Weberian terms, the Cultural Revolution represented an irreconcilable confrontation between Mao's "charismatic" leadership on the one hand and the "rational" bureaucrats of the new communist order on the other.

Whether we choose to frame the issue in Weberian or Chinese categories, the question remains: What are the origins and, more importantly, the consequences of different types of leadership? Lewis offers a functionalist explanation for the contrast between Mao and Liu: Mao's populism was an effective response to the requirements of rural revolution in the "red" base areas, just as Liu Shaoqi's authoritarian style was better suited to the difficulties of organizing in the "white" areas under Japanese and Guomindang control. But Mao's revolutionary tactics, Lewis cautions, lost their efficacy when confronted with the sober business of economic development.

Although historical experiences and exigencies undoubtedly do play a considerable part in accounting for the emergence and influence of divergent leadership styles, the explanation is not quite so simple. For as Mao's pivotal role in the Cultural Revolution suggests, leaders may exert enormous influence over the course of a social movement even when their methods seem woefully out of step with the "objective" demands of the day. A strictly functional answer is thus insufficient to make sense of the many instances in which forceful leaders redefine situational imperatives in keeping with their own idiosyncratic visions of the world.

That some individuals swim against the tides of history – and manage moreover to convince millions of converts to follow in their wake – calls for a closer look at the roots of rebel leadership. Why are some individuals self-confident enough to defy "objective" circumstances in a seemingly irrational bid to satisfy their political imaginations whereas others adopt a more risk averse approach? Common sense suggests that the answer must lie in part in the psychological makeup of the rebel leader him/herself. But social science offers few clues on how to follow up on this common-sense proposition. Political psychology, once a staple ingredient in theories of revolutionary movements, has fallen from scholarly grace. The amateurish manner in which psychological studies of revolutionary leaders were often conducted may have rightfully condemned them to the dustbin of theory, yet the result is that we find ourselves largely bereft of conceptual tools for probing one of the most fascinating issues surrounding social movements.

Studies of Chinese politics have often noted the differences in temperament between Chairman Mao and his rival, Liu Shaoqi. As Lowell Dittmer wrote at the time of the Cultural Revolution, "Mao seems to be a more spontaneously emotional person than Liu; in meetings with subordinates he has been known to weep or to become violently angry and curse his antagonist in blunt, colorful language . . . Liu, on the other hand, is emotionally withdrawn a 'cold fish' . . . Liu[s] political errors . . . usually consisted of excessive rigor in the enforcement of justice. He tries to display rationality and unbending rectitude . . . Mao evidently believes in his emotions as indicators of a more compelling truth. Liu . . . showed a constant preoccupation with the 'costs' of things" (Dittmer 1974:174–96). This oft noted difference between the "uptight" Liu and the unrestrained Mao was matched by stark contrasts in their style of leadership: Mao's conception of the proper relationship between leader and led is unmediated contact . . . Liu has a contrasting tendency to mediate and formalize relationships between people . . . While Liu's leadership style is formal and routinized, Mao's is episodic and provocative . . . Mao exhibits a flexibility in switching positions or allies that prevents any stabilization of expectations and leaves his colleagues in perpetual uncertainty (Dittmer 1974:181–185).

This polarity between "rebel" and "mandarin" styles of leadership goes well beyond the individual cases of Mao Zedong and Liu Shaoqi. In his detailed study of a Chinese village under communism, sociologist Richard Madsen comes up with a parallel dichotomy of leadership styles at the grassroots level. He finds that political life in Chen village was deeply influenced by competition between two leaders "committed to a distinctly different concept of local moral order" (Madsen 1984:34). One of these village leaders, whom Madsen characterizes as a "member of the Communist gentry" (246) – roughly equivalent to Lucian Pye's "mandarin," relied upon familiar methods of dispensing patronage to build up his power base. The other, whom Madsen dubs a "Communist rebel" (249), activated the resentment of marginal members of the village to strive toward a new, more egalitarian rural community.

The dualism has counterparts in other cultural traditions, as well, of course: the dichotomy in Greek mythology between Apollonian order and Dionysian disorder; the contradiction in Christian theology between upholders of church authority and adherents of antinomianism, and so forth. These binary oppositions point to fundamental tensions within the human psyche itself. If fruitfully combined, such seemingly contradictory – yet mutually constituted – tendencies can lend tremendous dynamism and dedication to collective action. The so-called "Yan'an roundtable," in which China's revolutionary leaders managed to transcend widely disparate backgrounds and mobilizational styles to cooperate in fighting first the Japanese and then the Guomindang, was a critical ingredient in the communists' impressive rise to power. By the same token, the unraveling of this collaborative effort spelled disaster for the revolutionary enterprise – as exemplified in the internecine conflicts that led directly to the Cultural Revolution (MacFarquhar 1974–77).

Although the Cultural Revolution is sometimes treated simply as a "two-line struggle" between rabble-rouser Mao Zedong and organization-man Liu Shaoqi, such conflicts within the political elite bespoke an equally deep cleavage cutting across society at large. China's Cultural Revolution was not simply a mobilization effort manipulated from on high, but a mass movement in which rival local leaders competed ferociously for control. Nowhere was this clearer than in the city of Shanghai, where worker rebels wielded enormous authority – first as instigators of popular unrest and then as officials in the newly constituted "revolutionary" order. But rebel hegemony did not emerge unchallenged. In Shanghai, as elsewhere in China, the early years of the Cultural Revolution were marked by battles between "rebels" (zaofan pai) seeking to overthrow local powerholders and "conservatives" (baoshou pai) struggling to protect them. All across the country, rebels challenged the revolutionary credentials of leading cadres whereas conservatives supported the powers-that-be. William Hinton, commenting on the ubiquity of this phenomenon, notes that the basic dichotomy occurred "with such regularity and persistence that it had to be recognized as some sort of law of the political sphere as universal as Boyle's law in chemistry or Newton's law in physics." (Hinton 1983:611)

The differences in personality and operating styles that helped to define the confrontation between Mao and Liu were mirrored at the local level. An examination of leaders of the two major worker factions in Shanghai reveals that such individuals were divided not only by competing political agendas, but by temperament and demeanor as well (Perry and Li 1997). Whereas the commanders of the rebel Workers' General Headquarters were known for their fiery personalities, the rival Scarlet Guard conservatives were a decidedly circumspect lot.

Rebel leaders were famed for profanity and violence – habits that long predated the outbreak of the Cultural Revolution. Many of them also favored personal hobbies and apparel that set them apart from the typical Chinese urbanite of the time. As one Workers' General Headquarters leader recalled his youthful exploits during this period of general conformity to drab Maoist standards:

I grew a beard and spend most of my non-working hours playing cards in the club. On Sundays I went to the suburbs to fish instead of engaging in proper duties. I even bought a necktie and then went to a shop that sold exotica to buy a used western suit. Sometimes I ventured to the city center in coat and tie. When I saw people wearing leather jackets, I spent more than 40 yuan to buy one. I was totally preoccupied with my playboy lifestyle. My frivolous habits gave the older workers a very bad impression. I organized dances and the like, which the older workers didn't appreciate. (Huang Jinhai April 5, 1977)

Although we now know that Chairman Mao himself was enjoying dance parties – and more – at this very time, such frivolity was not sanctioned for the populace at large (Li 1994:93–94, 280, 345–46, 356, 479). As political scientist Wang Shaoguang points out, the bleak economic situation following the Great Leap Forward had generated a strong ascetic tendency: "Now one might be considered backward if any aspect of one's life-style was out of the ordinary, such as wearing brightly colored clothes, applying hair oil, going to a restaurant, cultivating flowers, raising gold-fish, or playing chess" (Wang 1995:34).

Yet, years before the start of the Cultural Revolution, those who became the most prominent rebel leaders had already attained notoriety for a willingness to buck such social restrictions. Sociologist Gong Xiaoxia, who interviewed a number of Cultural Revolution leaders, observes that "most rebel leaders I met had some peculiar hobby, such as photography, writing, painting, singing, etc. . . . which I did not see among the conservative leaders I know . . . Evidence suggests that many early rebel organizations were formed on the basis of such shared personalities" (Gong, personal communication, November 2, 1995).

Rebel personalities are not born, but made. The wider social environment defines what is considered "rebellious" behavior, and it is only in the course of interacting with that environment that individuals develop defiant or compliant strategies. But this does not mean that explanations of rebel leadership can be reduced to environmental circumstances. For between environmental pressures and individual responses there lies a good deal of latitude for personal ingenuity and agency. Individual emotions and interpretations, while poorly understood by social scientists, figure significantly in this complex process. For some, social rules exist to be bent or broken – and the more cleverly one does so, the more elated one feels; for others, living by established rules is the sine qua non of self-respect. Although it is obviously emphatically not the case that "unruly" individuals turn inevitably to political rebellion, it does appear that such identities contribute to a particular style of rebel leadership.

Movements seeking radical social transformation need both rule breakers and rule makers. The former play an obvious role in persuading people to transgress prevailing norms in favor of new values and modes of behavior. For a movement to succeed in effecting genuine social change, however, it must also ensure a certain level of compliance to its own norms. The "commissar" performs a critical function in enforcing revolutionary discipline.

The Chinese communists' remarkable rise to power was facilitated by a conscious strategy of balancing these twin demands. In the revolutionary base areas, an audacious party secretary would be assigned a cautious deputy; a radical policy initiative would be followed by criticism of those cadres who had resorted to excessive force in carrying out the initiative;

138

and so forth. After the establishment of the People's Republic in 1949, this see-saw pattern continued in the numerous "mass campaigns" – from the effort to eradicate flies to the implementation of People's Communes – that marked the first seventeen years of communist rule. (Admittedly the see-saw began to list in an evermore leftist direction from at least the time of the Great Leap Forward in 1959. Yet as the retrenchment of the early 1960s – spearheaded by Liu Shaoqi – indicated, the teeter-totter was still in operation.) Thus it was only natural at the onset of the Cultural Revolution in 1966 that "conservatives" expected to play a key role in the eventual resolution of the movement.

The Cultural Revolution saw a dramatic change in the rules of the political game, however. Aware that he was entering his final political battle, an aging Mao Zedong abandoned his earlier commitment to "the correct handling of contradictions among the people" in favor of an all-out embrace of rebellion. The unrestrained inclinations of grassroots rebel leaders elicited a positive response from Chairman Mao, who stood as the ultimate arbiter of Chinese politics during the Cultural Revolution. By August 1973, the commander of the Workers' General Headquarters in Shanghai – Wang Hongwen – had gained a "helicopter" promotion to vice-chair of the Chinese Communist Party, tapped by Mao as his putative successor.

If Mao's approval ensured the dominance of the rebel faction (albeit only until his death in the fall of 1976), it also sealed the fate of the conservative Scarlet Guards. In Shanghai, the Scarlet Guard leaders – to a person – were drawn from the ranks of party activists. In contrast to the colorful rebels (some of whom were party members, others of whom were ordinary workers, and yet others of whom had been designated as "bad elements" prior to the Cultural Revolution), the Scarlet Guards were a rather bland lot who had gained their stake in the system by carefully toeing the party line. Their opposition to the rebels stemmed as much from differences in personal style as from any deep-seated ideological divide. As one Scarlet Guard commander put it, "I couldn't stand those Workers' General Headquarters leaders. They were rascals. We were, after all, party members and were used to strict demands on ourselves. During the Cultural Revolution I never could get along with those other people" (Tang Wenlan, May 17, 1992 interview).

The Scarlet Guards formed as an indignant reaction against what its members perceived as rebel excesses. Those who organized conservative groups were repelled by the lawless initiatives of those on the rebel side.

The worker rebels engaged in a series of sensational maneuvers – lying on the railroad tracks, stealing dossiers, assaulting leading cadres and work team representatives – that provoked the ire of many of the party activists among the workforce. As one Scarlet Guard leader recalled of the rebels at his factory:

> Those who put up big-character posters all belonged to a group of people whose demeanor (biaoxian) was usually pretty poor. Some of them were not diligent workers, who even after the Cultural Revolution didn't change their ways. They were careless and irresponsible . . . So at that time I was really dismayed. I felt that these people's basic character was bad and yet here they were, issuing commands and criticisms of the Shanghai Party Committee . . . Whenever they got off work they just went wild. (Li Jianyu July 3, 1992)

Conservatives were the obedient and risk-averse counterpart to the errant and reckless rebels. To some extent these polar identities were a product of different social roles. Whereas many rebels had been nurtured on the margins of Maoist society, conservatives were part and parcel of the party system itself. However, considering that a substantial proportion of rebel leaders (about one-third of the top commanders of the Workers' General Headquarters) were themselves party members, the fit between sociopolitical position and personality was far from perfect. Moreover, to the extent that this correlation did obtain (Scarlet Guard leaders were all drawn from the ranks of factory cadres), one is hard pressed to determine cause and effect. It is entirely conceivable, for example, that cadres had been promoted to their positions of authority precisely because of their restrained, disciplined temperament. As long as both sides of the revolutionary equation could be amply accommodated, the Chinese Communists compiled a stunning record of accomplishments: a decisive military victory that sent the American-backed Guomindang into permanent exile, a land reform that effectively eliminated the old rural elite, a socialization of industry that gave the state complete control over the industrial economy, and so on. When the leadership balance was broken by the Cultural Revolution, however, an unprecedented reign of terror ensued. The brutal death of Liu Shaoqi in 1969 symbolized the demise of restraining forces within the revolutionary leadership. Given the green light to proceed with abandon, those intent on eliminating the opposition unleashed a torrent of destructive violence whose repercussions reverberate to this day. The "One Strike Three Antis" Campaign, which rolled across the country in the early 1970s, was a terrifying expression of unbridled vengeance on both elite and mass levels.

Large-scale social movements are complex affairs containing deeply incongruous strains. The examples discussed above suggest that such contradictions may be promoted by contrasting leadership types reflective of basic tensions in the wider political culture. The cultural alternatives, moreover, seem to reflect fundamental differences in individual identities. If these assumptions are correct, they point toward a new direction for the study of movement leadership – a direction that lies in between the well trodden paths of a fascination with the uniquely (aberrant) personalities of individual leaders, on the one hand, and a fixation with social structure at the expense of human agency on the other. While the first approach, essential as it may be in the explanation of particular social movements, is usually too idiosyncratic to sustain wider generalization, the second underestimates the catalytic role that different types of leaders may play in giving rise to different forms of contentious politics. In "bringing leadership back in," analysts will be well advised to treat leadership as a variable that oscillates between certain culturally intelligible values, rather than as either an inimitable concatenation of individual eccentricities or an automatic outgrowth of environmental imperatives.

The Chinese experience indicates, furthermore, that the manner in which such contradictions are (or are not) resolved can tell us a good deal about the ultimate fate of social movements. So long as the paramount leaders of the Communist Revolution managed to harness their substantial differences to a common revolutionary cause, the movement was virtually unstoppable. An agreed-upon division of labor between "rebel" Mao and "mandarin" Liu fused populist spontaneity with party discipline into a powerful combination that helped ensure revolutionary success. But once that potent synthesis came unhinged – most notably during the Cultural Revolution – the enterprise careened out of control. A previously productive division of labor gave way to a destructive factionalism. Differences in personality and leadership style, once a source of constructive collaboration, were now a font of deadly strife. Whereas a movement able to contain such antinomies is capable of bringing about startling social transformation, a movement that allows but a single variant to predominate may be doomed to self-destruct.

The importance of harmonizing contradictory strains within the leadership applies in other countries and across other cleavages as well. In many social movements, gender is a significant dividing line. Although the top leadership of revolutionary and nationalist movements is typically dominated by men, during the early days of high-risk activism, women often play a central role in the day-to-day organizing tasks that build movements at the local level. Susan Geiger's (1997) study of the Tanganyikan nationalist struggle documents the importance of grassroots indigenous female organizers in the early mobilization of activists. In a situation of high-risk activism, where wage labor employment meant vulnerability and fear of employer reprisals, the independent and collaborative income-earning activities of women, coupled with strong informal social networks that cut across ethnic boundaries, enabled them to occupy leadership roles in the early nationalist movement. A similar pattern occurred during the early days of the Civil Rights Movement in the United States, also a period of high risk activism. "Men led, but women organized," argues Charles Payne (1990), not because of a difference in threats or exposure to reprisals, but because women had a stronger sense of efficacy fostered by religious beliefs and a greater sense of personal investment in kin and communal networks.

The authority exercised by the female leaders in the Civil Rights Movement in the United States and the nationalist movement in Tanganyika cannot be understood in terms of traditional sociological categories, such as Max Weber's concept of charismatic leadership. Weber conceptualized charismatic leadership in a manner that privileges masculinity, as based on actions that are heroic, disruptive, and removed from the mundane considerations of everyday life. The activities of these female activists correspond more closely to a form of charisma that is not detached from everyday life. This form of leadership, which Kathleen Jones (1993:116) labels "prudentialized charisma," involves mundane yet creative activities that foster dignity, build on daily survival and resistance strategies, challenge routine practices, and create and sustain dialogue and action networks. "Charismatic leadership," writes Jones (1993:115), "becomes not the isolated heroic action of the saint but the collective, creative, even mundane activity of an otherwise marginalized group to evidence grace under pressure as a way of securing dignity."

Again, our point is that successful movements tend to reflect a balance between disparate leadership styles, whether differentiated along lines of personality, gender, or other key cleavages. Such a division of labor allows a movement to appeal to a variegated constituency and to surmount a variety of organizational challenges.

Leadership Matters: Turning Points in the Struggle for Tanganyikan Independence

In highlighting the ability of successful movements to maintain a creative tension between potentially antagonistic leadership patterns, we do not mean to suggest that the importance of leaders in contentious politics can be understood simply in terms of generic leadership styles. Flesh and blood individuals do, indeed, make a difference.

The history of the Tanganyikan struggle for national independence illustrates the decisive role that a creative leader can play in determining the trajectory of a nationalist movement. In contrast to neighboring Kenya, where the violent Mau Mau uprising produced widespread bloodshed, the struggle for Tanganyikan independence was peaceful, in large part because of the leadership of Julius Nyerere. At key turning points in the struggle for independence, his leadership of the Tanganyikan African National Union (TANU) was a critical factor in determining the course of events, producing a nonviolent and racially inclusive path to national independence. In the absence of Nyerere's forceful leadership, proponents of an alternative racial nationalism would probably have triumphed, making the subsequent history of the Tanganyikan nation more similar to Uganda, where Asian residents were expelled in 1972. Although he later became the architect of an authoritarian state that repressed organized dissent, Nyerere was always a strong advocate of nonracial citizenship and the protection of minority rights.

Structural factors alone cannot account for this outcome. There were structural factors that help to account for the movement's nonracial nationalism and nonviolent character, including the absence of a large European settler community and Tanganyika's status as a United Nations Trust Territory. The former meant few potentially violent conflicts over land while the latter encouraged nationalists to pursue a nonviolent strategy of bringing international pressure to bear on British colonial officials. But there were more powerful structural forces encouraging a violent racialized struggle for independence, especially the class inequalities of a tripartite colonial racial order. This colonial racial system constituted Asians (that is, people of Indian and Pakistani origin), Europeans (that is, all whites), and Africans (that is, all blacks) as distinct races and relegated Africans to the lowest position in economic, political, and social hierarchies. Colonial economic policies effectively closed off commercial activities to Africans while a racial salary structure and segregated schools, hospitals, prisons, social clubs, and residences ensured that access to all scarce and valued resources was unequally distributed along racial lines. The top ranks of all state institutions were staffed by non-Africans, from the professional civil service to the military to the judicial system. This tripartite racial order produced nationalist leaders who espoused a racially exclusive vision of the nation as well as leaders advocating nonracial nationalism. As the following account suggests, the trajectory of Tanganyika's anticolonial struggle for independence was a product of intense conflict among nationalist leaders, not the inevitable result of inherited social structures. Decisive influences on this trajectory were Julius Nyerere's persuasive powers and his staunch commitment to nonviolence and nonracial citizenship.

The importance of Nyerere's charismatic leadership is evident in a major turning point in the nationalist struggle: the decision of January 1958 to participate in racially based elections. In response to a growing independence movement demanding majority rule, colonial authorities organized the first general elections, which were to take place in two stages, in September 1958 and February 1959. Each of the three racial groups received ten of the thirty contested seats in Parliament, but candidates had to compete for votes among all races since all voters were required to cast ballots for candidates of each race. Leaders of the organization directing the struggle for independence, the TANU, were divided over whether to participate in Legislative Council (LEGCO) elections based on a tripartite voting formula of "racial parity." The issue was heatedly debated at TANU's January 1958 Annual Delegates Conference at Tabora. For TANU, observes Judith Listowel (1965:303), this conference represented "a crossroads: it could either participate in the first general elections and follow the path of constitutional development; or it could boycott the elections, stage a general strike, and drift into violence."

Prior to 1958, TANU leaders had strongly opposed participation in any election based on a tripartiate formula. "We reject the principle of equal racial representation," wrote Julius Nyerere (1967:26) in 1952 "on the same ground on which we condemned that of European domination. It is a principle which in spite of its deceptive name assumes the principle of racial superiority." As late as April 1957, Nyerere advocated nonparticipation in racially based elections. But he changed his mind by January 1958, sensing that TANU could win an election even under conditions of restricted suffrage and racial parity and that a nonelectoral route to independence would probably be violent. In a critical strategic move, Nyerere decided before the conference to support TANU participation in the election, on the grounds that this concession would speed up the attainment of independence and avoid unnecessary bloodshed.

Divisions among nationalist leaders over participation in the 1958–59 election were rooted in contrasting visions of nationhood and citizenship. The group that coalesced around Nyerere favored electoral participation and advocated a nonracial nationalism that would grant citizenship to European and Asian residents. Nyerere was strongly in favor of allowing Europeans and Asians to join the nationalist movement but was unable to persuade his fellow nationalists to do so until after independence, in 1963. A decision to participate in the 1958 election constituted an opening wedge, since in order to win a majority on the Legislative Council, TANU would have to run Asian and European candidates sympathetic to their struggle, even though they were not allowed to join TANU. Those opposed to the decision to participate in the election demanded a redistribution of wealth and power along racial lines. Some insisted that self-government would mean the immediate forced departure of all Europeans and Asians. Opponents of participation included Zuberi Mtemvu, a TANU provincial secretary who, following the Tabora decision, went on to form an opposition political party, the African National Congress, which advocated "Africa for the Africans" and espoused a vision of racial nationalism that included citizenship for indigenous Africans only, a government composed only of Africans, an all-African civil service, and the redistribution of wealth and income away from the dominant European and Asian groups toward the historically oppressed and disadvantaged African majority (National Archives 1960–61: Accession 540, 17C).

At the outset of the Tabora conference, the majority of delegates favored boycotting the election. Many advocated launching a general strike (Listowel 1965:304). "There was considerable sentiment among the delegates for a boycott," writes Hugh Stephens (1968:142), "and it required the full use of his [Nyerere's] persuasive powers during the four-day meeting to carry his point of view." According to the account of one prominent delegate, Bibi Titi Mohammed: "Nyerere had a real problem, and I am sure he stayed for three days without eating anything and just drinking milk. Because people were saying we should fight, and Joseph Nyerere [his brother] said he would go and beat him up. Everybody was against him! . . . It was very chaotic. They were completely against this [tripartite voting] . . ." (Geiger 1997:100). The four days of lively debate among nationalist leaders included a good deal of shouting and screaming

145

in a boiling hot conference hall. The first delegate to speak in favor of participation, Adbulla Rashidi, was shouted down, jeered, and nearly chased out of the hall (Listowel 1965:305). Nyerere used his oratorical skills to persuade his fellow nationalist leaders that failure to participate in the election would put a conservative United Tanganyika Party (UTP) in office and provoke violence that would delay independence (Iliffe 1979:557). Outside the convention, in a public speech at the Police Grounds of Tabora, Nyerere defended his position in an emotionally charged anti-colonial speech denouncing foreign rule. "At the height of his speech," writes M.H.Y. Kaniki (1979:360), "he wept, igniting mass hysteria among the crowd who joined him in shedding tears." In a passionate concluding forty-five minute speech at the convention, Nyerere denounced political domination by foreigners and proclaimed: "We want that house in which [British Governor] Twining is now living. In order to get into it, we must dirty our feet by walking through the mud of an unfair election. What would you rather do? Keep your feet clean and not get the Twining house, or dirty your feet and get the Twining house?" (Listowel 1965:306) A majority of delegates (thirty seven out of sixty) then voted in favor of participation in the election.

The Tabora decision clearly shaped the trajectory of the nationalist movement, paving the way for a TANU electoral victory in the 1958–59 election and a subsequent shift in colonial policy, with the British backing away from their earlier insistence on racial parity to demand only that a postcolonial government guarantee the rights and security of the European and Asian minority communities. Tanganyika became the first country in British-ruled East Africa to achieve national independence, on December 9, 1961. The British decided to grant Tanganyika independence at an earlier date than anyone had initially anticipated in large part because of a desire to keep the racially moderate forces represented by Nyerere in control of the nationalist movement (Stephens 1968:145).

A second important turning point in the history of the Tanganyikan nationalist movement was the trial and conviction of Julius Nyerere in July of 1958, on charges of criminal libel against colonial district officials. The presiding magistrate sentenced Nyerere to either six months in prison or a fine of 150 pounds. Radical voices within the nationalist movement hoped that Nyerere, like many other African nationalist leaders, would go to prison and become a political martyr. His imprisonment would spark popular outrage and violent resistance to colonial rule. Some activists planned a procession to the prison, where they would break in and free

Nyerere. "Had he chosen to go to prison . . . ," writes Judith Listowel (1965:332–33), "there would have been a campaign of passive resistance (kugoma) . . . the military and the police would have had to be called out and from then on resistance would no longer have been passive." After receiving assurances from the new colonial governor, Sir Richard Turnbull, that the government was willing to work with TANU to prepare Tanganyika for self-government if law and order were maintained, Nyerere decided to pay the fine (Stephens 1968:144–45). He thereby defused the situation and channeled the nationalist movement along a nonviolent path.

The preceding account suggests that forceful leadership shaped the strategic choices that determined the trajectory of the nationalist movement. Contention over nonracial nationalism persisted during the postindependence period, but subsequent struggles among nationalists, including the 1961 conflict over whether to define citizenship in terms of race or residence, were profoundly influenced by the outcome of these earlier disputes. The structural legacy of a racialized colonial order ensured that the effort to create a new nation would also be a struggle over race, but whether a racialized or nonracial nationalist vision would prevail and become institutionalized was a contingent outcome, dependent on conflicts that were decisively shaped by the capacities and purposive efforts of dynamic leaders. This does not mean that we need to revive "great person" theories of history by limiting our attention to individualist accounts of the personal traits of influential leaders. It does suggest, however, that we need to recognize that in the fluid and often ambiguously defined situations facing activists, dynamic leaders can, at key conjunctures, determine the trajectory of a movement.

Indeed, whether a revolutionary struggle gives birth to democracy or dictatorship is decided not only by the class composition of the movement (as Barrington Moore demonstrated so eloquently), but also by the character and interactions among its leaders. We turn finally to the relationship between revolutionary leadership and regime result.

Revolutionary Leadership in the Americas: George Washington, Fidel Castro, Maurice Bishop, and Daniel Ortega

Washington, Castro, Bishop, and Ortega span a range of revolutionary types, and the movements in which they participated show a variety of outcomes. Examining their actions in the American, Cuban, Grenadan, and

147

Nicaraguan Revolutions displays the pivotal role of revolutionary leaders, and of variation in their abilities and character.

Washington had fabulous personal charisma, but no great conceptual or oratorial skills. As a general, his main talent was in holding his army together and inspiring loyalty. The vision that guided the American Revolution, and the populist rallying cries that mobilized the people, were articulated by Paine, Jefferson, Madison, Hamilton, Jay, and Henry. Yet Washington was an extraordinary bridge builder, political tactician, and institution builder. He was able to gather, and control, the talents of violently opposed men such as Hamilton, Jefferson, Burr, the Adams brothers, and the other Founding Fathers. His feat is clear in that although these men formed opposing political parties, and even feuded to the death in one case, he was able to keep them unified during the critical early years of the revolution and republic. As a political tactician, he carefully calculated his withdrawals and returns from public life to emphasize that he was not seeking personal political power. And in presiding over the Constitutional Convention, and as president over the early republic, he helped design and solidify the most successful and longest-lasting revolutionary institutions yet known. It is almost universally agreed by the early leaders of the United States, and their historians, that if not for Washington's leadership, the United States would neither have won its independence, nor been able to launch itself on a stable republican path after the revolution.

Fidel Castro too had fabulous personal charisma. But where Washington's appeal came from his incredible restraint and devotion to duty, Castro's came from fiery rhetoric and dashing, even reckless, bravery mixed with bravado. In his dedication to create a truly independent, self-sufficient Cuba, he repeatedly lived up to his slogan, "patria o muerte" (my country or death). In defying the dictator Batista, whom Castro saw as an oppressor in league with foreign powers, Castro first led a daring raid on the Monacado barracks, then after his release from jail, led a nearly suicidal marine landing on Cuba from Mexico, on the ship *Granma*. Of the aspiring liberators on the *Granma* over 80 percent were killed by Cuban troops, and it is something of a miracle that the survivors included Fidel and Raul Castro, and Che Guevara, who escaped to the hills.

Castro's daring won him a nucleus of supporters, and Batista's overbearing response to Castro's raids lost Batista support first at home, and then from the United States, which cut off Batista's supply of weapons. When Castro and his small band managed to intimidate the garrison at Santiago, and gain control of that city in eastern Cuba, Batista fled. But unlike Washington, Castro showed neither great institution-building ability, nor great restraint. Fidel and Raul Castro seized control of Cuba, and shortly thereafter – with the help of the Soviet Union – developed an ideologically closed Communist Party system and socialist economy. Raul was enough of an institution builder to develop a political system that kept the Castros in unquestioned supremacy. But the Castros were not great bridge builders and coalition makers. Castro alienated Cuba's bourgeoisie, most of whom fled the country, and the Catholic church.

While no one can question Castro's patriotism or inspirational abilities, the political and economic system he developed seems unlikely to outlast his own lifetime, in contrast to say, the institutions developed by the Sandinistas in Nicaragua. In this respect, Fidel Castro's strengths and weaknesses are similar to those of Mao Zedong, who also was unable to build a system that seems likely to long outlast his personal rule, and quite different from Washington, and even Lenin and Stalin, who managed to create powerful economic and political systems that lasted from one-half to two centuries beyond their deaths.

Maurice Bishop, after ten years of organizing and preparation, led a movement (the New Jewel Movement) that took power in the Caribbean island of Grenada through a revolutionary coup in 1979. However, Bishop is an example of a fairly complete failure as a revolutionary leader. Unable to even maintain loyalty and unity among his own supporters, he was murdered in 1983 by a breakaway faction of the New Jewel Movement. The chaos that followed his murder was so great that it provoked foreign intervention from the United States and neighboring Caribbean states, who in effect restored the old regime led by one of the older parliamentary parties. Bishop had sufficient tactical sense to take advantage of an opportunity to seize power, but he (and his lieutenants) lacked the skills to build a broad coalition or to create stable new institutions. As a result, his revolutionary movement remained narrow, and his achievement of power soon ended. Yet there was nothing structural, in the economy or institutions of Grenada, that could have foretold his failure to remain in power, as compared to Castro's success.

A striking contrast to both Castro and Bishop is Daniel Ortega, one of the key leaders of the Sandinista revolution in Nicaragua in 1979. The Sandanistas were a diverse lot, with several factions divided over how best to campaign against the dictator Anastasio Somoza. One group, or tendency, wished to slowly build power in the countryside, following the model of Castro in Cuba. A second group aimed to slowly build political

149

influence among the Nicaraguan populace. The third group, led by
Ortega, aimed to mobilize both urban and rural groups, and to boldly push
forward with acts of defiance. These included political kidnappings, and
even a brazen invasion of the national congress. Ortega's campaign of
sudden, surprise strikes was so successful that the "third tendency" prevailed. Somoza's clumsy responses to the Sandinista rebellion led to defections among his troops, and increased recruits for the Sandinistas. As the
number of fighters for the Sandinistas grew to several thousands, they
launched simultaneous attacks in several cities and on several rural fronts
against Somoza's forces. The latter crumbled, and the Sandinistas were
able to take the capital city of Managua, and seize power.

At the time of the Sandinista victory, structural conditions were even
less supportive of developing democracy than they had been in Cuba at
the time of Castro's victory. Cuba in 1959 was more urbanized, had a
higher literacy rate, and a greater history of experience with democracy,
than Nicaragua did twenty years later. In Cuba in 1959, urbanization was
55 percent, literacy 90 percent; for Nicaragua in 1979, urbanization was
50 percent, literacy 60 percent (World Bank 1998: World Development
Indicators). Yet Castro's interest in democracy was virtually nil compared
to his desire to remold Cuba in his desired image. For the Sandinistas, this
was not the case. In order to achieve their revolution, the Sandinistas –
especially the brothers Ortega and their religious coleader Ernesto Car-
denal – had to reach out and build coalitions with Nicaragua's business
community and traditional elite. The struggle to defeat Somoza was not
dominated by operations at one extreme end of the country, as was Castro's
campaign in Cuba, but extended throughout the country. Isolating
Somoza, and removing his U.S. support, required gaining the support of
business leaders for the Sandinistas' goals. The Sandinistas thus built
umbrella organizations before taking power, and a broadly representative
junta after taking power, to manage their strategy.

In the early years of the revolution, the pressure of dealing with the
counterrevolutionary efforts of the U.S.-supported "contras," and the
difficulties of realizing grand social projects while still maintaining a
substantially private and capitalist economy, led to splits among the
revolutionary leadership, and as in Cuba, many of the bourgeoisie fled to
the United States. But many also remained, and the Sandinistas – despite
sometimes extreme rhetoric – were not bound by their ideological cast.
They were more pragmatic than strictly socialist, and though their eco-

nomic policies were often questionable, they never resorted either to full party dictatorship or to complete socialization of the economy.

In fact, the commitment of the Sandinista leaders to democracy was so great that in 1984, while still in full power, they agreed to hold internationally supervised elections, in which Daniel Ortega was elected president. The turnout of these elections was some 75 percent of the potential voters, and they were judged fair by the international observers. More like Washington than like Castro, and like such other revolutionary leaders committed to democracy as Cory Aquino in the Philippines or Nelson Mandela in South Africa, Daniel Ortega (and his brother, the minister of defense and military commander Humberto Ortega) did not take advantage of either their military leadership during victory, or their leadership of the postrevolutionary junta, nor of Daniel Ortega's term as president, to permanently institutionalize their personal power. Instead, in the 1990 elections, the Sandanistas again stood in fair elections, and this time lost, with power passing to a member of the old bourgeois families, Violetta Chamorro. The Ortegas had not only won a revolution, they had managed to institutionalize a postrevolutionary democratic regime, that at this point, twenty years later, still appears vigorous and stable, and independent of the personal power of its founders.

The success of a protest or revolutionary movement, even given suitable structural conditions, thus depends on revolutionary leaders carrying out a complex array of tasks, calling for different abilities. If the revolution's main leader lacks some of these abilities, and cannot (or will not) find and support their exercise among his or her coleaders, then the revolution is likely to fail in some way. Moreover, the path of postrevolutionary regimes is never wholly determined by structural conditions. Maurice Bishop's New Jewel Movement, despite great hopes and considerable popular support, self-destructed in internal ideological and factional battles. The Sandinistas, starting with far less favorable conditions, including poverty, inequality, no recent history of democracy, and a violent counterrevolutionary war, nonetheless were able to institutionalize a democratic regime in Nicaragua, a sharply divergent outcome from that in Castro's Cuba. In all these cases, the choices, character, goals, and abilities of leaders were highly determining factors in their movements' success and outcomes.

In sum, leadership can fail. It can also determine the choice of dictatorship or democracy, and of communism or capitalism, in postrevolutionary regimes. If we assume that all the outcomes of revolutions are simply a product of structural conditions, it is because we have deceived ourselves by choosing a small number of cases in which structure and leadership both contributed to success, and not probed them deeply enough to learn how leadership decisions and character shaped their course and outcomes.

Conclusion: The Tasks and Character of Leadership in Contentious Politics

Launching a protest movement, and leading it to success, requires a variety of rhetorical, conceptual, organizational, and personal skills. Usually, these are not all found in one person; thus the need for a variety of leadership "types" to collaborate in making a successful protest or revolution. Assuming that "minimal" structural conditions for a protest or revolutionary movement to arise are present – that is, there is a segment of the population and/or elite that is disaffected from the status quo, and there are limits to what the state is able or willing to do, either to meet popular demands or repress opponents – then the role of leadership becomes crucial at several points in actualizing the potential for protest and social change.

Although this chapter has focused on revolutionary situations and formal leadership at the national level, we believe the same principles are equally true of a wide variety of settings for contentious politics, ranging over formal social movement organizations, oppositional networks, and local grassroots contention. Even though much grassroots and antiestablishment organizing aims for an absence of formal "leaders," preferring to disseminate authority in collective forms, the key leadership *actions* – people-oriented actions of providing motivation, building coalitions and commitment, and articulating a vision that draws an emotional and enthusiastic response; and task-oriented actions of plotting a movement strategy and assembling the resources and assigning responsibilities to see that strategy carried out – still need to be undertaken. How successfully these two types of actions are carried out, and what kind of conflicts or cooperation emerges in regard to these tasks, should tell us much regarding the dynamics and outcome of a variety of forms of contention. We also believe the phenomenon of individuals with various degrees of "self-effacing" versus "self-aggrandizing" leadership characteristics is likely to be encountered at a number of levels, and in a wide variety of movement settings.

152

Leadership Dynamics and the Dynamics of Contention

We thus argue that while structural factors may create greater or lesser opportunities for the emergence and success of social and revolutionary movements, and while cultural contexts and the incentives for action are important tools for mobilization, the detailed course and final outcomes of contention are *not* fully determined by such factors. Even if conditions are conducive to mobilization, a commitment of potential protestors to a movement must be forged, and this task requires people-oriented leadership at a variety of levels, from framing issues in a way that resonates with people (Gamson, Fireman, and Rytina 1982; Snow and Benford 1988; 1992), to building the bridges of community that tie individual protestors to the leadership and the movement (Robnett 1997). Often, the grassroots elements of this mobilization are undertaken by women, or leaders in existing community organizations, rather than formal national leadership (Kaplan 1997; Robnett 1996). But the task is no less important; the movement leader who fails in marshalling popular support will likely meet the fate of Che Guevara, isolated and easily liquidated by the authorities.

Once protestors have been mobilized for action, a plan of action must be chosen that maximizes the strength of the opposition, and identifies and targets the weaknesses of the status quo regime. The task-oriented choices of leadership here are crucial, not only in determining failure or success, but also in determining the future character of the movement and its outcome – will the strategy be violent or peaceful, inclusive or exclusive, moderate or radical, in its aims and tactics? Will the leadership unite or fall into conflict over these issues? The leadership skills called for here are those of the skilled politician or military commander planning a campaign: an ability to size up opponents, seize opportunities, force mistakes by enemies, and manipulate media. In some cases, the revolutionary campaigns are military, and military and guerrilla leaders such as Cromwell, Washington, Trotsky, Castro, Mao, Sandino, and Zapata, naturally rise to the fore. In other cases, the campaigns are more political, such as that of Robespierre and the Jacobins in the French National Assembly, or of Madero in Mexico, or of Julius Nyerere in Tanganyika.

Finally, once a victory over the status quo has been won, the new social order must be successfully institutionalized. How this is done, and how successfully, depends on how motivation and organization are carried beyond the revolutionary struggle, and how leaders orient themselves to the postrevolutionary institutions. In the American Revolution, talented but largely self-effacing organizational leaders, including Washington, Hamilton, Madison, and Jefferson, shared this role. In the French

Revolution, Napoleon combined the talents of military general and builder of a new centralized French bureaucratic system, but in a self-aggrandizing way that laid no building blocks for democracy. In Russia, Stalin's terror and restructuring of the countryside created an economic/institutional regime that lasted for two generations, but involved a cult of personality that eventuated in an authoritarian party-state. And in China, Zhou Enlai, Liu Shaoqi, and Deng Xiaoping took on the task of institutionalizing the revolution, often in the teeth of opposition from Chairman Mao. But not all major revolutions find such skills; in the English Puritan Revolution of the seventeenth century, although Cromwell's skills as a military leader produced a victory of Parliament, neither Cromwell nor any other leadership figure in Parliament could institutionalize the Commonwealth, which deteriorated into a detested military rule, and led to the old regime monarch being welcomed back into power by the British people and elites after Cromwell's death.

Because the study of revolution and social protest has tended to focus exclusively on successful movements, there has been a tendency to confound the role of structural conduciveness and effective leadership. Since successful revolutionary leaders are precisely those individuals who plan strategies that maximize the weaknesses of the status quo, and seize upon the opportunities presented by structural conditions, one will indeed generally be able to find structural reasons for a successful leader's accomplishment. But that does not mean that the quality and choices of movement leadership are not crucial to that success, or that outcomes would have been the same regardless of the ability or character of movement leadership. Such a determination can only be made by looking at the *process* of contention, and seeing how movements that develop in similar structural conditions can give rise to *different* outcomes due to different tactical choices or character in revolutionary leaders. In this chapter, we have made a first attempt at exploring just such processes and outcomes.

6

The Sacred, Religious, and Secular in Contentious Politics: Blurring Boundaries

Ron Aminzade and Elizabeth J. Perry

Introduction: Religion and Politics

Theories of social movements have been built, for the most part, from studies of western democracies in which the differentiation of secular and religious institutions and norms is unusually pronounced. The result of focusing on such secularized societies has been a tendency to see religions as furnishing social movements with organizational (and occasionally ideological) resources – but little more. Thus scholars have often emphasized ways in which churches serve as mobilizing networks, and have sometimes also noted the importance of religious beliefs and symbols as a source of collective action framing. Less frequently, however, have they ventured beyond a purely instrumentalist perspective to explore the expressive dimensions of religious conviction in processes of contention.

In this chapter our focus is on cases drawn from Chinese and African societies that have diverged from the secularized path of change in the West. China (in both its communist and precommunist incarnations) has not institutionalized the sort of church-state separation and attendant freedoms of religion that are taken as hallmarks of liberal democratic polities. In Africa, even where institutional differentiation and religious freedom are evident, popular beliefs about other-worldly entities and sacred legitimations of secular authority continue to inform routine and nonroutine politics. The reasons for these distinctive patterns of church-state relations and belief systems need not concern us here, but one result is that the intersection of religion and politics assumes quite different – and in some respects more transparent – consequences in our cases than may be evident in many western democracies. We highlight a variety of ways in which religious and sacred elements figure centrally in social movements and other types of contentious politics. Although we draw liberally from both African and Chinese examples, we do not undertake a systematic comparison of these two very different cultural regions (each of which, of course, is also marked by tremendous internal diversity). That important task awaits future consideration.

Our purposes here are twofold. First, we wish to introduce less familiar, but extremely rich, cases for analysis. Second, we explore the boundary between the sacred and secular in order to understand the implications of the fluid nature of this boundary for secularized and nonsecularized polities alike. In the conclusion, we propose some general (if speculative) lessons that we believe apply across the divides of culture and regime.

Let us begin with a few definitions. By *religion*, we refer to the beliefs, practices, rituals, and social organizations of people who are drawn together by a religious tradition. Such traditions offer other-worldly, transcendent answers to fundamental questions concerning the meaning of life and death (Kurtz 1995). Religious communities stand in contrast to *secular* entities whose basic operating principles are not justified by religious convictions. *Secularization* is the process by which religious and secular institutions and norms are differentiated into separate spheres. This process, it is important to emphasize, does not necessarily involve a diminution, marginalization, or privatization of religious beliefs and practices (Casanova 1994). Moreover, both religious and secular groups designate certain things as *sacred*, or worthy of awe and veneration (Koenker 1965).

In this chapter, we examine the role of the religious and the sacred in a variety of movements, some of which are generally thought of as basically secular in character. We hope to underscore the importance of nonmaterial factors in cases that have usually been understood largely in terms of economic grievances. Let us be clear that we are not proposing some new framework for explaining movement emergence; we believe that the familiar concepts of opportunities, networks, and framing are as useful for religiously based movements as for their secular counterparts. But we do insist that attention to the religious and sacred dimensions of contentious politics provides important clues in solving the puzzle of how movements interpret opportunities, appropriate and build mobilizing structures, and capture and sustain popular commitment over time. Dynamic models of contention (McAdam, Tarrow, and Tilly 2001; as well as other chapters in this volume) highlight the significance of certification, brokerage, and the social construction of opportunity and threat as key mechanisms in the development of collective action. Religious and sacred factors often play a major part in all of these mechanisms.

Of course, religions are seldom inherently or exclusively subversive (Smith 1996). Religious beliefs contain multiple contradictory messages that can be appropriated for conservative as well as revolutionary purposes. Religions have diverted people's attention from their misery and supported an oppressive status quo, just as they have also encouraged people to collectively challenge injustice and oppression. There are numerous, well-documented instances of the stabilizing role of religions, from Confucianism in traditional China to catholicism in medieval Europe to contemporary southern African Zionist churches whose healing systems individualize and depoliticize social problems (Schoffeleers 1991). These exist alongside millenarian, messianic, and heretical religious movements that have enabled people collectively and disruptively to challenge their oppression (Adas 1979; Kobben 1960; Lanternari 1963; Lewy 1974; Wallace 1956). Scholars have delineated ideal types of religions of the status quo, religions of resistance, religions of revolution, and religions of counterrevolution (Lincoln 1985:266–92) and documented how different interpretations of the same religion can produce acquiescence alongside rebellion and generate conflicts between "official" and "popular" religion (Garrett 1985). For example, Dwight Billings (1990) shows that evangelical protestantism in the United States fostered militancy among coal miners in central Appalachia but inhibited labor activism among textile workers of the Carolinas. Religion, in short, can serve as either an "opiate of the masses" or "amphetamines of the people" (Stark and Christaiano 1992).

Our concern is not to analyze the heterogenous political character of religions or the sociopolitical conditions under which religion fosters quiescence or opposition. Our goal rather is to examine, in a preliminary and suggestive fashion, the features that distinguish religious and secular contentious political claims making, the sacred dimensions of secular forms of contentious politics, and the implications of these differences and similarities for the concepts informing current studies of social movements and revolution.

Scholars of revolution have investigated the politically disruptive potential of religion for decades, documenting the religious content of the English Civil War and the French Revolution and the revolutionary impact of early protestantism. But social movement studies only recently have begun seriously to analyze religion and contentious politics. Reasons for the silence include the influence of structural–functionalist theory in the social sciences, fragmented subfields that make possible the divorce of the sociology of religion from political sociology, and the overly rationalist and instrumentalist assumptions of much of social movement theory.[1] In addition, research on social movements has been carried out by secular academics laboring in highly secular institutions, where religion is sometimes dismissed as epiphenomenal.

The limited research on religion and politics that has been done by social movement scholars highlights the role of religious organizations in the mobilization of various movements and the ways in which religious resources and institutions have been appropriated by movements with secular goals, such as ending racial segregation or achieving national independence. Less attention has been paid to ways in which the cultural dimensions of religion inform secular claims making, including the role of the sacred in shaping oppositional identities, emotion rules, temporal orientations, logics of action, and perceptions of threat, opportunity, and success. In this chapter, we hope to redress the imbalance.

The Distinctiveness of Religious and Secular Contentious Politics

Is there anything to the distinction between religious and secular contentious politics? Despite many similarities (which we will explore in greater detail), we believe that certain features of religiously inspired collective action do distinguish it from its secular cousin, if not categorically, then at least by degree. Though our answers should be taken as provisional, we think that there are both organizational and cultural features of religious-based contention that differentiate it from more secular forms. These include the unusual institutional legitimacy of religious-based organizations, which creates distinctive threat and opportunity structures, and the ability of religious movements to appeal to an other-worldly, transcendental ontology, which has implications for commitment processes, challenges to authority, and logics of action.

---

[1] Sociologists of religion have studied a wide variety of different types of groups that embrace a transcendent vision and hold their enterprises to be sacred in some collectively deviant way. Our concern is with those groups that engage in contentious politics, that is, "the public, collective making of claims that would, if realized, affect the interests of people other than the claimants." (McAdam, Tarrow, and Tilly 1996) Thus, our purview encompasses "preapocalyptic" warring sects that engage in a holy war against the "forces of evil," but not "postapocalyptic" other-worldly communal sects that seek sanctuary by establishing "heavenly kingdoms" beyond the reaches of the secular world (Hall 1978:206–07).

Blurring the Sacred, Religious, and Secular

In many societies, religious groups enjoy a unique institutional legitimacy that translates into a number of distinct advantages when it comes to contentious politics. The character of opportunities facing religious and secular movements may be very different due to recognition by state authorities of the sanctity of religious spaces where they cannot intervene, even if they suspect these to be sites of oppositional political mobilization. This recognition often constrains state repression of church-based movements, as was the case in Poland under the communist regime and in Central and Latin American states, where authoritarian regimes were limited in their ability to repress political dissidents who used the church as a base of resistance (Smith 1991). During the Iranian Revolution, observes Salehi (1996:51, 54), politicized Shiia clerical leaders "would preach emotionally and fearlessly, delving into issues that people would not otherwise have dared to discuss in public" but "these leaders were untouchable, unless the government was prepared to face large and immediate riots." In the case of contemporary China, Tibetan lamaseries and Xinjiang mosques, while not beyond the reach of the communist state, provide some shelter for separatists seeking both religious and political autonomy. When religious leaders associated with these institutions enjoy an international reputation and following (as has certainly been true of the Dalai Lama since his receipt of the Nobel Peace Prize), the stakes are raised for government interference in their activities.

Church-based movements may enjoy other opportunities deriving from their religious connections. For example, to the extent that such movements can maintain their religious status while pursuing secular goals, they may benefit from exemptions from taxation and conscription. Their tax-exempt status may allow them to mobilize financial resources more easily than overtly "political" organizations, while their followers' claims of "conscientious objection" may enable activists to avoid military service and hence continue their oppositional political activities.

The opportunities available to movements are temporally structured by social calendars, but the nature of these calendars may differentiate religious-based and secular movements. For secular movements, political calendars based on election dates or larger societalwide cycles of protest (Tarrow 1998b:141–60), have been linked to the opportunities that shape the temporal pattern of protest activities. For religious-based movements, calendars based on holy days and months may play a more important role in structuring political opportunities. During the Iranian Revolution, protest followed a temporal pattern set by such a religious calendar. Islamic ceremonies performed on the seventh and fortieth day after the death of those killed in demonstrations, as well as ceremonies and mass gatherings associated with the sacred months of Moharram and Ramadan, structured the protests of 1977–78, providing the occasion for political preaching and confrontations with security forces (Salehi 1996:54–57). A similar pattern is observable in the case of Bolivian tin miners, whose days of traditional religious observances have become identified with political events that express class consciousness and solidarity. "The ritual calendar," observes June Nash (1989), "becomes a schedule for acts of protest that have frequently upset governments and disturbed a covenant in industry." The outbreak of many White Lotus-inspired rebellions in China, as Susan Naquin (1981) has noted, is better explained by the calendrical implications of sacred scriptures (*baojuan*) than by prevailing economic or political conditions. Masters of the White Lotus teachings (a folk Buddhist millenarian faith) would predict the coming of a new age (or *kalpa*) based upon their interpretation of scripturally specified astrological and other omens. During the passage to this new epoch, in which it was believed that the Buddha of the Future (Maitreya) would finally reign supreme, only the faithful could escape death from the accompanying calamities. The call to meet the kalpa, like the call among christian millenarians to prepare for an imminent Second Coming and thereby avoid the perils of Armageddon, created a frenzied sense of urgency.

The resource opportunities available to church-based movements may differentiate their temporal pattern of growth and decline from that of secular movements. The support of congregations and church leaders, more than shifts in public opinion or divisions among secular political elites, often pattern the temporalities of religious movements. "A social movement which is church-based (such as the sanctuary movement)", writes Barbara Yarnold (1991:x), "may have a longer life span than other social movements, losing momentum not due to a lack of public support, but due to a loss of interest on the part of religious leaders."

But the distinctions between religious and secular movements go beyond such instrumentalist factors as access to organizational opportunities and material resources. The central way in which religious-based political movements differ from secular ones concerns claims to an other-worldly, transcendental ontology. Religions posit the existence of an invisible spiritual world and "a more or less hidden causal relation between human events and supernatural determinants" (Lanternari 1985:153). The issue is not whether such a supernatural world actually exists. As long as people believe it does and act accordingly, invisible spirits can shape political life. In Soweto, Johannesburg, dead people ("shades") are widely believed to affect the living directly, serving as intermediaries between humans and the supreme being (West 1975). Adam Ashforth's (1996) study of witchcraft in Soweto documents how beliefs and discourses about unseen powers help to shape community power relations and constitute the boundary between public and private realms.

Religion is based on faith and supernatural knowledge. Dreams, visions, trances, and bodily shaking are often accorded a privileged status as guides to the spiritual world. Religious leaders do not have to rely only on rational persuasion since their followers can be "moved by the spirit" rather than persuaded by rational arguments. Religions offer adherents comprehensive answers to fundamental questions about death and the meaning of human existence. Given the highly salient nature of these beliefs and their imperviousness to falsification, they often sustain the level of commitment required for high-risk activism and violent challenges to secular authority.

A transcendental ontology that includes belief in an afterlife allows leaders to make extraordinary demands on followers, whose interpretations of opportunities, threats, successes, and failures may not be firmly grounded in "objective" political conditions. The altered sense of costs, benefits, and possibilities made possible by a transcendental ontology and supernatural powers can create intensely committed followers willing to sacrifice for the cause, including willing martyrs with altered understandings of obstacles and opportunities. "For many religious believers," writes Christian Smith (1996:10), "the overwhelming intractability of the world as it is can, in some circumstances, melt into pliant transience before the face of the holy, the sacred, the eternal. Divine imperative . . . can, under some conditions, . . . relativize what might otherwise seem insurmountable." For example, members of the faith-based peace organization Pax Christi USA have an attitude toward success that does not reflect a utilitarian cost-benefit logic, as is clear from a popular saying in their ranks: "We are called to be faithful, not effective" (Pagnucco 1996:218).

The existence of a religious ontology that recognizes spiritual forces beyond the material world also makes possible appeals to a transcendent authority. Such appeals may support the status quo, as in the case of European monarchs' claims to rule by divine right, but they can also provide the basis for challenges to secular authority. "Much of the struggle around religion and politics," observes Daniel Levine (1985:99), "centers in some way on legitimation. Legitimation is contested at many levels, in struggles to claim the moral authority of religion and divine will (however defined) for different sorts of group practice and commitment and for alternative structures of power." Religious change can have important, often unintended and indirect, political consequences, legitimating new forms of authority and political participation. The prophets of African traditional religions have frequently appealed to divine authority to challenge secular leaders and call for moral restoration in response to crises associated with colonial conquest. As divinely inspired critics claiming transcendental authority, they were relatively immune from the traditional authority of the elders and able to challenge the secular authority of colonial rulers. Acting more in accordance with religious prophecy than in response to an open political opportunity structure, they inspired their followers to think and behave in politically disruptive ways.

Religious claims of sacred transcendence can alter logics of action by providing an expanded sense of the possible, enlarged notions of space, and extended time horizons (Hall 1978). The means–ends calculations that scholars often assume inform the behaviors of actors may not be applicable to those whose logics of action privilege the existence of nonmaterial, or spiritual, forces and domains. The conviction that redemption awaits in the hereafter has served to bolster the commitment and courage of believers as disparate as medieval crusaders and kamikaze pilots. The explicit invocation of the supernatural contributes to an enlarged sense of possibilities that can at times become politically threatening. As Nancy Chen (1995) has shown in her investigation of "qigong" (Chinese breathing and martial arts routines), practitioners feel transported into an otherworldly realm, an intangible, spiritual zone into which the communist authorities cannot intrude. That this escape to a supernatural realm is potentially subversive is indicated by the government's much-publicized establishment of special hot lines where alert citizens are requested to report their suspicions of dissident "qigong masters" (Perry and Fuller 1991). Similarly, the recourse of some contemporary sectarian movements (for example, Heaven's Gate followers in southern California) to the use of outerspace and cyberspace represents a search for alternative (if scientistic) zones of nonstate interference.

Spirit possession is another way in which logics of action can be transformed by the creation of altered spatial, and often temporal, boundaries, as members of the faithful find themselves taken over by other beings who may issue from radically different times and places. In the case of Melanesian cargo cults or the Sioux Indian Ghost Dance, long deceased ancestors were considered the source of spirit possession. Their return to earth, it was believed, would augur a total reversal of familiar spatial patterns: Fish would suddenly fly in the air and birds would swim in the sea. Political hierarchies would be similarly overturned; the natives would henceforth rule over the white man (Mooney 1991; Worsley 1968). In Zimbabwe, leaders of the struggle for independence espoused a socialist ideology, but spirit mediums provided nationalist forces with a system of ritual practices to gain the protection of the ancestors and guerilla fighters described experiences of being saved by ancestors and supplied with goods by their ancestors' spirits (Lan 1985). Anticolonialist movements were often buttressed by invulnerability cults in which it was held that spirit possession and other somatic rituals – such as qigong routines in the case of the Chinese Boxers or war medicine (maji maji) in the case of East African resistance to German colonialism – would ensure imperviousness to bullets. This belief, although seemingly easily disproved, has enjoyed a remarkably wide currency in nativist movements around the globe.

That these spiritual accoutrements can be very helpful in launching and sustaining resistance movements has certainly not been lost on state authorities, who have often moved decisively, even precipitously, to contain them. Thus the very factors that provide special opportunities for the religiously inspired can also provoke special dangers. The threat of state repression is ever present, especially in less secularized societies where the permitted sphere of religious activity may be unclear. Indeed, more than a few religiously inspired rebellions have (ironically enough) been triggered by state suppression efforts; groups with no initial hostility toward the authorities find themselves forced into a battle for their very survival. This was the situation of numerous sectarians in imperial China, whose uprisings were frequently a response to state-sponsored persecution of heterodox beliefs (Overmyer 1976). And it remains true in contemporary China, as the draconian repression campaign against Falun Gong practitioners makes clear.

Blurring the Boundary: Resources, Rituals, Ideologies, and Identities

While the distinctions between religious and secular movements are, we think, significant, there are also large areas of overlap. Many scholars have pointed out that a similar process of resource mobilization underpins

163

the activities of secular and religious-based movements. The sources and availability of resources may differ, with religious-based movements having ready access to assets unavailable to secular movements, including established church leaders who can effectively mobilize their "flock" should it turn its attention to contentious politics. But the process itself appears to be similar. Scholars have noted the many organizational resources that church-based movements receive from religious institutions, including trained and experienced leaders, financial resources, congregated participants, solidarity incentives, preexisting communications channels and authority structures, deviance-monitoring mechanisms, and equipment and facilities (Smith 1996:13–16). Aldon Morris (1984) has shown how the black church provided the U.S. Civil Rights Movement with critical resources, including an organized mass base, leadership, finances, meeting places, and a rich culture. Liebman and Wuthnow (1983) analyze the new religious right in the United States using the conceptual tools of resource mobilization theory. Scholars have also documented the role of religious organizations and communication networks in spreading the core ideas of the sanctuary, peace, and fundamentalist christian movements in the United States (Yarnold 1991) and the contribution of pacifist religious organizations to sustaining the American peace movement during times of war (Kleidman 1993). Mayer Zald (1982) proposes a marriage between resource mobilization theory and world systems theory to fine tune our understanding of the rise of major religious movements.

Secular movements of protest also frequently appropriate emotionally powerful symbolic resources from religious communities. Scholars studying collective-action framing have documented the uses of religious symbols, icons, music, and rituals in many movements and revolutions, including the French Revolution (Vovelle 1976), the Revolution of 1848 (Berenson 1984), the American Civil Rights Movement (McAdam 1982; Morris 1984), the Iranian Revolution (Arjomand 1988; Moaddel 1993; Salehi 1996), and the Solidarity Movement in Poland (Osa 1996; 1997). Edward Tiryakian (1988; 1995) treats revolutions in Iran, Nicaragua, and the Philippines, as well as the "velvet revolutions" of 1989 in various Eastern European countries, as analogous to religious revivals, as moments of collective effervescence and social renewal when the social order is delegitimated and the profane becomes transformed into a sacred context. Secular nationalist movements often invoke myths of origin that link participants to an imagined past commemorated with quasisacred symbols and rituals. The observance of national holidays, such as Bastille Day in

France, Fourth of July in America, and October 1 in China, in a fashion not unlike the celebration of religious festivals, is one manifestation of this broader phenomenon.

The Chinese communist movement, while staunchly antireligious in its official Marxist ideology, offers a rich illustration of how secular revolutionary movements can draw on indigenous religious symbols and rituals. As noted in the chapter on leadership, one of the key tasks of revolutionary leaders is to provide meaningful frames for collective action; often such schema are derived from religious traditions. Similarly, as Daniel Levine (1985) has observed, leadership legitimation frequently hinges on religious sanction. During China's revolutionary struggle, recourse to religious symbolism was sometimes a self-conscious instrumental strategy by leaders seeking to mobilize mass support for their cause. Communist strategist Liu Shaoqi conceded that religious myths could prove useful in attracting sectarians to the revolution. Liu (1938) noted with evident approval that in those places where rumor held that Red Army Commander Zhu De was a direct descendant of the Ming founder, Triad and White Lotus believers were inclined to lend their support to the communist cause. Similarly, one of the early leaders of the peasant movement, Peng Pai, encouraged the popular belief that he was a quasidivine bodhissatva as a means of recruiting the Buddhist faithful to his enterprise (Marks 1984). The phenomenon was not unique to China, of course. Kenyan nationalists glorified their leader, Jomo Kenyata, in a hymn book that included the song "Come unto Jomo," sung to the tune of "Come unto Jesus" (Mazrui 1972:6). In Zaire General Mobutu referred to himself as "the Father and God of the nation" (Sanneh 1991:208).

Often, however, the resort to religious symbols and practices is not a calculated tactic by clever leaders, but an unwitting expression of deep-seated cultural influences. The political rituals of the Chinese Cultural Revolution, a movement whose goals included the suppression of all vestiges of religion, evidenced the unconscious appropriation of much older modes of religious worship. As Anita Chan and her coauthors (1984) describe Cultural Revolution routines in one South China village: "Before every meal, in imitation of the army (where the Mao rituals were reaching extraordinary proportions), Chen Village families began performing services to Mao. Led by the family head, they intoned in unison a selection of Mao quotations; sang 'The East is Red'; and as they sat to eat they recited a Mao grace." Similarly, in his memoir of the Cultural Revolution, Liang Heng (1983) describes how his father – an urban intellectual sent

165

down to the countryside for "reeducation" – conveyed urban secular customs to his new peasant neighbors. After converting an old Confucian ancestor-worship shrine into a place of adulation for Mao Zedong, "He put up fresh posters of Chairman Mao and [Defense Minister] Lin Biao wearing soldiers' uniforms . . . Then he turned to face the Great Helms-man and the Revolutionary Marshal and bowed, with utmost gravity, three times to the waist. There was a general titter of nervous laughter. Father looked so serious, and the peasants had never seen anyone bow to any-thing except the images of their own ancestors. But they were eager learn-ers, for they loved Chairman Mao."

The prophetic traditions of traditional religions are often appropriated by secular revolutionary movements. In China, as Maurice Meisner (1986) has noted of the Long March, "the survivors' consciousness that they had lived while so many more had perished lent a sacred character to their rev-olutionary mission and gave rise to an almost religious sense of dedication . . . Mao was the prophet who had led the survivors through the wilder-ness." It was during the Cultural Revolution, despite the movement's avowed hostility toward religion, that adoration of "prophet" Mao Zedong attained unprecedented heights. Adaptation of the prophetic traditions of indigenous religion is also evident in African anticolonial struggles, in which prophet mediums have played an important role. At the end of the nineteenth century, spirit mediums were military leaders and advisors in southern Rhodesian revolts and in the Maji Maji uprising in Tanzania (Iliffe and Gwassa 1972; Ranger 1967; Wright 1995).

Secular movements frequently use sacred documents or icons to mobilize popular support and legitimize their power. During the Cultural Revolution, the so-called "little red book" containing quotations from Chairman Mao was treated as tantamount to holy scripture. Zealous young Red Guards waved copies of it when launching their persecution drives against alleged counterrevolutionaries. And across much of the country-side, peasants earned extra compensation from their production teams if they could recite passages of the little red book by heart. In Eastern Africa, Julius Nyerere, leader of Tanzania's nationalist struggle for independence and subsequently of a secular socialist state, never appeared in public without his famous magic cane, widely believed by supporters to give him supernatural powers. Charisma, as Weber recognized, has a seemingly magical aspect that surfaces even in highly secular movements.

Commemorative events often take on a sacred character in revolution-ary nationalist movements. (On the key role of events in movement development, see the chapter on temporality.) In China, the Long March (1934–35), a saga in which the Red Army retreated some six thousand miles from its Jiangxi Soviet base area to a new revolutionary capital in Yan'an, acquired a legendary fame that resembled a religious milestone. Although the Long March was prompted by military defeat, it became an inspirational symbol of the revolutionary endurance and heroic self-sacrifice that would ensure eventual victory. More than thirty years later, student Red Guards during the Cultural Revolution commemorated the event by undertaking ritualistic "new long marches" in an attempt to establish their own revolutionary credentials. In Kenya, nationalists planned to celebrate Kenyatta Day on October 20, 1965 with a "last supper" commemorating the last meal that President Kenyatta had before his arrest during the Mau Mau uprising, but the event was altered due to protests from Christians (Mazrui 1972:6).

Pilgrimages, an important feature of religious observances, have been popularly appropriated by oppositional political forces to venerate secular leaders whose memory may serve as a reminder of prior alternative policies. In contemporary China, for example, in Mao's home province of Hunan, a monastery dedicated to the deification of the chairman has attracted tens of thousands of pilgrims in recent years. The devotees, who come from hundreds of miles away, undertake a three-day fast before the journey to demonstrate their piety. Once at the monastery, "some pray for the safety and harmony of family members while others ask Mao to cure chronic diseases. The latter group are given a glass of 'holy water' after their prayers. Those who feel Mao has listened to their prayers thank him for the kindness received" (*Eastern Express* 1995:39). When more than 1,000 armed police stormed the monastery in a drive to expel the throngs of pilgrims lodged at the temple dormitory, peasants from surrounding counties rushed to defend their sacred site. Local government authorities considered blowing up the temple, but later dropped the idea for fear it might trigger civil unrest.[2]

---

[2] That such fears are not unfounded is suggested by an intriguing resistance movement in which the 29-year-old peasant leader claimed to be Mao Zedong's son who had come forward to lead a new rural uprising. The would-be Mao penned treatises on the "thirty great relationships" (Mao Zedong had limited himself to ten) and assumed the titles of party chairman, military commission chair, state chairman, political consultative conference chair, and premier. The imposter also sent letters to various government offices praising the radical ideas of the Gang of Four, attacking Deng Xiaoping's market socialism, and calling for armed rebellion, student boycotts, and workers' strikes (Li Kaifu 1992:132–33).

Scholars have also highlighted striking parallels between religious and secular ideologies. Said Arjomand (1993:52), among others, characterizes communism and fascism as secular salvations, "nontheistic political religions of the twentieth century." As Robert Tucker (1961) astutely observed, Marxism, although ostensibly opposed to religion as the opiate of the masses, nonetheless bears a striking resemblance to elements of the Judeo-Christian faith. Karl Marx's own upbringing within this religious tradition surely helped to shape his vision of communism as a kind of paradise in which people would finally reclaim their lost (alienated) human nature. Although the proletariat, rather than the risen Lord, served as the messiah in Marx's framework, there remained the familiar promise of salvation (or liberation) for the faithful (revolutionaries) and damnation (or liquidation) for the infidels (counterrevolutionaries). Common to both philosophies is a belief in the inevitable march of history to ward a utopian future in which only the true believers will inherit the earth. Since faith – based on either secular beliefs about the inevitable laws of history or sacred beliefs about divine purpose – is probably the sine qua non of the kind of personal commitment and sacrifice called for in revolutionary and religious crusades alike, the similarities are not surprising.

Nationalist ideologies often emphasize faith as a powerful weapon in the arsenal of those whose material armaments lag far behind those of their opponents. Anticolonialist nationalisms, observes Calhoun (1997:109), often produce or reproduce a division between spiritual and material life, recognizing the military and technical strength of foreign powers while valorizing the spiritual realm, where the moral and cultural strengths of the nation are located. Indian nationalists, for example, proclaimed "the domain of the spiritual its sovereign territory" (Chatterjee 1994:5). In constructing new political communities, nationalists frequently asserted their cultural independence from colonial powers in terms of religion.

It is also not uncommon for religious-based political ideologies pragmatically to incorporate secular elements. The Islamic traditionalism, or "fundamentalism," that informed the Iranian Revolution, for example, was heavily influenced by secular models of constitution making and produced a synthesis of radically different legal traditions (Arjomand 1993). The Taiping Rebellion (1850–62), which resulted in the deaths of some twenty-five to thirty million Chinese, rendering it the costliest civil war in human history, was based on a syncretic ideology that borrowed elements from its targets. Led by a disappointed Confucian examination candidate by the

168

name of Hong Xiuquan who subsequently declared himself the younger brother of Jesus Christ, the Taipings evidenced a complex amalgam of beliefs and practices. Ostensibly committed to ridding China of its heathen traditions, the "God Worshippers" (as the early Taipings were known) attacked ancestral shrines, Buddhist temples, and other non-Christian vestiges. In many ways, however, they also drew actively upon these pre-existing institutions. The Taiping land reform program, although claiming authority on the basis of God's gifts to His children, was nonetheless squarely within the tradition of generations of Confucian reformers. And, once settled in their "Heavenly Capital" of Nanjing, the Taipings instituted a bureaucratic examination system which, albeit drawing in content upon the Bible and the religious writings of Hong Xiuquan, was in form strikingly reminiscent of Confucian exemplars. Moreover, the Taipings' representation of their Manchu opponents as pagan goblins was modeled in no small measure on Buddhist demonology. The free-wheeling theology of the Taipings led to the undoing of the movement when one of Hong Xiuquan's chief lieutenants, claiming to be possessed by no less a spirit than the Holy Ghost, challenged Hong's dominance and triggered a frightful internal bloodbath. Repression of the rebellion by combined Manchu and British forces followed.

A distinct advantage of religious-based movements, observes Christian Smith (1996:17–18), is that shared religious beliefs can readily provide "a sense of ease, trust, and loyalty that greatly facilitates group communication and solidarity" and expedites "the process of coming to a shared 'definition of the situation.'" Yet a similar process of identity formation and framing characterizes the formation of movements espousing secular revolutionary ideologies. Although secular revolutionary movements do not appeal primarily to other-worldy, spiritual sources of authority, political ideologies rooted in teleological beliefs, such as the inevitable historical demise of capitalism and triumph of the revolution, can create ardor akin to the fervor motivating participants in religious movements. The identity transforming experiences of dedicated movement activists who acquire a staunch belief in the inevitable triumph of their cause often resembles religious conversion. Although their identities and goals remain secular in character, the belief that they possess superior knowledge about the inevitable course of history constitutes a quasireligious grounding for their revolutionary identity and commitment.

The boundary between secular and religious protest is further blurred by the reality that activists in secular movements do not lead compartmentalized lives with rigidly separated political and religious identities. Furthermore, premovement identities typically inform political activism. People usually join social movements not as isolated individuals, but as prior members of communities or as activists who remain embedded in communities that continue to encourage religious identities. Given the common phenomenon of bloc recruitment, and the fuzzy boundaries often separating religious and secular within local communities, recruits to nonreligious movements often bring important aspects of their identities and cultures from preexisting religious communities with them. This is the case even for activists in ostensibly highly secular political movements, such the South African Communist Party. Africans who joined this party and rose to leadership positions within it were the products of mission education. They did not sever their ties to missionary cultures, and oppositional theologies informed their work within this avowedly secular political movement (Kelly 1991:7). The Bolivian tin miners studied by June Nash (1989) combined ideologies of socialism and communism with traditional rituals and beliefs based on a world of devils, deities, and enchanted beings, making use of longstanding religious observances to build class solidarity. "Popular religion," observes Clarke Garrett (1985:71), "does not make a clear separation of the religious from the secular. It is so much a part of daily existence that it can appear to outsiders like clergy and historians not to be religious at all."

The boundary between religion and politics is socially constructed and only makes sense within the framework of a given ideological order. In less secularized polities in which routine exercises of political power are embedded in religious symbols and beliefs, the distinction between heresy and rebellion dissolves. In African societies where British colonial officials bolstered the powers of traditional chiefs via a system of indirect rule, the exercise of chiefly political authority was closely connected to traditional religious ideologies and practices. Participants in religious movements and colonial authorities both correctly understood religious challenges to the symbolic and ideological dimensions of chiefly authority – such as the destruction of ancestor shrines or disruption of communal rituals – as political, as well as social and cultural, rebellion. Karen Fields (1982) carefully documents how the Christian millenarian Watchtower movement of Latter Day Saints inspired the insurrection of 1917–19 in Zambia (formerly Northern Rhodesia). Prayer meetings, hymn singing, speaking in tongues (*chongo*), prophetic preaching, drumming, and mass baptizing became seditious expressions of civil disobedience. "By the very act of being baptized," writes Fields (1982:345–46), "converts received a new form of government . . . accepting baptism in 1917–19 from a Watchtower preacher was the same as transferring one's ordinary political allegiance."

There are few systematic comparisons of faith-based and secular social movement organizations, but those that have been done in secularized societies find similarities as well as differences. Ron Pagnucco's (1996) comparison of the political behavior of 273 faith-based and secular peace groups in the United States found that faith-based organizations were just as likely to use conventional tactics of political bargaining but more likely to also embrace unruly tactics of nonviolent direct action and "moral witness." Brenda Donnelly's (1987) comparison of Christian and non-religious organizations involved in social protests in the post-Civil War United States found that religious organizations were less likely to be successful than nonreligious groups but that religious identification and ideology does not directly account for the difference. In her account, the disparity in outcomes was connected to the multifaceted goals of the Christian challengers, which were more difficult to attain. Religion did, however, indirectly affect the outcomes, for church-based groups' embrace of multiissue concerns was connected to their pursuit of "universalistic" goals whose primary beneficiaries were not members of the organization.

Further Blurring the Boundary: Moral Domains, New Social Movements, and Science

Religions have always served as major sources of moral codes and injunctions, providing people with ethical standards by which to assess their own and other peoples' behaviors and with meaning systems that offer comprehensive answers to fundamental questions about life and death. Not surprisingly then, even in highly secularized capitalist societies, religions have often served to fuel social movements. As Sidney Tarrow (1998a) notes of the United States, "separation of church and state and the free coinage of religious denominations in the presence of an expanding capitalist society . . . created a durable religious movement sector in shifting relations with the political struggle." In contemporary secularized polities, the multiplicity of secular movements with predominantly moral agendas and the development of new technologies concerning life and death further blur the boundary between secular and religious movements.

171

Even when framed in a rhetoric of rights suggesting state-based claims, ostensibly secular movements, such as those advocating gay rights, animal rights, abortion rights, or womens' rights, are advocates of moral imperatives about sexual conduct, marriage, dietary restrictions, and how to live one's daily life, thereby encroaching on ethical domains that are also the province of religious authorities. Blurring the boundary between the religious and the secular, these movements place in the public sphere contentious issues that implicate the state and its regulatory apparatuses as well as church authorities.

A number of scholars have identified a form of religious consciousness in the "new social movements" of advanced industrial societies (Beckford 1990; Hannigan 1991) Many so-called "new social movements," they point out, contain certain tendencies or branches, such as ecofeminism or deep ecology, that are holistic in their visions and explicit about their spirituality. Hannigan (1990; 1991) argues that the new social movements, like the new religious movements, are a product of eroding boundaries between the private and public domains. In his view, new religious movements are attempting to "sanctify" the secular public realm while new social movements are trying to democratize activities once considered to be in the private sphere.

As we have endeavored to show in this chapter, there is nothing "new" about the blurring of private and public, or religious and secular, domains. The centrality of the sacred in religious and secular movements alike has long called into question such distinctions. Although the ramifications may be more obvious in nonsecularized polities, they apply to secularized societies as well. In the case of the United States, the abolitionist movement, the suffrage movement, the temperance movement, the civil rights movement, and the antiwar movement all demonstrate the blurring of such boundaries well before the advent of the so-called new social movements.

In secularized settings, social movements have often spoken not only to issues of citizenship and the distribution of scarce resources, but also to control over the moral domains implicated in decisions about life, death, and human freedom. Recent scientific developments have only intensified the tendency of both church-based and secular movements to contest or support the state's authority to regulate such matters. Late twentieth century technological developments have meant the growing intrusion of scientific technology in the creation, manipulation, or prolongation of life and the prevention or hastening of death. As science intervenes in birth and death via new fertility drugs, abortion pills, genetic engineering, artificial insemination, and euthanasia, movements and the state are forced to address issues concerning the meaning and value of life – a centerpiece of religious concern. With contentious claims making encompassing the assertion of moral codes that challenge decisions and legitimations based on technical expertise, the boundary between secular and religious movements is likely to become – if anything – even more blurred.

Conclusion: Conceptual Implications and Future Prospects

A good deal of research remains to be done before we can conclusively identify differences between secular and religious-based contentious politics, although the preceding survey suggests more similarities than differences. One potentially fruitful area of comparison concerns the emotion climates, feeling rules, and ritualistic repertoires of religious-based and secular movements (see Chapter 2). Scholars of contentious politics have typically treated activists as disembodied rational actors, but bodily experiences and intense emotional performances often play an important role in securing peoples' commitments to faith-based movements. Somatic rituals may be more pervasive and better developed in faith-based movements. However, there is wide variability in emotion rules and climates across religious denominations, with some emphasizing decorum and others stressing emotional experience. This suggests that there may be as much variation in emotional climates within as between religious and secular movements, but further research is needed. A number of studies have also documented the way in which religious commitments and processes of conversion and deconversion are gendered (Neitz 1993). However, scholars have not yet addressed the question of whether there are gender differences between faith-based and secular movements, with the former perhaps appealing more to "an ethic of care" and the latter more to "an ethic of rights" (Gilligan 1982). The influence of regime type is another promising area for future work. In what ways do different kinds of secularized and nonsecularized states contribute to different patterns of religious contention?

The concepts informing contemporary social movement theory were typically founded in modernist assumptions of a secularized society with fairly sharp boundaries between church and state and declining religious beliefs and practices. What does our preceding discussion of the ability of religion to dramatically reconfigure time and space and to alter logics of

173

action imply for key concepts like cycles of protest or political opportunity structures? It suggests, for example, that religious movements may follow temporal trajectories based on religious prophecies rather than rising and falling as part of a cycle of protest rooted in secular political events. Religious movements, like secular movements, are shaped by social schedules embedded in routines and networks that connect participants, but the institutional and ideational bases of these connections are not the same.

Our discussion also suggests that appeals to, and legitimations of, sacred authority may challenge conventional rationalist understandings of how political activists perceive the opportunities facing them. Belief in an afterlife, in the existence of spirit worlds, or in the intervention of spirits in the world, creates logics of action that concepts like "political opportunity structure," which are based on rationalist and instrumentalist assumptions, fail to capture. Perceptions of opportunities and threats systematically structure collective political action, but we cannot unproblematically infer such perceptions from "objective" political conditions.

Perhaps the greatest contribution of a religious sensibility lies in spotlighting factors that enable sustained commitment to movement causes. In studying religion, we are inevitably drawn to questions of faith, inspiration, and sacrifice. All of these factors figure centrally in the dynamics of contention, whether ostensibly religious or not, but they have been downplayed in instrumentalist models that emphasize grievances, resource mobilization, and political process. Attention to religious dimensions reminds the researcher of the powerful role that nonmaterial forces play in the growth and development of movement identities, as demonstrated, for example, in the 1989 Tiananmen uprising in China (Calhoun 1994).

In speculating about religion and politics in the twenty-first century, we must be attentive to the ongoing repercussions of a number of late-twentieth century developments, especially the fall of communist regimes, the end of the Cold War, and the spread of neoliberal "free market" ideologies and practices. Historically, large-scale religious movements have emerged during periods of crisis and transition in the expanding capitalist world order and shifts in relations between the core and periphery (Wuthnow 1980). Given the rapid spread of neoliberal ideology and market institutions at the end of the twentieth century in areas of the "developing world," from China to Africa, that had once pursued state-led development efforts resistant to the capitalist world order, we should expect a surge of nativistic, revivalistic, millenarian, and messianic movements to mark the early twenty-first century. The character of their claims will vary across contexts, but some will undoubtedly generate demands for political as well as social change. This is most likely where traditions of political engagement from the prior era of socialist reconstruction persist or where religiooppositional subcultures drawing on the popular merger of nationhood, language, and national church are appropriated by secular dissident groups (Johnston 1993).

In many parts of the world, neoliberal policies advocated and enforced by global institutions, such as the World Bank and International Monetary Fund, have meant reduced-state capacities, as structural adjustment policies produce a decline in state provisioning of education, health care, and welfare services. As state-based development projects (for example, those inspired by socialism) are displaced by globally organized economic growth, religious-based conflicts for control over formerly state-run services have increased. Religious-based institutions and movements have used the provision of social services to win new converts or secure the commitment of the faithful, thereby fueling the growth of Christian-Muslim conflict in sub-Saharan Africa and the expansion of Islamic fundamentalist influence and power in Northern Africa. By creating a more diversified multifunctional role for religious institutions, and downscaling secular state activities via the privatization of schools and hospitals, such policies are likely to generate conflicts between church and state as well as among religious-based movements. The phenomenon is already visible in both "advanced capitalist" and "developing" countries.

The globalization of culture is another likely source of future political contention. Globalization is not synonymous with a happy homogenization of religious values; the process also evokes heterogeneity and resistance (Robertson 1989b). The spread of Western-based mass media in Eastern Africa, for example, has stimulated calls from Christian and Muslim clerics for greater state regulation of the distribution of immoral videos from overseas in a time of decreasing state willingness and capacity to regulate markets (Ponella 1996). Globalization is likely to generate contention by simultaneously fostering secularized global identities as well as traditional religious identities. Global movements of migrants are likely to continue to produce more religiously diverse populations in the countries of Western Europe, thereby making civic consensus about the activities of a secular state difficult to attain.

In the West, the decline of Marxist-Leninist ideology has prompted many on the Left to embrace more modest, often local, goals, to recognize the dynamism, complexity, and uncertainty of late capitalism, and to be wary of claims concerning superior knowledge about the ultimate course of history. Millenarian secular political ideologies may thus play a less important role in left-wing Western political contention of the twenty-first century. Scientific developments, however, are a probable source of future contention between right and left, as movements stake out moral claims about life, death, sexuality, and the natural world that have typically been the domain of religious authorities.

A fundamental tenet of modernist philosophies and the social science theories influenced by them was that cultures were becoming increasingly "scientific," and therefore less religious, in orientation. Whether the disappearance of the spiritual and magical was to be lauded or lamented, intellectuals since the Enlightenment have tended to accept it as an inevitable byproduct of scientific and technological advance.[3] At the beginning of the new millennium, however, earlier reports of the death of religion seem grossly exaggerated. Revolutionary movements from Iran to Poland have shown that dramatic political change in the late twentieth century can still be fueled by religious conviction. Looking toward the future, Samuel Huntington forecasts a "clash of civilizations" in which Christianity, Confucianism, and Islam will vie for supremacy. Likewise Ken Jowitt predicts a "new world disorder" in which movements of hatred and rage, often excited by religious creeds, will supersede the Cold War rivalry between communism and capitalism. Mark Juergensmeyer (1993:2) writes of a new Cold War between the secular West and new religious nationalisms, in which "the confrontation between these new forms of culture-based politics and the secular state is global in scope, binary in its opposition, occasionally violent, and essentially a difference of ideologies." As Roland Robertson (1991:289) observes, "grand narratives are not dying in Latin America or Asia, and indeed their (religious) vitality is probably in part a response to a precarious state of the grand narrative in the West."

Even in countries that remain staunchly secular in their political ideologies, such as communist China, something of a religious resurgence is underway. The remarkable growth of protestant christianity has been

---

[3] The term *secularization* is used in three different senses in the literature. Although secularization as a differentiation of church and state is certainly visible in most liberal democracies, other connotations of secularization – involving either the decline or the privatization of religion – do not necessarily follow. See Casanova 1994.

noted by many outside observers in China, Eastern Africa, and Central and Latin America. Less recognized, but perhaps more socially significant, is the widespread revival of folk religion. In both urban and rural China, the rebuilding of ancestral temples and refurbishing of ancestral graves, installation of altars for the worship of household deities, reemergence of shamanism, geomancy, fortune telling, and other varieties of "feudal super-stition" (as the regime derisively characterizes all such practices) is occur-ring at a head-spinning pace. Albeit small in scale, rebellions inspired by popular sectarian religion have proved to be a persistent headache for the Chinese government during the post-Mao reform era. Of even greater worry to Chinese state authorities are the religiously based separatist movements in Tibet and Xinjiang, both of which have grown larger and more vociferous in the reform period. In view of the ethnic conflicts that have crippled much of the formerly communist world, Chinese leaders are understandably nervous about similar challenges from Buddhists and Muslims within their borders.

Although there is a common perception among twentieth-century Americans that some religious traditions (for example, Islam) tend to spawn contention and violence, whereas others (for example, Buddhism) are more pacific in effect, a cursory survey of the historical record suggests that few religions are immune to strife. Within religious traditions, however, it may well be the case that certain strains, especially millenar-ian and syncretic variants, are particularly likely to generate contention.[4] Millenarianism, with its prediction of an imminent transformation of the world under the guiding hand of a messianic figure, encourages both a crisis mentality and passionate loyalty to the prophetic leader. As Eric Hobsbawm (1959) and Norman Cohn (1970) observed, millenarianism shares with secular revolutionary movements a utopian commitment to immediate and total change. The promise of divine assistance only strengthens the former's hold upon its followers. At the same time, move-ments inspired by syncretic belief systems, which draw inventively upon multiple religious traditions, seem especially conducive to militancy. Whether this is primarily because of the bold, free-spirited inclinations of

---

[4] We use the word *syncretism* with caution in view of the criticism that it has drawn in recent postcolonial discourse. Of course, all religions – like other belief systems – are to some extent syncretic in origin. We are referring here to a melange of religious beliefs and prac-tices, constructed through the creative combination of elements taken from previously dis-tinct religious traditions.

the individuals who launch such movements or whether there is something inherently destabilizing about the ideological melanges themselves is difficult to say. In any event, syncretism, and syncretic millenarianism in particular, is likely to remain a prominent feature of religiously inspired contention in the twenty-first century.

7

Threat (and Opportunity): Popular Action and State Response in the Dynamics of Contentious Action

Jack A. Goldstone and Charles Tilly

As compared with the fiercely repressive 1970s, the 1980s opened more opportunities to South Africa's black activists. International support for their cause was rising, black educational enrollment was increasing, color bars on employment were disappearing, and black trade unions had become legal. The South African government's abortive attempt to coopt mixed race (Coloured) and Indian citizens through the creation of separate, subordinate parliaments, furthermore, made blanket repression more difficult for the state to manage. Still, up to the decade's end threats abounded. The Black Authorities Act (1983) spurred local councils to raise rents, evict defaulters, and raze illegally constructed shacks; governmental forces tightened their surveillance of militants; and in July 1985 beleaguered premier P. W. Botha declared a state of emergency.

In the face of significant repression, the early 1980s saw widespread formation of local civic associations and significant expansion of worker militancy in general (Price 1991:162–82). The banned African National Congress (ANC) and Black Consciousness (BC) movement joined forces in the creation of a vast United Democratic Front (UDF) from 575 disparate organizations. The UDF drew on connections established by the BC and ANC, but went well beyond them. In 1985 a similar (and, in fact, overlapping) coalition of trade unions formed COSATU, the Congress of South African Trade Unions. Those well-connected organizations coordinated widespread resistance to the regime. Despite the state of emergency in most industrial centers, despite banning of many community organizations, and despite detention of thousands of activists without trial, black mobilization accelerated during the 1980s.

In Diepkloof township, Soweto, youth activists and civic organizations involving older citizens mobilized extensively between 1982 and 1984.

179

There, the Black Authorities Act spurred popular resistance: calls for councilors to resign, rent boycotts, school boycotts and much more. By 1985, local young people were organizing clandestine UDF neighborhood committees. One militant later reported that:

Before the banning and the state of emergency, we in Cosas [Congress of South African Students] used to meet as big groups of students. After, we had to develop sub-structures in different schools and each sub-structure would delegate two trusted people to go to general meetings where most things would be planned and evaluated . . . Before meetings we would all meet at a point and then move to a secret venue . . . Only about two or three people would know where the secret venue would be. (Marks 1996:6)

These "comrades" became the core of Soweto's street activists. As many of them went to jail, others – many of them more inclined to violent reprisals – sprang up to replace them. Indeed, in the 1980s, the response to state repression was not less protest, but more and more violent waves of protest in the townships.

Over South Africa as a whole, this sort of interaction between repression and local activism produced a surprising pattern: When governmental threats increased, so did popular opposition (Olivier 1990; 1991). While we can point to the new forms of organization and the new opportunities for action that entered the South African scene during the 1980s, we must recognize that threat itself was focusing resistance. According to prevailing theories of contentious politics, such an effect is an anomaly.

Opportunity and Threat

The usual story of political opportunity goes basically in one direction – from opportunity to action. Political opportunity increases, whether by external or internal factors that weaken the state, or by changing social conditions that increase the resources and confidence of popular groups seeking change, or some combination of both. This leads some groups to take overt actions challenging the state; the latter responds with some mix of concessions and repression, trying to roll back the rising opportunity. But the state's weakness or rising popular strength sustain the movement, and taking advantage of the increased political opportunities, the movement succeeds. Or at least, it does so until such time as the conditions that brought forth the opportunity recede. As opportunity expands, actions mount; as opportunities contract, action recedes (McAdam 1996;

McAdam, Tarrow, and Tilly 1996). So the model suggests; but the reality is rather more complex.

As Karen Rasler (1996) and others (Gartner and Regan 1996; Hoover and Kowalewski 1992; Jackson et al. 1978; Lichbach 1995) have clearly shown, the expanding opportunities model "overlooks the pattern of tactical moves and countermoves" between regime and challengers, as both sides engage in a series of choices regarding actions, repression, and concessions (Rasler 1996:149). Moreover, if there is only a single dimension captured by "rising opportunities," such that increased repression by definition reduces opportunity, then this view is inconsistent with the repeated *empirical* finding that in many situations, even after controlling for other factors, increased repression leads to *increased* protest mobilization and action. Khawaja's (1993) study of Palestinian protest in the West Bank, Rasler's (1996) study of Iranian protests in 1977–79, Francisco's (1996) study of protest in Germany, and Olivier's (1990) study of Black protest in South Africa all find, as the latter clearly states, that "the effect of repression on the rate [of collective action] is not negative! Repression led to a significant increase in the rate of collective action" (Olivier 1990:99). As a number of analysts have pointed out (Francisco 1996; Lichbach 1987; 1995; Tsebelis and Sprague 1989), this result requires a complex, dynamic view of the role of repression and opportunity in contentious collective action.

While the literature on contentious politics is not silent on threat, referring often to costs of action, costs of mobilizing, and the risks and incidence of repression, we believe that "threat" has not been explored as extensively as "opportunity." Indeed, "threat" is often treated as merely the flip side of opportunity, a negative measure of the same concept, so that "increased threat" simply equates with "reduced opportunities." We believe this is mistaken, and that "threat" is an independent factor whose dynamics greatly influence how popular groups and the state act in a variety of conflict situations. If this is true, much more needs to be said about how "opportunity" and "threat" combine to shape contentious action.

Consider three episodes of protest activity in which action, mobilization, and success were *not* simply proportional to opportunity. In China in 1989 a decade of economic and administrative reforms, a huge expansion of the university population, and a visit by President Gorbachev of the U.S.S.R. that brought the world's media to Beijing, clearly provided

181

heightened opportunities for student mobilization against the dictatorship of the Chinese Communist Party (Zhao 2001). Weeks of mobilization involving up to a million individuals in complex networks, with extensive symbolic actions and media support aimed at reframing the legitimacy of the regime, plus clear wavering among the military defenders of the capital, made some sort of change look increasingly inevitable. But Deng Xiaoping snatched victory away from the students and their supporters, marshaling provincial troops to swiftly crush the movement, as repression trumped opportunities (Calhoun 1994). In Iran a decade earlier, political opportunities were fleeting: A few consoling words by President Jimmy Carter regarding human rights hardly made up for the overwhelming military and secret police forces and oil revenues enjoyed by the Shah. Yet elites and popular groups challenged the Shah and, despite a flow of martyrs produced by state repression, continued to mobilize and frame the Shah's regime as an anti-Islamic, traitorously pro-Western abomination. In so doing, they managed to gain the initiative, transform the opportunity structure as more and more elites and popular groups defected from the Shah, and create a triumphant revolution (Kurzman 1996). In France from 1789 to 1793, peasants and elites responded to waves of political opportunity, then to fears of war and invaders, then to fears of the centralization of the church and state under the revolutionary government, with waves of revolutionary and counterrevolutionary mobilization. Rising political opportunity surrounding the calling of the Estates General may have provoked antiseigneurial uprisings, but it was fears of invaders and pillage that provoked the peasant mobilization of the Great Fear, fears of royal reprisals that sparked the Paris crowds on the 14th of July and succeeding *journeés*, and fears of taxation and conscription and loss of local clergy that sparked the massive counterrevolutionary mobilizations throughout France (Markoff 1997). Much of the popular mobilization during the French Revolution was defensive in inception, responding to threats of growing danger, not a matter of groups seeking change and seizing growing opportunities to achieve it. In short, not all mobilization for contentious politics follows rising opportunities; nor do rising opportunities – even with successful mobilization and brilliant framing, as in Tiananmen – always lead to successful contention.

We suggest that one way to approach these complexities is to separate "opportunity" from "threat." Let "opportunity" be the probability that social protest actions will lead to success in achieving a desired outcome. Thus any changes that shift the balance of political and economic

182

resources between a state and challengers, that weaken a state's ability to reward its followers or opponents or to pursue a coherent policy, or that shifts domestic or outside support away from the regime, increases opportunities. Under these guidelines, the usual markers of rising "political opportunities," such as a defeat in war, elite divisions, state fiscal problems, a rising but disenfranchised middle class, international pressures, and weak or divided state leadership, fit nicely (Tarrow 1998b).

But the chances for success are analytically distinct from the risks and costs that a social group will experience if it acts – or doesn't act. Let us label the costs that a social group will incur from protest, or that it expects to suffer if it does not take action, as "threat." The way that "threat" and "opportunity" combine, rather than shifts in the chances of success or the costs of action alone, will shape decisions regarding action. A group may decide to bear very high costs for protest if it believes the chances of achieving success are high; but the same group may decide to avoid even modest costs of protest if it believes the chances of succeeding are low. Thus protestors in East Germany and Czechoslovakia in 1989, in Estonia in 1990, and in Moscow at the White House in August 1991, took great risks in demonstrating against the regime; not because they believed they were not taking such risks (they were and did, as the security forces acted firmly in the initial confrontations), but because they believed the chances of success were greater than they had yet seen in their lifetimes (Karklins and Petersen 1993; Opp, Voss, and Gern 1995; Pfaff 1996). A group may also decide to risk protest, even if opportunities seem absent, if the costs of not acting seem too great. Thus the mobilization of blacks against apartheid by the ANC in South Africa from the 1960s to the 1980s, or of Indians against the British to force independence after World War II, or of French peasants in Brittany and the West resisting the reorganization of church and state by the Jacobin regime, were mobilizations in the face of repression in the hope of changing a feared and hated status quo or resisting unwelcome changes, not simply responses to rising opportunities.

A Simple Model of "Opportunity" and "Threat" Interaction

"Opportunity" and "threat" can thus take various combinations to shape contentious action. Nonetheless, this formulation is still too vague. We can add more precision by breaking each of these terms down further into components. For the moment, let us assume that individuals

183

contemplating protest are rational, and try to assess the potential costs and gains of protest; we will return below to the fact that all such assessments depend on perceptions and framing. It is important to realize that people do not make these choices simply as isolated individuals – a person's relationships to other people within important groups, their assurances that others in their networks will support their actions, and expectations about what other groups will do all enter into perceptions of whether a protest will be successful, and its expected costs (Goldstone 1994; Opp, Voss, and Gern 1995; Pfaff 1996). With these caveats in mind, we expect protest actions to occur if the expected results are a net gain. The expected gains (G) equal the value of the gains that would result from success (V, which may be new advantages obtained or current or prospective harms avoided) times the probability of success, or "opportunity" (O), minus the costs incurred from protest (C, which include time and resources expended, and the repression incurred. For simplicity's sake, let us say that these costs are dominated by the costs of repression). We then have the simple formula

$$G = (V \times O) - C. \tag{1}$$

Of course, this formula involves yet another simplification – that the costs of repression do not depend on the chances for success. In some cases, this is clearly false – those leading a rebellion are likely to suffer far greater costs if the rebellion fails than if it succeeds. However, if we focus on the ordinary protestor, say the person who helped defend the Russian Parliament in 1991, or the civil rights protestor who risks a beating or arrest, for them the eventual result days or weeks later will not change whether a bullet finds them on the barricade, or lighten the beating, or avoid the arrest. For them, the immediate risks involved with the act of protest itself are what counts – which is to say that leaders and followers may have a separate calculus of prospective gains and risks, with both being much greater for those in charge.

We can then break down our terms in equation (1) still further. The probability of success depends on state weakness (for example, fiscal problems, elite divisions, military defeat), and on popular support for the protest, and on the power of nonstate opponents or allies, at home and abroad. These are the "opportunity" dimensions. The value of achieving success depends on whether things might be gained by action, but this includes both new advantages (A) and avoiding harms that are currently experienced or anticipated; such harms under the existing regime are one kind of "threat" which we may label "current threat" (T_c). There are also costs of repression if protest is undertaken; this is another kind of "threat," which we may label "repressive threat" (T_r). What is interesting and important to observe is that *the state has substantial control over both kinds of threat*. That is, the state can increase prospective or current harm by increasing taxes, increasing violence against the population or specific groups, taking away rights or property, or other such actions. The state can also decrease current or prospective harm by making concessions, that is changing its policies to improve conditions for popular and/or elite groups. In addition, the state can choose to respond to protest action with varying levels of repression. Thus the state, in choosing a mix of concessions and repression, can manipulate both the value of success, and costs imposed by various threats.

To restate the model, we now have the more complicated expression:

$$G = [O \times (A + T_c)] - T_r \tag{2}$$

where $O = k_1$ (state weakness) + k_2 (popular support)
$\qquad\qquad + k_3$ (strength of nonstate allies and opponents)

and where protest actions are expected if the gains (G) are greater than zero.

It may seem that we have a needlessly complicated and useless expression. However, if we focus on how states and groups may respond to the conditions in this model, we find a far richer range of dynamics for state contention than is found in the simple "rising opportunity leads to rising protest" model.

Let us first focus on the options for a protest group. In the short run, the group and the state probably can do little about state weakness, which depends on structural conditions or events, such as financial weakness, elite divisions, or military defeat. However, both the group and the state can appeal for popular support and the alliance of specific groups, by both framing the options of change and the status quo, or (for the state) by offering concrete concessions to the population at large, or to targeted groups. The latter, however, requires some financial resources on the part of the state. This formulation already shows the intermingling of framing and opportunity, the way that group actions and framing can influence opportunity, and the ways that state concessions can also shape opportunities.

The state, however, has additional options, namely its ability to manipulate the current threats to the protest group, and the level of repression that follows on protest action. Here there is room for effective action by the state, but also room for great errors. Both concessions to alleviate current threats, and repressive threats to respond to (and deter) protest actions are costly, but the costs will differ greatly depending on the size of the group, the nature of the current threats, and the costs of repression. For example, in South Africa, the ruling Afrikaner party long deemed the costs of imprisoning black leaders and maintaining a repressive domestic military were less than the costs of alleviating the apartheid regime that pressed on blacks but preserved a privileged position for whites. Thus considerable expenses were undertaken to create a level of repressive threat large enough to counter the mobilizing effects of the large current threat imposed by apartheid on nonwhite groups. In the U.S.S.R., Mikhail Gorbachev faced a different situation. In his effort to reduce the costs of military competition with the West, it was crucial to reduce tensions and show a "reasonableness" in his regime. Thus using a high level of repressive threat to counter the rising opportunities created by *perestroika* was ruled out. Instead, Gorbachev tried to offer concessions to various groups, and alleviate some of the evils imposed by the state-socialist system and one-party rule, in the hopes of winning enough support to sustain his reforming regime. But he failed, because the opportunities for fundamental change, and the gains to be had from eliminating the party altogether, continued to outpace his concessions and mild repression. The terms in equation two (O and A) grew, while Gorbachev could not reduce current threats, or increase repressive threats, enough to prevent growing protests for change. Perceiving this, conservatives in the military launched a coup aiming to greatly increase the level of repressive threat to preserve the domination of the Communist Party. But the repressive threat failed, while heightening the sense of harm that would be experienced if the party remained in power, thus sealing the abolition of one-party rule.

If we focus for the moment on the ability of the state to manipulate both current threats (by concessions to alleviate current or future harm) and repressive threats (by choosing how much force to use in response to protest), we can diagram the state's options as choosing a point in a two-dimensional space, as shown in Figure 7.1.

In facing any protest, the state must choose some combination of concessions and repression. Clearly, for a given level of opportunity and prospective advantages of success, a variety of levels of concessions (T_c) and repression (T_r) will combine to offset expected gains and eliminate the motivation for protest. We can draw such a boundary of sufficient com-

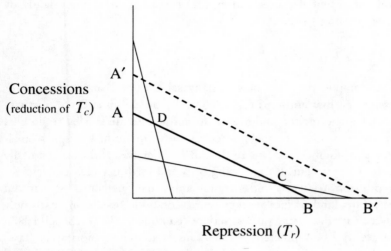

Figure 7.1 Concessions and Repression

bined actions regarding threats by connecting the point at which concessions alone (point A) or repression alone (point B) would discourage
protest. For a given level of opportunity, any points in this diagram under
the line AB would be insufficient to discourage protest, and any points
along or slightly above the line would discourage it.

How does the state decide which combination of concessions and
repressions to choose along this line? That depends on the costs of concessions and repression. We can draw a "constant cost" line for the state.
If repression is cheap compared to concessions, then the line will be relatively flat, and intersect the necessary level of threat boundary at a point
of mainly repression (for example, point C); if concessions are cheaper, the
line will be relatively steep, and intersect the necessary level of threat
boundary at a point of mainly concessions (for example, point D).

Now let us take things a step further. In most situations, the state has
at best imperfect knowledge about the level of popular support for protestors; it may overestimate its own support. It may also overestimate its
own strength, and thus arrive at a different estimate of opportunity than
that held by the protest group. Thus the state, in general, will have a hard
time picking the right level of concessions and repression to respond to a
group. This creates both considerable hazards for the state, and a rich

dynamic of potential routes and cycles of contention, driven mainly by actions regarding "threat."

Scenarios

As one example, the state may initially set the level of concessions or repression too low, and thus find itself under the AB line. Protest activity will then start to mount, and the question for the state is what to do next – increase repression, or increase concessions, or both. One problem is that the state is uncertain where the AB frontier lies, and thus can easily fail to find its way out. It may swing back and forth between concessions and repression, trying to find a combination that quells protest, without success. This kind of inconsistent repression and concession is strongly associated with increasing protest actions (Kurzman 1996; Lichbach 1987). Or a state may be "addicted" to one kind of action. Authoritarian states tend to be highly reliant on repression, while democratic states more often are inclined to a mix of concession and repression, or to greater concessions (Davenport 1995; Gurr 1986). Authoritarian states may thus, if they overestimate their support and underestimate that of the opposition, rachet up repression slowly and insufficiently to halt mobilization, while refusing to make concessions that would relieve the current threat imposed by existing conditions.

A further problem – and here the dynamics become interesting indeed – is that repression or concession *can themselves move the AB frontier*. That is, repression that is excessive can create a perception of increased current threat under the status quo, due to greater illegitimacy and violence from the regime. As Khawaja (1993:67) points out, on the West Bank from 1976 to 1985, "in their micromobilization efforts to gain popular sympathy for the collective cause, [*intifada supporters*] point to repeated acts of repression, as these acts ease their task of constructing a 'bad profile' of the authorities. . . . They reframe the repression action of authorities as . . . endangering people's existence and survival." In general, as Gartner and Regan (1996:278) argue, "if the repressive tactics are considered overly severe relative to demands [to maintain order], the domestic costs begin to increase. Too much repression may leave the opposition little alternative to revolt."

In addition, modest concessions can lead to increased demands for further change, either because of the de Tocqueville effect – minor changes made by the regime are an advertisement of its illegitimacy, but do not fully correct that illegitimacy, and thus lead to greater demands for elimination or transformation of the regime – or because the concessions attract other supporters who now feel that they too can extract more from the regime. Rasler (1996) has shown how concessions by the Shah of Iran in response to protest led to escalation and diffusion of a variety of protest actions. Thus, acts of repression or concessions can shift the AB line outward, requiring still greater repression or concessions to halt a mounting protest.

Looking back at equation (2), we can see that a state's response to protest can alter an initial situation in several ways. Weak repression or concessions can increase perceptions of state weakness, or raise popular support for an opposition movement, or cause nonstate groups to favor the opposition over the state. Excessively strong repression can raise the perceptions of current threat, and also cause the opposition to gain allies. All these shifts increase O, meaning that higher levels of concessions and repression will be needed to supress protests. Thus the effect of state actions in response to protest may be to shift the suppression line AB outward to A′B′.

For example, in Figure 7.1, if a regime that favors repression acts in a manner that puts it somewhere to the left of point C – that is, a response that includes some modest concessions, but rather more repression, yet still not quite enough to stamp out the opposition movement – the result may be to increase demands for more concessions and to make the opposition willing to suffer even greater costs to remove the regime. The required level of concessions and repression to suppress the movement may then move out to the new line A′B′. In this particular example, if the regime is bound by the flatter line through point C as its frontier for action, it has doomed itself; it is now neither capable of enough repression, nor willing to provide enough concessions, to halt the movement. That is, there is no point on the line through point C that is above the new suppression line A′B′.

By contrast, if a different kind of regime, bound by the more vertical line through D, had initially responded with actions somewhat below point D – not quite enough repression or concessions to halt the movement, but encouraging the opposition and gaining it popular sympathy, and thus moving the suppression line out to A′B′ – this regime can still halt the movement. Note that there is a region on the more vertical line through D, toward the top of that line, that is above A′B′, where the level of concessions is still great enough to stop the movement. Thus if the regime moves far enough in giving substantial concessions, the regime could survive, although with significant reforms.

Of course, different regimes will have different boundary lines governing their possible responses to protest, and different conditions of conflict – that is, various levels of resources and popular support for the regime and opponents – will determine how much in the way of concessions or repression will be needed to suppress a challenging movement. Thus the dynamics of opposition action, state responses, and renewed action can take a variety of pathways.

Mounting protest, severe repression. In many cases, where authorities have responded to protest with rapid and overwhelming repression, protest was damped down. Even though the regime might have lost support, moving the AB frontier outward, the initial repression was so great that even under an extended AB frontier, the current level of repression still suffices to halt protest. Examples include the Tiananmen massacre in China in 1989, the PRI assault on students in Mexico city in 1968, and the peasant massacres in El Salvador in the 1930s.

Mounting protest, repression initially leading to greater protests, but then damped down by much greater repression. In some cases, where authorities respond to protests with repression, the result is distress and anger among the population which creates more opposition supporters, increases the perceived threat of the status quo, and thus leads people to be willing to bear greater costs to overturn the regime. The repression thus acts to move the AB line outward, and it may initially move further and faster than the regime's repression can keep pace with. For example, in Russia in 1905, the murderous suppression of a peaceful, priest-led protest in Moscow on "Bloody Sunday" outraged the Russian population, leading to hundreds of thousands of workers striking and protests throughout rural Russia. Only a truly massive national repressive effort – "jumping" to the far side of the new A'B' boundary – restored order.

Mounting protest, repression initially leading to greater protests, then further repression and/or concessions leading to still greater protests, and so forth: the classic "spiral" of revolutionary conflict. In many cases, the regime was never able to get back "on the other side" of the advancing AB boundary. This might be because after some initial rounds of inadequate repression or concessions, the newly required level of repression was too costly, or the regime was constrained by internal or external factors, or it exceeded the capacity of the regime to implement. In Iran in the late 1970s, concessions to protestors led to more demands for change but then repressive measures that were strong enough to create popular distress, but too weak to suppress mobilization, provoked still more opposition. Each zig and zag in the Shah's policies created more opposition supporters, so that further concessions and repression proved inadequate to halt the escalating mobilization. Constrained by the need to maintain U.S. support, the Shah could not implement ruthless all-out repression early, seeking instead piecemeal efforts at repression and concession, but after several rounds of these, opposition grew to such levels that the Shah (and many of his U.S. supporters and domestic military personnel) could not stomach the degree of repression that would have been required to restore order. In Cuba in the late 1950s, Batista reacted to Castro's relatively weak opposition with a degree of random and severe repression that alienated Cubans, but as Castro's support grew, Batista was unable to coordinate and mount the repressive effort that would have been required to stop him.

And in a particularly revealing case – the Soviet Union in the late 1980s – the need to maintain peaceful relations with the United States and expand trade and borrowing with Europe greatly constrained Soviet repression in the face of mounting nationalist and anticommunist protests (Dunlop 1993; Urban et al. 1997). While conservatives in the Soviet regime did seek to impose sufficient repression to halt the protests (as in the massacres in Georgia and Estonia), Gorbachev blocked them from doing more, thus creating the situation of repression that was sufficient to increase demands for change but not to stop it. At the same time, conservatives blocked Gorbachev from making greater concessions, to the point of launching a coup against him when it appeared he was willing to deal with Yelstin to remove the Communist Party from its position of unchallenged authority. The overall result was again a zig-zag of concessions and repression, with Gorbachev, Yelstin, and communist conservatives each seeking to limit the others. Throughout this process, protest mounted, was stimulated by concessions and limited repression, but could not be effectively suppressed (although the if the anti-Gorbachev coup had succeeded, certainly massive repression of anticommunist mobilization would have followed).

A spiral of protest, repression, and expanding protest, but ending in massive concessions. In a manner similar to the dynamics of the cases in the revolutionary spiral, in British India in the late 1940s, in the U.S. South during the Civil Rights Movement of the 1960s, and in South Africa in the 1980s, repressive actions against protest did more to discredit the regimes than to suppress mobilization, inasmuch as the mores of the ruling authorities and world opinion imposed considerable constraints on the levels of repression that could be employed. As the costs of repression and the constraints of external opinion limited repressive strategies, while mobilization and protest continued, the regimes adopted massive concessions to avert revolutionary conflict.

Protests leading to concessions. This is the antithesis of the revolutionary pattern, but this model is simply another variation of the same underlying dynamics, only with different regime responses. In this case, the regime largely (although not entirely) refrains from violent repression, preferring to offer concessions. In some cases, the concessions may be insufficient, leading to more and more protests until massive reforms occur. This was the case in the British Reform Movement from 1817 to 1832, and in the Workers' Rights Movement of the Depression era. In other cases, modest concessions are sufficient to defuse, or at least to institutionalize, protest activity, as is the case with most social movements in modern democratic polities.

Regime Type and Patterns of Contentious Politics

Note that this model also predicts different dynamics of contentious politics for different types of regimes and protest groups. In liberal democratic regimes in wealthy countries, for groups seeking modest goals, the costs of repression are likely to be higher than the costs of concessions. Thus for most issue-oriented groups, concessions and mild repression rather than reverse are the likely pattern of protest. This is the pattern shown by the more vertical line through point D in Figure 7.1. The dynamic pattern here is that if modest levels of concessions and repression are not sufficient to halt the movement, the system will implement large concessions and preserve itself through reforms. An exception would occur, however, for groups to whom concessions would be exceptionally costly (for example, socialist groups seeking to overthrow capitalism); in these special cases a strong effort at repression and not concessions is the more likely response.

In contrast, for authoritarian regimes, concessions to any groups challenging their monopoly of power is likely to be more costly than repression; thus repression is more likely to dominate protest in these settings (as in the flatter line through point C in Figure 7.1). However, repression has its costs as well, particularly if it alienates aid donors and trading partners. Such regimes are therefore likely to swing between token concessions and repression, as their estimates of the costs of each fluctuates (for example, China today). Such regimes also run the risk of becoming habituated to repression as a preferred response to protest; if their repressive capacity should ever fall, they then are vulnerable to a massive eruption of protest.

We should also note that these dynamics in response to changes in threat lend themselves to producing quite nonlinear responses to critical events, as one would expect from the "eventmental history" approach of William Sewell, Jr. In the above model, increased repression needn't simply reduce the likelihood of protest, as an opportunity model that treats repression mainly as a decline in opportunity would suggest. A critical event that changes perceptions of state strength or of popular support, or of the current level of threat from the existing regime, can suddenly shift the calculus of a protest group or groups, moving the A′B′ line outward (or inward), thus creating a suddenly new set of conditions for protests and state-protester interactions. Thus, for example, the response to "Bloody Sunday" was not the expected "opportunity response." Instead, the violent repression shifted perceptions of current harm from the continuation of the existing regime, increasing the motivation to protest.

Conclusion

Does rising opportunity portend rising protests? In many cases yes, but that is too simple; if that is all that were involved, we would have a fairly linear and continuous response of protest to opportunity, and we should see protest move smoothly in arcs of rise and fall, in response to opportunities waxing and waning. In fact, we see sudden eruptions, reversals, cycles, and critical events, with states sometimes being successful and sometimes self-destructing. An increase in repression or concessions is often followed by more protest, rather than less. This can only be explained by realizing that opportunity is always in interaction with current and repressive threats, and that this interaction gives rise to varied dynamic patterns of protest and contention.

Once the range of these dynamics is appreciated, we can see that a wide variety of patterns of contentious politics – failed revolts, revolutionary spirals, protests leading to massive reforms, and more conventional social movement protests – are not radically different processes. Rather, each represents a possible outcome of opposition and state actions under a specific configuration of movement suppression boundaries and regime choice frontiers, within a single model of dynamics of contentious politics. Greater attention to "threat," and to its interaction with changes in "opportunity," thus gives insights into the often swirling dynamic patterns of contentious politics, and reveals the basic underlying structure behind a wide range of its forms.

8

Contention in Demographic and Life-Course Context

Jack A. Goldstone and Doug McAdam

To call a concern with demographic and life-course processes a silence in the study of contentious politics is something of an exaggeration. It would probably be more accurate to term it a muted voice in contemporary scholarship and, sticking with the auditory analogy, a faint echo from older research traditions. If we consider only contemporary scholarship, there has been a low-level, but persistent, interest in the long-term biographical impact of social movement participation (DeMartini 1983; Demerath, Marwell, and Aiken 1971; Fendrich 1977; 1993; Fendrich and Tarleau 1973; Marwell, Aiken, and Demerath 1987; McAdam 1988; 1989; McAdam, Van Dyke, Shockey, and Munch 1998; Sherkat and Blocker 1997; Whalen and Flacks 1989). On the "independent variable" side, there has also been a stress on the role of "biographical availability" as a factor mediating recruitment to individual activism (McAdam 1986; Snow and Rochford 1983; Wiltfang and McAdam 1991).

Besides these contemporary emphases, several older research traditions also stress the role of demographic or life-course processes as either causes or consequences of individual activism. Perhaps the most enduring of these traditions is rooted in Mannheim's influential concept of the "political generation" (1952). Political generations emerge when particular birth cohorts are exposed to highly distinctive life experiences during adolescence or young adulthood. Mannheim clearly counted generalized social and political unrest – what we might now call a "protest cycle" – among these "distinctive life experiences." Such experiences are thought to mark these cohorts for life, leaving them with characteristic world views, and political orientations and commitments. But it was not simply on the outcomes side that Mannheim discerned a link between life-course factors and political contention. He also believed that, because of their need to define and differentiate themselves from their elders, youth cohorts were receptive to radical ideologies and therefore more disposed to political activism as well. Mannheim's general approach to the demographic structuring of protest behavior has lived on in the work of Richard Braungart (1984; 1971), Joe DeMartini (1983), and others. In addition, though stressing different mechanisms than Mannheim, a host of classic works also asserted a developmental disposition toward activism on the part of the young (for example, Feuer 1969; Klapp 1969; Le Bon 1960).

Virtually all of the work reviewed above is concerned with the *micro* determinants and consequences of *social movement* participation. The literature on demography/life course and contention is a good bit "quieter" on the *macro* dimensions of the relationship and, what macro work does exist, is primarily concerned with the role of demographic processes in the origin of *revolution*. But some such work does exist; indeed, in assigning central explanatory significance to this factor, Goldstone (1991; 1997) has revisited – while greatly refurbishing – one of the oldest lines of theory on the social causes of unrest. Thomas Malthus' [1993] famous theory *cum* cautionary tale on the destabilizing effects of unchecked population growth remains one of the standard citations in the history of the social sciences. Consistent with Goldstone's work, but somewhat narrower in its empirical focus, is the specific literature on land pressure and the rise of peasant revolts (Jones and Kuhn 1978; Lefebvre 1973; Midlarsky 1986; Mousnier 1970; Paige 1975; Whitmeyer and Hopcroft 1996; Wolf 1969). Finally, in stressing the important role that migration processes can play in exacerbating conflict between spatially proximate ethnic groups, certain competition theorists have also fashioned a partially demographic account of the origins of contention (Weiner 1993).

Given this smattering of contemporary and more temporally distant scholarship on the link between demographic and life-course processes and contentious politics, readers would be forgiven for wondering why we have chosen to take up the topic at all. The reason is simple. For all the merits of the extant scholarship, we think contemporary work on social movements and revolutions continues to seriously undervalue the role of demographic factors and life-course processes. There are two problems worth noting in this regard. First, while one can identify, as we have, specific literatures that, in piecemeal fashion, grant some importance to the topic, there is nothing like a sustained demographic/life-course perspective on contention. Secondly, what fragmented work exists on the topic betrays the general asymmetry noted previously. That is, most work

Table 8.1 *Silence and Voice in the Study of Democracy, Life-Course, and Contention*

	Emergence/Development	Decline/Outcomes
Macro	*Demographic pressures and the emergence of contention*	*Contention as a force for aggregate change in life-course patterns*
	Land pressure and peasant rebellion	
	Migration and the rise of ethnic competition	
Micro	*"Biographical availability" or other life-course factors mediating entrance into activism*	*Biographical consequences of individual activism*

by social movement scholars is pitched at the *micro level* and concerned with life-course *outcomes*, while students of revolutions reverse the two emphases, focusing on the *macro determinants* of contention. The aim of this chapter is to redress these two lacuna. Table 8.1 will simultaneously serve as a convenient road map for this effort and a conceptual mapping of the discrete literatures touched on previously.

The italicized entries in the table represent our attempt to locate all of the literatures touched on above within our two-by-two framework. More importantly, by combining these two dimensions, we have generated the four issues we want to focus on in this chapter. But in concentrating on these four topics, we aspire to something more than a dry tour of our two-by-two table. Rather we want to use the four topics to animate a distinctive demographic/life-course "reading" of two broad and highly consequential episodes of contention: the decomposition of the former Soviet Union and the American new left. More generally, we think that any systematic effort to understand the complex relationship between demographic and life-course processes and political contention will necessarily need to simultaneously address these four topics.

The Decomposition of the Soviet Union

The Soviet Union did not collapse simply because of gross population pressures. Rich in resources, and with slow population growth in its core regions of Russia, the Ukraine, Belarus, and in the Baltic states, the story of the Soviet Union's collapse in the 1980s is far different than the story of the collapse of the empire of the Tsars, in which one critical blow came from a dramatically expanded and impoverished peasantry (Robinson 1967). Yet an essential element to understanding the Soviet decomposition is still population *processes*. These include shifts in the allocation of people to various sectors of education and the economy, processes of social mobility (and frustrated mobility), changes in the demographic profile of the elites, imbalanced population growth and development between the slavic and nonslavic regions of the Soviet Union, marked changes in demographic variables – most notably infant mortality, the rise of distinct countercultural groups in Soviet society, and the generational impact of such events as the Afghan War. The result of these macro and micro processes was to fissure the Soviet elite, fuel popular discontent and nationalism, and create divisions in the army and the party hierarchies. In combination with a fiscal crisis that led Mikhail Gorbachev to seek economic and political reforms, these processes turned efforts at reform into an uncontrolled stream of protest, electoral surprises, attempts at coup and counterreform, and finally, to revolution. Indeed, we believe that without attention to all of these demographic processes, one gains only a partial view of the complex processes behind the collapse of the Soviet Union.

Macrodemographic Processes in the Decomposition of the Soviet Union

In the 1950s and 1960s, the Soviet Union enjoyed both a high rate of economic growth, and a shift in its population away from farming to urban and industrial employment. In the 1940s, 46 percent of the Soviet population worked in agriculture (including forestry, fishing, and miscellaneous rural employment); by the 1960s, this fraction of the workforce had fallen to 23 percent, with large increases in the clerical, professional, and service sectors (Goldstone 1998b:107). This shift was accompanied by changes in education: There were huge increases in the percentage of the population gaining secondary and postsecondary education, with the number of those qualified as "specialists" by higher technical or college training rising from about 1 million 1940 to 10 million in 1970 (Remington 1990:190). This combination of changes in the education of the population, and changes in the composition of the workforce, produced substantial economic mobility.

But in the 1970s and 1980s, these population changes began to fall out of synch. Educational access continued to grow: Whereas in 1959, only 2 percent of the population had postsecondary degrees; by 1989 this had risen to 9 percent. Yet the composition of the workforce remained "stuck" in a predominantly blue-collar, early industrial mode – throughout the 1970s and 1980s, two-thirds of the workforce remained in agriculture, mining, and manufacturing, with only 19 percent in educational and service positions; only 5 percent of the workforce was professional and managerial, a proportion unchanged since the 1960s (Dunlop 1993:68; Goldstone 1998b:107). Thus while the number of college graduates rapidly increased, the proportion of entry-level positions in managerial professional and service positions did not.

Moreover, the nature of postsecondary education changed as well. The vast majority of those going on to college were assigned to "technical institutes" where they received engineering or other technical training. These "specialists," as they were called, emerged overqualified for the kind of routine factory work to which they were assigned, but underqualified for the elite managerial and party political positions, which were reserved for graduates of the major universities. What's more, even the most advanced and honored university graduates, professionals, and managers of academia, services, and industry were excluded from the political hierarchy of the Communist Party, who recruited from provincial university graduates who built their careers mainly in Party jobs (Lane and Ross 1994). By the late 1980s, one could identify three distinct career tracks leading out of postsecondary education: technical specialists who were assigned mainly to factory work; graduates of universities in Moscow and Leningrad in the scientific and professional fields (known as the intelligentsia) who took urban and managerial jobs but were mainly outside the party power structure; and graduates of provincial universities who mainly studied engineering and agriculture and worked their way up the party hierarchy through jobs in Komsomol (the Communist Party youth league) and provincial Party posts (both Gorbachev and Yelstin came from this latter group).

Thus the pattern of social mobility changed completely from the 1950–70 period to 1970–89. In the earlier period, an expanding educational and university system fed mobility into an expanding industrial and urban workforce and a growing party elite. Social mobility was widespread, and the elite fairly unified. But in the later period, a still-expanding educational and university system had nowhere to send its technical graduates, except into jobs for which they were overqualified, as the economy remained stuck in a preservice, heavy, industry-dominated mode. Moreover, the higher education system itself bifurcated, so that career tracks within the universities that prepared the top elite became more discrete. Thus in the later period, the elite "as a whole was fragmented and lacked moral cohesion" (Lane 1996:6). The views of the intelligentsia, professionals, and managers diverged from that of most of the Party elite, while an overtrained and underemployed corps of technical specialists chafed under the commands of Communist Party leaders.

This situation in the Soviet Union of the late 1980s was not unlike that in prerevolutionary France in the late 1780s. In France, the period of the 1750s and 1760s had seen an expansion and reform of the military, and an expansion of the economy, that provided for substantial social mobility. But in the 1770s and 1780s, the numbers of those gaining higher education or seeking higher positions based on their economic fortunes grew even faster, while the number of elite positions was restricted by the fiscal problems of the Crown and the demands of the older nobility. As a result, France in the 1780s, though coming out of period of substantial social mobility, still had large numbers of educated professionals who faced limited opportunities to get ahead, and resented the increasingly closed circle of nobility who retained command of the key institutions of society (Goldstone 1991:28–249). It was these professionals that led the Revolution of 1789. The Soviet Union in the 1980s held a similar cadre of frustrated professionals, who resented the Communist Party's control of the key institutions of Soviet society. And it was these professionals who provided the key support for the assault on the Party.

This demographic transformation is clear in Lane and Ross's analysis of the leadership of the Supreme Soviet of the USSR in 1984 versus 1989 (after Gorbachev's first efforts to create partially freed elections). In the period from 1984 to 1988, 23 percent of the officers and committee chairmen in the Supreme Soviet were still of the Bolshevik Revolution generation, having been born before 1920; only 8 percent had been born since 1940. But in the period 1989–91, only 2 percent of the elite of the Supreme Soviet had been born before 1920; and the number of those born after WWII had doubled to 16 percent. The shift in occupational background is even more marked. In 1984–88, 69 percent of the officers and committee chairmen in the Supreme Soviet were former members of the Supreme Soviet or newly elected officials with jobs in Komsomol and the Communist Party; managers and professionals comprised only 8 percent. But in 1989–91, former managers and professionals made up 47 percent of the Supreme Soviet elite; this was now a larger portion of the elite than the 36 percent who were drawn from jobs in the Supreme Soviet, Komsomol, and the Party (Lane and Ross 1994:456). "The ascendant political elites are persons with a professional background educated primarily in Moscow and Leningrad" (Lane and Ross 1998:49). The demographic analysis makes clear that "a new elite in terms of its generational, occupational, and institutional background had replaced the professional politicians of the Breshnev era" (Lane and Ross 1994:437).

While it was certainly reformers within the Party such as Yelstin and professionals and members of the intelligenstia who took leadership roles in the anti-Soviet movement, the core of their support was provided by technical specialists and professionals who made up *Democraty Rossiya* (Democratic Russia). It was this party that organized demonstrations in Moscow and Leningrad, that won the elections for anticommunist candidates to the Soviet Congress and the presidency of the Russian Republic (Urban et al. 1997).

Gorbachev had called for popular elections to the Congress of People's Deputies to gain support for reform *within* the Communist Party. But the professionals and specialists knew precisely how badly the Party had been managing the economy of the country. They saw the Party itself as the problem. Initially, opposition focused on environmental issues and corruption. But when Gorbachev asked Party candidates to stand in elections, anti-Party candidates also came forth, and in spite of election laws designed to favor the Party, in the urban prefectures where the professionals and specialists were strong, the Party candidates suffered humiliating losses.

The anger of urban technical and professional workers was supported from another quarter – the rising nationalist sentiment in the Caucasus, the Baltics, and in Central Asia (Carrere d'Encausse 1991). Nationalism in the Baltics was an old phenomenon, but was prompted in part by demographic processes – the vast migration of Russians placed as "colonists" in the Baltic states. Not bothering to learn the language of their new region, while taking many of the better jobs, their incursion was resented. Although the Soviet Union professed to honor its nationalities, and did try to fill the top leadership positions in its various regions with natives, the professed honor given to nationalities clashed with reality. In fact, the Soviet program of incorporating its various national regions was a policy of Russification, encouraging Russian inmigration and promoting Russian families. Moreover, Stalin had freely deported and transferred whole ethnic groupings within the Soviet Union, giving rise to a mix of ethnic enclaves, such as that of Armenians in Azerbaijan and Abkhazians in

Georgia. Yet despite this, the Soviets maintained national borders, and subsidized national "cultural" festivals. This policy reaped the worst of both worlds – it nurtured a sense of nationalist identity while also exploiting and discriminating against the nationalities (Beisinger 1996; Brubaker 1994).

Although during the 1950s and 1960s the Soviet Union poured great resources into the Central Asian and Eastern Republics, the sharp fall-off in economic growth in the 1970s led to a sharp fall in their support. The rapid population growth of these regions since World War II then ran smack into a wall of declining resources, a poisoned environment, and shortages of everything from cleaning supplies to medicines. Changing levels of infant mortality are one of the best indicators, not only of overall health, but also of propensity for civil violence (Esty et al. 1998). In Central Asia, infant mortality soared. In Turkmenistan, "the official infant mortality rate was 54.2 infants [dead] per 1,000 births, ten times higher than in most West European countires . . . about on a level with Cameroon" (Remnick 1994:205). Remnick adds that experts in Moscow said that the Central Asian Republics regularly underreported their infant mortality rates by as much as 60 percent. Throughout Central Asia, the diversion of rivers, the devotion of land to cotton monoculture, all at the directive of Russian party leaders, deadened the land and support for the party. Thus when the weight of the party was lifted even slightly by Gorbachev, a surge of nationalism joined the stream of opposition and discontent coming from the urban specialists and professionals.

Even in Ukraine (damaged by Chernobyl) and the Baltic states (outraged by revelations about the Ribbentrop pact and Stalin's plans to incorporate them into the Soviet Union prior to WWII), nationalism surged. True, Central Asia bore the brunt of economic decline with expanding populations and a sharper contraction in resources. But in all the regions of the Soviet Union, the basic demographic processes were the same: Ethnic Russians came in and reorganized economic life to their advantage, while pretending to hold up the national cultural traditions of the regions they took over. When poverty, pollution, and rising mortality resulted from economic mismangement and centralized policies, it was the Party and the Soviet system that was held responsible. (For example, in Latvia, by the late 1970s the U.S.S.R.'s careless construction of a heavy chemical industry created such pollution that only 50 percent of all pregnancies went to term and resulted in normal births; in the United States the comparable figure is 90 percent [Cullen 1991:118].) Even in Russia, Russian nationalism was turned against the Soviet system. Whether it was the peaceful nationalism in the Baltics and the Ukraine, or the violent nationalisms in Georgia, Armenia, Azerbaijan, and Tajikistan, anticommunist sentiment turned into regional separatism, which further undermined Gorbachev and helped to literally tear the Soviet Union apart.

Microdemographic Processes and the Decomposition of the Soviet Union

Overproduction of educated specialists and professionals; a fragmentation of the elites; invasions of Russians into ethnic regional republics; soaring infant mortality – these macrodemographic processes were visible all across the Soviet Union. But how did these changes penetrate everyday lives? What happened in the socialization processes of millions of individuals that allowed the rule of conformity to the Party to be replaced by new individual initiatives?

The answer is that the generation of Soviet men and women who came of age in the 1980s were a wholly new generation, the "thaw" generation as Remnick (1994) labels them. Born after Stalin and after the binding horrors of WWII – the "Great Patriotic War" – as it was known in the Soviet Union – their loyalty to the Party was based on expectations of prosperity, rather than on terror or enthusiasm born in war and revolution. This was a generation that was more urban and educated than any in Soviet history, and whose experiences in the 1980s with rock music and the Afghanistan War were not unlike those of the U.S. youth of the 1960s. The major differences were that the U.S. youth of the 1960s and 1970s enjoyed an era of expansive economic growth, and a political system that was, however reluctantly, able to respond to popular pressures to extend civil rights and end the Vietnam War. The Soviet youth of the 1970s and 1980s faced an era of dramatic, even desperate, economic contraction, and a political system that – until Gorbachev took power in 1985 – defended its past errors and refused to even consider the need to change. Thus when given the opportunity to finally make changes in the late 1980s and early 1990s, this generation in the Soviet Union grabbed its opportunity.

One striking new development in the Soviet Union of the 1970s and 1980s was the development of a youth counterculture, similar to and partially based on those of the West (Bushnell 1990). Though not actively opposed to the Communist Party, these groups represented something like a "drop-out" attitude, pursuing grafitti, rock music, and aberrant dress to mark their nonconformity to Party and Soviet norms. Indeed, their defiance of those norms, in their own apolitical way, won the admiration of some mainstream dissidents; thus the association of dissidents like Vaclav Havel of Czechoslovakia with heavy metal bands and rock musicians is not just a matter of taste; it represents an affinity among those who in their own different and personal lifestyles were seeking the common goal of escape from the stifling prescribed life of the "Soviet man."

A more important development was the generational experience of the Afghan War, an event that left its impression throughout Soviet society, from military officers to raw recruits to the mothers of those who were killed or mutilated as victims of that conflict. Just as the Vietnam war in the United States produced not only an alienated generation, and a demand for greater professionalization and reform in the U.S. military, it had similar, perhaps even stronger effects in the Soviet Union. The legitimacy of the Communist Party, already weakened by economic slowdowns and the alienation of specialists and elites, was dealt another blow by the sacrifices demanded in Afghanistan. A war fought in a distant land, for disreputable allies, and without victory despite overwhelming technical superiority, left the same disgust in the generation of those who fought it in the Soviet Union as the Vietnam War did in the United States. Not only did mothers of war victims and disillusioned veterans of the war support the anticommunist movement of democratic Russia, veterans lent their military skill to the defense of Yelstin and the Russian parliament during the attempted countercoup of 1989. And it was the defection of senior military officers of the younger generation who had fought in Afghanistan – Alexander Lebed, Boris Gromov, Pavel Grachev, Anatoly Salayev, and Yevgeny Shaposhnikov – from the attempted coup that sealed its failure (Remnick 1994:482–83).

In sum, at the micro level, the population of the Soviet Union was undergoing a generational shift. Lifestyles, key events, and allegiances were all shifting. Even within the party, the younger generation had members within the media and the government who were forming a network of those questioning the system. As Len Karpinsky, one of the leaders of the "thaw generation" within the Party, put it, within the Party there was "a layer of Party intellectuals. To be sure, this layer is thin and disconnected; it is constantly eroded by cooperation and promotion and is thickly interlarded with careerists, flatterers, loudmouths, cowards, and other products of the bureaucratic selection process. But this layer could move toward an alliance with the entire social body of the intelligentsia if favorable conditions arose." (quoted in Remnick 1984:176).

The collapse of the Soviet Union was the result of reformism and nationalism, elite divisions and popular disillusionment with the Party. The collapse was not simply a revolution from above led by a reforming elite; nor was it simply a set of nationalist movements from below. It was a much broader and deeper movement; rooted in sweeping demographic changes at the macro level, and changing lifestyles, networks, and allegiances at the micro level, it amounted to nothing less than a societywide rejection of domination by the Communist Party and all that it stood for.

Macrodemographic Outcomes of the Soviet Collapse

The most obvious macrooutcome of the collapse of the Soviet Union is the end of the "Soviet Man." Where once there were citizens of the U.S.S.R. of dozens of nationalities, today there are only Russians, Latvians, Georgians, Uzbecks, Khazaks, Lithuanian, Moldovans, Ukrainians, Armenians, Azerbaijanis, and many others. Everywhere, nationalism and nationalist conflicts have grown more intense, as Abkhazis, Chechens, Tatars, and other minorities within newly independent national states struggle for their own independence. The Russians living outside the territory of the Russian Republic are now ethnic minorities in foreign countries, with all the tension that entails.

A second, and even more striking and regrettable, demographic change is the sharp deterioration in all indices of morbidity and mortality. While health conditions were appalling in the late years of the Soviet Union, since its decomposition conditions have grown even worse. Pollution, of course, continues largely unabated, and economic crisis has prevented any refunding of the wretched infrastructure of medical facilities and supplies. But something more seems to be in the air. The collapse of the superpower Soviet Union, and its replacement by – what? – a series of political and economically struggling states, with mixed populations, unruly and ineffective police, corrupt and often bankrupt governments – has produced an apparent collapse in people's will to live.

From 1990 to 1994, the mortality rate in Russia has increased by 33 percent (Notzon et al. 1998). This seems not to be simply a matter of poverty or infrastructure breakdown, as the change has been least marked in outlying regions and among the elderly and the poor. Instead, the change is sharpest among people in their 30s and 40s, and in the most urban and developed areas of European Russia. Thus male life expectancy has dropped by 8 years in Moscow and by over 7 years in St. Petersburg, compared with the average decline of 6.4 years for Russia as a whole. The impact of these changes is startling: "In 1994 a Russian man aged 20 years would have only a 1 in 2 chance of surviving to age 60 years, compared with a 9 in 10 chance for men born in the United States or Britain" (Leon and Shkolnikov 1998:790). There has been a sharp decline in fertility as well (Heleniak 1995). Thus at the macro level, the collapse of the Soviet Union has given people new national identities, with associated gains in ethnic tensions and conflicts; but for many it has also taken away their sense of purpose and hope, leading to skyrocketing mortality among those who were in the prime of life, mainly from stroke, heart attack, and alchoholism.

Microdemographic Outcomes of the Soviet Collapse

At the individual level, the effects on people, particularly on the very technical specialists and intelligentsia who led the overturning of the old system, have been similarly severe. People appear to have lost their moral compass. Under Soviet rule, you either went along with the closely prescribed program of contributing to Soviet progress, or you fought for your individual integrity and identity. Either way, your life was clearly mapped out; a modest but survivable and widely shared poverty was your lot, and your friends were important primarily for their connections or their trust.

The collapse of communism has turned all this helter-skelter. Communism is gone, but what identity has replaced it? What does it mean to be "Russian?" Do you identify with the Russia of the Tsars? With the Russia of Old Believers and devoted slavophiles? Or is Russia "just another nation," and not a very successful one at that? People are neither for nor against the system; they are now out for a dollar, and against everyone and everything else. The intellectual and technical skills that once helped secure at least a stable livelihood are now useless unless harnessed to foreign or private capital. In the chase for dollars, "the intelligentsia is bewildered by it all and incapable of providing moral guidance. They struggled for a new life and it turned out that this life deceived them" (Remnick 1994:340).

The professionals and scholars and managers who took over the Congress of Soviet Deputies and the Supreme Soviet could not stay in power.

The state institutions that had sustained them fell into decay; universities and government offices were no longer receiving even regular salary payments. In addition, the wild inflation of the ruble destroyed any savings accumulated by the middle and professional classes. By the mid-1990s, although Boris Yeltsin remained president, Yelstin's allies lost control of the Soviet Parliament, where a revived Communist Party became dominant, flanked by radical nationalists and a host of petty factions. The government has shown neither stability nor authority. In the absence of either moral leadership from the intelligentsia, or political leadership from the government, a sense of illegitimacy and lawlessness has spread throughout the society.

Thus unlike many countries in Eastern Europe, the collapse of the Soviet Union has meant neither the reclaiming of a former historical identity, nor enthusiasm for embarking on a new economic and political path. Instead, as inflation has wiped out savings, as pensions and salaries go unpaid, and as vast fortunes are made in a new sector – private enterprise – that most of the population neither imagined nor was prepared for, most people have suffered a tremendous disruption of their expected life course. And they have no clear vision of what should replace it.

Into this vacuum of authority has stepped organized crime (Potelchina and Belykh 1994; Satter 1998). Life is now cheap in Russia, violence all-pervasive. Ministers, journalists, and political figures, as well as the economic rivals among the leading banking and commodities dealers, are frequently assassinated and travel everywhere only with bodyguards. Former KGB (intelligence) agents and military officers have become security forces-for-hire for those who can afford them.

Interestingly, at the micro level, the demographic characteristics of life in Russia – especially in its major cities – is similar to those in gang-troubled inner cities in the United States: high rates of mortality, especially from drinking and interpersonal violence; high rates of unemployment; and poor health indicators, especially those associated with extreme stress, such has high blood pressure and high rates of cardiovascular disease (Hertzman et al. 1996). Breakdown in the social order precipitated by the dissolution of the Soviet Union thus seems to have affected individuals' lives in much the way as the breakdown of social life in America's inner cities, and with a similar outcome in the rise of "gangs" as social organizations bringing some order – although very much on their own terms – into lives and communities that lack it.

The American New Left

We now turn our attention to a very different, but equally interesting, case of political contention; that involving the rise, development, and decline of the American new left. We begin by sketching the macro demographic context in which the new left emerged and by calling attention to the specific processes which would appear to have facilitated its rise.

Macro Demographic Processes in the Rise of the New Left

The term *new left* has typically been used as a broad designation for the set of left/progressive movements that developed in the United States in the 1960s and early 1970s. These movements would certainly include: the antiwar movement, women's liberation, the direct action wings of the environmental and antinuclear movements, the Chicano and American Indian movements, and the student movement, among others. The issue of whether to include the Civil Rights Movement under the broad new left umbrella is tricky, but need not concern us here. Our own view, though, is that the movement as a whole does not merit the designation, but that the Student Nonviolent Coordinating Committee (SNCC) and the Black Power wing of the struggle (which SNCC helped to inspire) were certainly a part of the broader new left. Indeed, one can argue that no organization was more critical to the rise of the new left than SNCC.

More relevant than these definitional matters are the demographic roots of the new left. In this regard, it strikes us as no accident that this "movement family" (della Porta and Rucht 1991) developed during one of the defining demographic "events" of the twentieth century in the United States. We refer, of course, to the post-World War II "baby boom." During the last year of World War II, slightly more than 2.8 million babies were born in the United States. Through the first six months of 1946, the rate of increase hovered around the 1945 average. Over the last half of the year, however, the birth rate accelerated rapidly. By year's end, a record 3.4 million babies had been born.

Initially, the "boom" was not recognized as such. Given the interruption in people's lives occasioned by the war – and before that, the Depression – the sharp rise in the birth rate was plausibly interpreted as a short-term response to pent-up demand. After a few years of "unnaturally" high birth rates, the demographers predicted a return to the long-term trend of declining birth rates established in the 1920s and 1930s. The

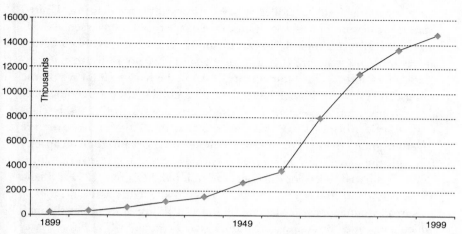

Figure 8.1   College Enrollment in 4-Year Higher Education Institutions in the United States, 1899–1999 (*Source*: National Center for Educational Statistics, Washington DC. *Digest of Education Statistics 1998*. Table 3.)

demographers were wrong. The annual number of births in the United States continued to soar into the 1960s. The "few years" predicted by the demographers turned into nineteen.

But what did the baby boom have to do with the rise of the new left? In our view, a great deal. Though it would certainly be wrong to say that the boom *caused* the new left, it is debatable whether the left protest cycle would have developed in its absence. The boom helped to set in motion a set of critically important economic, social organizational, and social psychological processes that, we think, facilitated the rise of the new left. In the remainder of this section we will confine ourselves to a discussion of three such processes.

The Growth in Higher Education   Figure 8.1 reports the number of students enrolled in four-year institutions of higher education and in the United States at the beginning of each decade of the twentieth century.

The remarkable growth in number of students after World War II is the dominant trend in the figure. But, for our purposes, this trend is no mere statistical curiosity. From the perspective of "mobilization capacity," the explosive growth in higher education in postwar America had real implications for the likelihood of significant student protest activity. Some have attributed the political significance of the trend to the liberal socializing function that colleges have historically served in the United States. We demur. For us, the significance of the trend is more social organizational than ideological. To put it simply, if one were asked to design an institutional structure that was ideally suited, ecologically, to the generation and spread of protest activity, it would be hard to improve on the American system of higher education. The combination of ecologically dense concentrations of people on single campuses with the highly elaborated latticework of weak bridging ties that binds the entire structure together grants the overall system a unique social organizational capacity for both the generation *and* spread of protest activity. If initial mobilization is facilitated by ecological concentration (c.f. D'Emilio 1983; Lofland 1969; McAdam, McCarthy, and Zald 1988; Tilly, Tilly, and Tilly 1975), its spread would appear to depend on the availability of weak ties through which new lines of action can diffuse (c.f. Freeman 1973; Granovetter 1973; Jackson et al. 1960; Marwell and Oliver 1993). The American system of higher education grants student activists both kinds of facilitative structures. And the postwar growth in both aggregate student enrollment and total number of four-year institutions only magnified the social organizational advantages inherent in the system.

Prosperity, Optimism, and Risk Taking But the unique structure of higher education in the United States only creates a certain "structural potential" for student protest activity. Whether or not that potential will be realized depends much more on broader political and cultural trends that shape both the substantive content of student concerns and the shared sense of efficacy and generational identification needed to act on those concerns. But the baby boom influenced these more amorphous "requirements" of mobilization as well. It did so primarily by helping to trigger and sustain the extraordinary economic prosperity that characterized the postwar period. It was not the only cause of this prosperity to be sure. America's assumption of the role of "policeman for Democracy" assured a level of defense production that far exceeded previous peace time levels. The onset of the Korean "conflict" only edged those levels higher. However, well before the first U.S. Marines set foot on Korean soil, the economic effects of the baby boom were being felt. Demand for all types of goods and services rose sharply as the birth rate soared. And as each year's birth cohort exceeded the previous one in size, the economy surged forward at an unprecedented rate. Between 1946 and 1964 the annual rise in domestic GNP averaged 6.5 percent (U.S. Bureau of the Census

1975:228). Unemployment over the same period averaged just 4.8 percent per year.

This sustained economic prosperity gave the baby boomers – or, more accurately, the oldest and more class advantaged of the boomers – an abiding confidence about the future. Why was this important? Serious activism involves taking risks. When confronted with those risks, most of us will abstain from activism. But the "chilling effect" that risk normally exerts on activism (or any other form of "risk taking") can, as Aminzade and McAdam note in their chapter on emotions, be overcome by the play of either of two emotions. The risks we associate with activism are apt to be discounted or ignored when the potential recruit is either buoyed by hope or gripped by fear. For their part, the oldest and most advantaged of the baby boomers (and indeed many born just prior to the onset of the boom) were a uniquely "hopeful" lot, and given to risk taking as a result. Activism was one of the expressions of this willingness to take risks. Consider the following quote from one of the 1,000 or so primarily white, northern college students who volunteered to take part in one of the earliest new left campaigns: the 1964 Mississippi Freedom Summer Project:

I never really weighed going South against any risks to my future . . . career wise . . . I'd like to think that was because I was so totally committed to the struggle. You know, 'I'm not into worrying about such crass shit, man; justice is at stake here.' But I think it was more complicated than that. The point is, I didn't *have* to worry – or at least I didn't *think* I had to worry – about a job or career. Man, I was getting teaching offers when I was in my second year of grad school! . . . there was this general feeling that you were invulnerable; there would always be a job for you. Jobs or material success – all that stuff – were sort of a given. So I never felt it was one or the other [a job or participation in Freedom Summer]. (quoted in McAdam 1988:16–17)

Prosperity, Generational Identification, and Felt Efficacy It was against this backdrop of diffuse optimism that the new left first developed. But the baby boom and the related postwar prosperity shaped the psychology of the baby boomers in another way as well. It did so by creating a strong sense of generational identity and "history making" potency among the young. Underlying these perceptions was the experience of having participated in the first real youth market in U.S. history. Instead of waiting to grow to adulthood to occupy center stage, as most generations have to do, the postwar generation had the stage turned over to them at an early age.

Or perhaps more accurately, they had a stage constructed especially for them. Initially, this stage took the form of a specialized youth market that saw children targeted as a mass consumer group for the first time in history. New products – from children's cereal to Davy Crockett coon-skin caps – flooded the market, reversing the traditional direction of cultural diffusion in American society. "Fads used to be started by young adults and then spread up and down to younger and older people. But the fads of the Fifties, almost without exception, were creations of the children. They flowed *up*" (Jones 1980:49–50).

The psychological effects of this world turned upside-down were twofold. First, the extraordinary cultural attention lavished on the young gave them a strong sense of generational identification. This was especially true for that segment of the postwar generation that contributed the vast majority of those who became active in new left groups. It was the off-spring of the American middle and upper-middle classes who comprised the core of the youth market in the postwar United States. It was they, or their parents, who had the discretionary income to support such a market. In turn, it was they who came to identify most closely with the distinctive youth culture that developed out of that market. Whereas adolescence has – in most industrialized nations – typically been experienced as a kind of limbo existence sandwiched between the ordered and meaningful worlds of child and adulthood, this segment of the postwar generation found it a very different experience indeed. Far from feeling culturally marginal, the well-to-do young experienced themselves as very much at the center of everything. For many, it was a dizzying, euphoric feeling. As a student remarked to Thomas Cottle (1971:267) in conversation recorded for his book *Time's Children*:

We're right at the center of everything. You remember when you're a child and your older brother is the big star, or your big sister is doing all the things? Now it's us, we're right in the center reading about ourselves in the newspaper. It's youth. Everything is youth and us.

This strong and positive identification with youth was crucial in devel-oping, among the class advantaged baby boomers, the capacity to act as a conscious political group. So too was its collective sense of its own potency as a cultural and political force. This was the second psychological effect of the unique position middle- and upper-middle class youth came to occupy in postwar America. It wasn't just that the privileged among the young saw themselves as where the action was, but as the *creators* of that action. This sense of generational potency, when coupled with the unbridled optimism of the period, made the earliest baby boom cohorts prime candidates for collective political action, especially when "called" to it by the political idealism characteristic of the period.

Micro Life-Course Processes and Recruitment to the New Left

C. Wright Mills (1959) described human existence as shaped by the "intersection of biography and history" nested in social structure. In the previous section we sketched the demographic component of the historical context in which the new left emerged. In this section we take up the biographical, or life-course, side of the equation. For if broad historical trends – including demographic trends – condition the likelihood of collective action, individual biographical factors mediate entrance into activism. And so it was with the new left. The richest source of data that bears on this topic comes from McAdam's research on recruitment to the aforementioned Freedom Summer Project (McAdam 1986; 1988; McAdam and Paulsen 1993).

McAdam's data is useful because it comes, not just from those who participated in the project, but from *all* those who applied to take part. It therefore allows for a more fine-grained analysis of the way life-course processes shaped both the application process and participation in the Summer Project. McAdam's work has typically been read as supporting a strong network account of movement recruitment and, indeed, strong ties to other applicants are among the strongest predictors of who did and did not go to Mississippi that summer. But, the impact of network ties, is played out against a very clear backdrop of strong life-course effects.

This is true whether one looks at the total pool of applicants or compares the volunteers with the "no-shows." Regarding the total pool, the information taken from the applications yields:

a reasonably coherent portrait of the applicants. The central theme of that portrait is one of biographical availability. For all the social-psychological interpretations that have been proposed to account for the conspicuous role of students in social protest . . . there may be a far more mundane explanation. Students, especially those drawn from privileged classes, are simply free, to a unique degree, of constraints that tend to make activism too time consuming or risky for other groups to engage in. Often freed from the demands of family, marriage, and full-time employment, students are uniquely available to express their political values through action. (McAdam 1988:44)

213

This perspective certainly applies to the Freedom Summer applicants. As a group they were extraordinarily class privileged, obviating the need to work during the summer. Barely 10 percent were married, typically to another applicant. And only 2 percent were parents. The point is, from a life-course perspective, the applicants were hardly a representative sample of even that most "biographically available" segment of the population; that is, all college students. If college students are uniquely free of life-course impediments to activism, the Freedom Summer applicants were freer still. And the actual volunteers were the freest of all.

After network ties to other applicants, the best predictor of participation in the Summer Project is age. McAdam (1986:84–85) explains:

The important idea reflected in [the comparative] data [on the volunteers and no-shows] is that biographical availability bears a curvilinear relationship to age. It is ordinarily assumed that young people are more available for activism than older persons. But clearly there is an age below which this simply is not true. Below a certain age, parental control limits one's availability for activism, even in the absence of such adult responsibilities as family or full-time employment. For most people, then, biographical availability is [perhaps most] evident in that narrow range of years marked by the confluence of relative independence from parental authority and the absence of intense adult responsibilities. Of the two groups of applicants, participants fall more clearly in this range than do [no-shows].

It would be nice, of course, if we had systematic life-course data on participation in a range of new left movements, but we suspect that the patterns discussed here would apply broadly across these movements. Indeed, since Freedom Summer served as a major source of the earliest activist cohorts in the student movement, the antiwar movement, and women's liberation, these findings have implications beyond the project itself (McAdam 1988:ch. 5).

So much for the role of demographic and life-course processes in shaping both the favorable historical context in which the new left was nurtured and the more idiosyncratic biographical context out of which individual new leftists were recruited. We now want to reverse the order of our variables and ask two related, yet distinct, "outcome" questions. First, can we discern, in the "demographic record," any long-term effects of the new left protest cycle? And, second, what, if any, life-course consequences can we attribute to participation in new left activities? Since the latter question has stimulated a fair amount of work, we will summarize that research first and then move on to the more interesting and little

214

studied question of the broader demographic implications of political and cultural contention.

The Micro or Biographical Impact of New Left Activism

At the outset of this chapter, we briefly touched on the one aspect of demographic or life-course processes that has received a fair amount of attention from social movement scholars. This concerns the biographical impact – both short and long-term – of movement participation. Indeed, there has been a number of systematic follow-up studies of former activists conducted to date (DeMartini 1983; Demerath, Marwell, and Aiken 1971; Fendrich 1977; 1993; Fendrich and Tarleau 1973; Fendrich and Turner 1989; Marwell, Aiken, and Demerath 1987; McAdam 1988; 1989; Whalen and Flacks 1989). Conveniently, all of these studies have taken some segment of the new left as their source of subjects, so they are clearly grist for our analytic mill.

Together these studies reveal a significant and enduring effect of movement participation on the subsequent biographies of their subjects. To summarize the findings, the former activists have tended to: (1) remain politically active and leftist in their political orientations; (2) be employed in the "helping" or social service professions; (3) have lower incomes; and are more likely than their age peers to have (4) married later; (5) been divorced; and (6) to have experienced an episodic or nontraditional work history.

Alas, all of the studies cited above share a significant deficiency: The former activists singled out for follow-up study were drawn from decidedly nonrepresentative slices of the total population of new left activists. So McAdam's work (1988; 1989) focused on the subsequent lives of those who took part in the aforementioned Freedom Summer Project. Whalen and Flacks' (1989) subjects were drawn from among those who had been arrested in connection with the 1970 burning of a bank in Isla Vista, California. James Fendrich's (1977; 1993) ground breaking work involved samples of black and white activists involved in an early civil rights campaign in Tallahassee, Florida. For their 1987 article, Marwell, Aiken, and Demerath surveyed 145 persons who had taken part in the 1965 SCOPE voter registration project organized by Martin Luther King's Southern Christian Leadership Conference.

In short, all of the former activists whose lives have served as the empirical bases of these studies, were drawn from the high-risk end of the activist continuum. That is, if we were to array all activism along a continuum ranging from the most fleeting, low-risk forms of participation (for example, monetary contributions to movement organizations; involvement in petition campaigns, and so on) to sustained involvement in intense high-risk ventures, we would find that the follow-up studies mentioned above would cluster at the latter end of the scale.

Fortunately, two recent studies have gone a long way toward remedying this deficiency by studying the long-term effects of more modal, low-risk forms of activism. Using data from the Youth-Parent Socialization Panel Study, Sherkat and Blocker (1997) show, in the first of these studies, that "'run-of-the-mill' participation in the antiwar and student protests of the late 1960s had an impact" on various aspects of their subject's lives. In similar fashion, the second study (McAdam 1999; McAdam, Van Dyke, Shockey, and Munch 1998) sought to assess the biographical impact of more modal forms of activism on a random national sample of U.S. residents born between 1943 and 1964. The significance of these recent studies stems from the fact that both have yielded results consistent with the findings generated by the aforementioned studies of nonrepresentative, high-risk activists. So, for example, like their high-risk counterparts, the subjects in these recent studies are:

1. more likely to have been divorced (McAdam, Van Dyke, Shockey, and Munch 1998);
2. more likely to have married late (McAdam, Van Dyke, Shockey, and Munch 1998; Sherkat and Blocker 1997);
3. more likely to have cohabited outside of marriage (McAdam, Van Dyke, Shockey, and Munch 1998);
4. more likely to have experienced "an extended period of unemployment" since completing their education" (McAdam, Van Dyke, Shockey, and Munch 1998);
5. less likely to have had children (McAdam, Van Dyke, Shockey, and Munch 1998; Sherkat and Blocker 1997);
6. and less likely to have ever married (McAdam, Van Dyke, Shockey, and Munch 1998).

By showing that these striking life-course effects generalize to more representative samples of new left activists, the recent studies raise a more general issue that, while consistent with Mannheim's notion of a "political generation," has never been explicitly addressed by either social movement or life-course researchers. The issue in question is the role of social

216

movements or revolutions as a force for aggregate level shifts in life-course patterns.

Macro Outcomes: The New Left as a Force for Aggregate Change in Life-Course Patterns

Is it possible that social movements and revolutions exert an impact on life-course patterns beyond the effect they apparently have on individual activists? That is, can activist networks sometimes serve as the locus within which alternative conceptions of the life-course and related behavioral norms develop and subsequently diffuse to the broader public? It seems especially plausible that we ask this question in regard to the impact of the new left on life-course dynamics in the United States. We say this for two reasons. First, the movements that comprised the new left embodied a powerful (and especially in the case of women's liberation, explicit) critique of what, in the postwar years, were viewed as the key components of the "normative life-course." Second, as various studies have shown (Rindfuss et al. 1987), conformity to the "normative life-course" has declined sharply since 1960. Is it merely coincidence that the emergence of these "deviations" from the "normative life-course" (for example, cohabitation, increased childlessness among married couples, delayed onset of childbearing, and so on) occurred during and immediately after the peak period of new left activity and influence?

Where did the life-course deviations we associate with the baby boomers come from? Reflecting the relative lack of interest among demographers in the question of aggregate level change in life-course patterns, few scholars have sought to answer this question. One notable exception to the rule is the economist, Richard Easterlin. In his provocative book, *Birth and Fortune*, Easterlin (1980) argues that these deviations were largely a function of the size and sequence of the baby boom cohorts. Benefitting from the rapidly expanding boom-fueled economy and the relatively small size of the Depression and World War II birth cohorts, the early boomers confronted unprecedented occupational opportunities which, in turn, allowed them to conform to the normative sequence defining the transition to adulthood. The younger boomers were not so lucky. Confronting an increasingly stagnant economy and intense competition for the attractive positions to which they were attuned, the younger boomers found paths to satisfying full-time employment blocked, thereby prompting them to delay or deviate from the normative transition to adult roles.

217

Easterlin's account is a powerful one and one that no doubt tells us much about the unique demographic profile of the baby boomers. We wonder, though, if it is the whole – or perhaps even the most important part – of the story. While demographically produced market pressures no doubt had something to do with the distinctive life-course patterns that emerged among the baby boom cohorts, a great deal of attitudinal and economic heterogeneity remains within these cohorts (Cooney and Hogan 1991; Elder 1978). Indeed, we suspect the effects of cohort size were, in part, mediated by the values and related political and cultural experiences of the baby boomers. Our own reading is that the rise of the new left and the attendant development of a "youth counterculture" exposed a good many baby boomers (and some preboomers) to very different socialization processes than the ones that had previously sustained the traditional transition to adulthood. In turn, these new socialization processes granted those exposed to them very different images of the life-course. Thus the political and cultural ferment of the period selectively altered socialization practices, resulting in more heterogeneity in life-course images and outcomes. Modell (1989) has interpreted this process as one in which large numbers of persons born during this period came to take personal control over their life-course processes. Or it may be, as we are inclined to suspect, that this segment of the baby boom generation was not so much taking demographic control of their lives as they were conforming to alternative life-course patterns.

Where did these alternative patterns come from? We do not know for sure. We can, however, sketch a plausible answer to the question based on work in which the second author has been engaged (McAdam, Van Dyke, Shockey, and Munch 1998). The findings from that work suggests a three-stage process by which these alternative patterns were first established and later made available to a significant minority of the baby boom and later birth cohorts. The first stage involves a conscious rejection of life-course "norms" in favor of a more "liberated" set of alternatives. The architects of these alternatives were pioneering activists in both the political and countercultural movements of the period. Drawing upon a diverse strand of critical perspectives on mainstream America, these activists sought to make the personal political by fashioning what they came to regard as more humane, just, or personally fulfilling alternatives to the traditional life-course statuses. Many of the Freedom Summer volunteers gave explicit voice to this process, acknowledging that such life-course "deviations" as cohabitation, childlessness (or communal child rearing), and episodic or

218

otherwise nontraditional work histories were consciously chosen as alternatives to traditional patterns that they perceived to be personally constraining or politically suspect.

The second stage of the process involved the embedding of these alternatives within that diverse set of geographic and subcultural locations that came to be the principal repositories of the "60s experience" within the United States. So in their capacity as centers of new left activism and counter cultural experimentation, college campuses – especially elite public and private institutions in the North and West – came to serve as home to the new life-course alternatives. So too did self-consciously counter cultural neighborhoods – Haight Ashbury in San Francisco, Greenwich Village in New York – in virtually every major city in the country. Gradually, upper middle class suburbs – first on the two coasts and later elsewhere – also came to "house" the new alternatives through the socializing force of older brothers and sisters and the tacit "sponsorship" of liberal parents.

In the third stage of the hypothesized process, through broad processes of diffusion and adaptation, these alternative patterns became available to an increasingly heterogenous subset of American youth. In the process, however, the alternatives were largely stripped of their original political and counter cultural content and came instead to be experienced by those exposed to them as simply a new set of life-course norms. Thus the increasing heterogeneity in life-course patterns noted by researchers owed, we think, more to variability in the options to which different subgroups of young people were exposed rather than any significant increase in the percentage "taking control" of their lives. Those who were exposed early on and fairly intensively to the alternatives were apt to conform to them; those who grew up in settings where the traditional patterns remained intact were likely to adhere to them. This is the process, we hypothesize, by which the new left came to influence the shifting normative contours of the life-course.

The question is, are the available data consistent with this account? The best answer is probably a cautious "yes." As part of the study mentioned previously, the second author and colleagues (McAdam, Van Dyke, Shockey, and Munch 1998) have presented data that would appear to show that the spread of at least one alternative life-course pattern – delayed birth of first child – was mediated by the kinds of processes and social locations touched on above. But, these data apply to only one life-course status and a single contentious "moment" (for example, the new left protest cycle of

219

the 1960s). In summarizing these results, then, our intent is not to pronounce definitive conclusions about the issue, but rather simply to flag the topic as one that would seem to merit further attention by both demographers and scholars of contention alike. If the latter have been slow, as a number of analysts have charged, to theorize and study the long-term outcomes of contentious politics (Giugni 1998; Gurr 1980) the macro level demographic impact of social movements and revolutions has been an especially neglected area of inquiry.

Conclusion

In closing we wish to invoke the synthetic spirit that has, from the start, animated this project. The title of the volume is, after all, silence *and* voice in the study of contentious politics. The point is, in sketching our two cases in demographic/life-course relief, we are not arguing that other factors were unimportant in shaping the origin and impact of the American new left and Soviet decomposition. In particular, the stress in much recent theory concerning the role of "political opportunities" and "mobilizing structures" strike us as clearly relevant to the two cases. What we *are* saying is that to assert the importance of "opportunities" or "mobilizing structures" without simultaneously examining the complex *processes* that shaped their development is to truncate an understanding of the unfolding dynamics of political contention. More germane to this chapter is the additional claim that in our two cases – and, we suspect, many others – the opportunities (or threats) that helped trigger mobilization and/or the settings within which it occurred were themselves shaped by important demographic or life-course processes.

In the Soviet Union, economic failures and divisions within the elite provided opportunities for protests and networks of party reformers and intelligentsia led the anti-Soviet movement. But these elements do not begin to explain the depth of the rejection of communism throughout multiple strata of society, or why and how the divisions in the Soviet elite arose, and then reached out to join with national fissures and the discontent of specialists, and then workers, miners, Afghan War veterans, and others who joined the tide of anti-Soviet movements. Without seeing the stark deterioration of demographic and health indices, the generational impact of such events as the death of Stalin and the Afghan War, and the changing patterns of education and mobility; without laying out the sharp change in the age, occupational, and geographic origins of the Soviet elite in the last years of the U.S.S.R. and the nature of the migrations and deportations that characterized the various Republics, it is difficult to understand why support for the Party collapsed so suddenly, why internal reformism coalesced with nationalism and populism in rejecting party authority, why even military officers turned against the Party. And of course, without seeing the astonishing rise in mortality after the Soviet decomposition, it is impossible to grasp the degree to which this transition found the Russian and many other post-Soviet peoples unprepared, disoriented, and unable to restore order and meaning to their lives.

A similar interaction between demographic and life-course processes and other theoretically salient factors is evident in the case of the American new left. In particular, to say that college campuses were the central "mobilizing structures" of new left activism, tells us little about the combination of economic and demographic factors that shaped the explosive growth in institutions of high education after World War II. Again our point is not to discount the importance of the concept of "mobilizing structure," but to try to develop a better understanding of the range of *dynamic processes* that strengthen, weaken, or transform the settings within which groups tend to mobilize. It should be clear from our selective, but purposeful, reading of these two cases that we regard certain kinds of demographic and life-course dynamics as among the most important of these processes.

9

Harmonizing the Voices: Thematic Continuity across the Chapters
Doug McAdam

Throughout this volume we have deployed auditory images and analogies to suggest what we are up to. We have talked of silences that have developed in this or that field; viable scholarly topics that have been drowned out by the dominant voices within a particular scholarly community. Our aim in undertaking this volume – and one of the central goals of the broader project in which the volume was conceived and nurtured – was to mute these voices and, by crossing narrow subfield boundaries that have developed in the study of political contention, reclaim some of the silences that seem especially central to a broader, more comprehensive understanding of contentious politics in all its rich variety. The preceding chapters represent an illustrative sampling of the analytic riches we think are available to anyone willing to think beyond the dominant concepts and perspectives that animate their particular part of the topical elephant and to think more synthetically and creatively about the broad topic of contentious politics.

But in calling for a larger chorus of voices than the ones we typically hear in any given subfield, who is to say we are not simply encouraging more noise; merely promoting a confusing analytic cacophony at the expense of the admittedly narrower, but also more coherent, theoretical motifs developed within these distinct scholarly literatures? One need only reflect on the Old Testament story of the Tower of Babel; of how an ambitious building project collapsed amidst the chaos and confusion of too many voices and the absence of a unifying language. The dangers suggested by the story are real and have clear implications for academic theorizing. But let us clearly state our intent in this volume. We are not interested in subverting the narrower intellectual agendas being forged in the various subfields which comprise our scholarly terrain. Rather we encourage researchers working in these coherent traditions to stay the course and see what their efforts yield. But there is also much to be gained from periodic stock taking and synthesis designed to blur academic boundaries and to import insights from proximate subfields. This is what we have tried to do here.

Moreover, we have never been interested in encouraging new voices for the sake of diversity alone. Rather our synthetic efforts at subfield bridging reflect our desire to forge a broader, more comprehensive understanding of the dynamic processes that we believe shape only nominally different forms of contention. In our view, any such understanding will necessarily reflect several important unifying themes. In bringing the volume to a close, we want to articulate four themes that seem especially critical to us in this regard. For in taking up the seemingly disparate topics covered by our chapters, we had these themes very much in mind. In short, the volume is not so much a fantasia of exotic topics as a collective effort both to give voice to important silences in the literature and to demonstrate the analytic merits of a set of broader unifying themes that we think are critical to an understanding of political contention. The four themes are: (1) micro/macro links; (2) the constructionist roots of contention; (3) the mutually constitutive relationship between institutionalized and contentious politics, and; (4) contention as a force for social change.

The Links Between Micro and Macro

One theme or aspect of contentious politics that we have tried to address in these chapters is the all important link between micro-level factors or processes and the generation of those meso and macro-level dynamics that figure so prominently in social movements, revolutions, and the like. Obviously, these contentious episodes are consequential to the extent that they are experienced as broad macro-level phenomena. At the same time, it should be just as obvious that movements and revolutions are not, in any simple sense, born at the macro level. This is not to discount the critically important role of broad macro processes – for example, population pressures, shifting political alignments, economic crises, and so on – in shaping the likelihood of contention. But, in our view, environmental factors should never be viewed as determinant. Rather the beginnings of contention must properly be located in the collective interpretations and resulting actions that people fashion in response to perceived environmental conditions. While occurring at the meso level, these all important *mobilization* processes are themselves shaped by both micro- and macro-level factors and processes.

Of the three broad theoretical traditions evident in the study of contention – rationalist, structuralist, and culturalist – it is the rationalists who have devoted the most attention to the question of micro–macro links. Representing individual interests as the motivational bedrock for all of social life, the rationalists see such interests as both the basis for, and chief impediment to, collective action. The key to whether individual interest facilitates or constrains contention is held to lie in various meso-level solutions to the "free-rider" problem. But it seems to us that the rationalist take on how individuals are transformed into an emergent collective, is only one theoretical response to the question of micro–macro links. In these chapters, we have sketched several other suggestive takes on this all important topic.

The Role of Individual Emotions in Motivating Action

In their chapter on "Emotions and Contentious Politics," Aminzade and McAdam argue that emotion has been generally overlooked as a micro-foundation of contentious politics. This is not, as they are at pains to acknowledge, to set up some false antagonism between rationality and emotion. They argue instead for "the power of emotions to shape both the assessment of potential gains and costs involved in any line of action the individual might take and perhaps to motivate action directly quite apart from any instrumental calculus of risks and rewards" (p. 17). Both possibilities suggest a very different micro–macro link than the one generally proposed by rationalists. In the first instance, emotion is seen as powerfully influencing the calculation of interest. One concrete example they offer of this concerns the role of fear in motivating individual participation in collective action as a means of safeguarding the various member benefits controlled by a solidary group that has adopted activism as a kind of behavioral proscription. This interpretation accords nicely with the consistently strong network effects yielded by various studies of movement recruitment (Bolton 1972; Fernandez and McAdam 1988; Gould 1993; 1995; McAdam 1986; McAdam and Paulsen 1993; Orum 1972; Snow, Zurcher, and Ekland-Olson 1980; Walsh and Warland 1983). Instead of selective incentives being offered to induce calculating "outsiders" to affiliate with a burgeoning movement, it may well be that it is the threatened loss of member benefits – and the powerful emotions associated with this anticipated state of affairs – that typically facilitate the emergence of contention.

In the second scenario the authors are attributing a direct motivational role to the play of individual emotions. Here emotions do not so much modify or shape individual interest as supplant it. In support of this possibility, Aminzade and McAdam offer a powerful and poignant example: protest by protestant and catholic wives against the internment of German-Jewish husbands at the height of Nazi rule. There can be no talk of "selective incentives" here, nor of any dispassionate calculation of interest. It is simply very difficult to make sense of this instance of activism from a narrow rationalist perspective. But empathetically, one can easily imagine a broader emotional "logic" operating here. Motivated by love and the stark fear which the abduction of ones mate must surely arouse, these women found the courage to act, even when confronted by the terrifying power of the Nazi regime and the seeming hopelessness of their plight.

Personality as a Causal Force in Contention

In their chapter on leadership, Aminzade, Goldstone, and Perry offer another interesting, and quite different, take on the issue of micro–macro links. While few doubt the importance of leaders and the exercise of leadership to the unfolding of political contention, the tendency, as the authors note, has been to either ignore the topic or to view leaders as an inevitable byproduct of more general mobilization processes. Aminzade, Goldstone, and Perry take issue with this latter view, daring to raise the hoary micro issue of personality. In their own words, leadership cannot "be reduced to environmental circumstances. For between environmental pressures and individual responses there lies a good deal of latitude for personal ingenuity and agency. Individual emotions and interpretations, while poorly understood by social scientists, figure significantly in this complex process" (p. 138). Could we ever really understand the origins of the Cultural Revolution without reference to Mao's personality? Or the rise of the Nazi's without invoking Hitler's personal attributes? To answer these questions affirmatively is not to reinvigorate the classic image of movements as the product of evil demagogues and psychologically needy followers (c.f. Adorno et al. 1950; Hoffer 1951; Le Bon 1960). The contemporary dominance of rationalist and structuralist perspectives on contention rests on the entirely sensible rejection of such overly psychological accounts of collective action. But in reacting against such extreme views, scholars of contention have perpetuated certain fictions of their own. Among the most untenable of these would seem to be the claim that the personalities of those who take part in movements and revolutions – and especially those who emerge as leaders during struggle – are irrelevant to an understanding of the phenomena.

In recent years, calls to fashion a more viable social psychology of collective action to replace the irrationalist presumptions of classic collective behavior theory have been voiced by any number of theorists (Gamson 1992b; McAdam and Paulsen 1993; Snow et al. 1998). In the same spirit, it now seems entirely reasonable to call for more attention to the ways in which the personalities and other psychological attributes of both "leaders" and "followers" may not only reflect broader macro processes, but simultaneously constitute an independent force shaping the emergence and ongoing development of contention. To invoke this possibility, suggests another line of inquiry into the complex relationship between the micro and macro in contentious politics. In addition to interests, identities, and emotions, personality represents another possible microfoundation for the study of social movements, revolutions, and the like.

The Importance of Collective Interpretation/Construction to Contention

Despite the cultural turn in the social sciences over the past twenty years, we think it fair to say that the dominant perspectives on contentious politics remain primarily structural. This would certainly appear to be the case in the study of revolutions where, despite recent efforts to fashion more culturalist alternatives (c.f. Goodwin 1994; Selbin 1993), the generally structural arguments advanced by Goldstone (1991), Skocpol (1979), Tilly (1978; 1993), and others continue to hold sway. The same is true for the study of social movements, with political process and resource mobilization theories being cited as the dominant approaches in the field by proponents (McAdam, McCarthy, and Zald 1996; Tarrow 1998b) and critics (Goodwin and Jasper 1998) alike. The study of democratization has yet to yield a strong culturalist alternative to the currently dominant structural accounts offered by the likes of O'Donnell and Schmitter (1986), Rueschemeyer et al. (1992), and others. Indeed, if there is a current cleavage in the field, it is between those who grant to popular movements an important causal role in episodes of democratization (c.f. Bermeo 1997; Collier 1999; Tarrow 1995), and those, such as O'Donnell and Schmitter, who do not. But all the major parties to this latter debate share a common structural approach to the study of contention.

For the most part, the coauthors of this volume, have been strong proponents of the structural approach to the study of contention. Nor are we prepared to abandon this stance in favor of some of the more radical "poststructural" perspectives currently being used to "deconstruct" this or that instance of contention. At the same time, we think it fair to say that the importance of collective processes of interpretation, social construction, and attribution, have been undervalued in the dominant theoretical works noted above. Accordingly, one of the central animating themes that runs through the chapters in this volume is the critical importance and ubiquitous nature of these "cultural" processes to the unfolding of contentious politics. We highlight the theme by revisiting just two of the numerous examples of such processes touched on in the individual chapters.

Events, Interpretation, and the Onset of "Unsettled" Times

If culture, in Ann Swidler's memorable phrase, really were a "tool kit" (Swidler 1986), we could expect people to avail themselves of the empowering possibilities inherent in that tool kit far more often than they do. In fact, most of the time people experience culture as a set of binding cognitive, affective, and behavioral strictures. The question then becomes, under what conditions are we likely to transcend these strictures and to rediscover the toollike promise of inherently ambiguous cultural texts or other materials? Swidler never addresses the question directly, but in her 1986 piece she offers what we regard as a promising start down that road. There she draws a distinction between culture's role during "settled" and "unsettled" times. As she writes (1986:278), "there are . . . more and less settled lives, and more and less settled cultural periods. Individuals in certain phases of their lives, and groups and entire societies in certain historical periods are involved in constructing new strategies of action." It is during these "less settled" or more uncertain periods, then, that we are apt to engage in more creative, toollike, cultural practices. But how are we to account for the onset of these "unsettled times?" Part of the answer to this question would seem to be structural. That is, the kind of destabilizing change processes (for example, war, economic crisis, population pressures, and so on) documented in the work of the aforementioned "structualists," may well constitute the proximate source of Swidler's turbulence. But as McAdam and Sewell argue in the chapter on temporality, "as compelling as the relationship between long term change processes and the onset of popular contention might appear to be, it is . . . clearly incomplete as an account of the origins of movements and revolutions. Absent the collective processes of interpretation, attribution, and social construction, our current models of contention are incapable of explaining *how* these various change processes conduce to popular struggle" (p. 158). Among the central processes mediating the relationship between long-term change processes and contention, according to McAdam and Sewell, are the kind of catalytic "events" they focus on in their chapter.

The important point for our purposes is that the broader significance of these events derives in large measure from the processes of collective interpretation, construction, and attribution they help set in motion. Indeed, the collective designation of an event as significant is inseparable from these culturalist processes. This is not to raise the postmodern specter of reality as simply another constructed text, corresponding only loosely, if at all, to events in the "real" world. Ours is a Weberian world of probabilistic contingency. All events are *not* created equal; instead they vary, both in the attention they demand and the interpretive leeway they grant those who seek to make sense of them. It would have been hard for those who were party to the taking of the Bastille to have interpreted the event as "routine" and otherwise nonsignificant. Similarly, events that we experience as conforming to the taken-for-granted assumptions of everyday life will be very difficult to represent as constituting any significant break with the past. Difficult, but not impossible; the point is, the meaning of an event never inheres in the event itself. Rather it is temporarily conferred on the event through an ongoing, and often contested, process of social interpretation and construction. It is this process, rather than the occurrences themselves, that accounts for the catalytic potential that McAdam and Sewell ascribe to events. It is the shared understanding of the event as "turning point"; as constituting a decisive break with the past, that very often marks the onset of an episode of contention. It does so by dramatically increasing the general sense of uncertainty on which such episodes turn. Variously interpreted as constituting a decisive opportunity to remake the world or as a profound threat to group interests, this palpable sense of uncertainty is the cognitive and affective hallmark of Swidler's "unsettled times" and of all manner of contentious politics.

The Cultural Legitimation of Contention: The Case of Religion

Our discussion of the crucial role of "catalytic" events in the onset of contention addresses the issue of *when* people are apt to start engaging in the kind of creative, cultural processes described by Swidler. But *what* materials are they likely to use in fashioning the new conceptions of politics, themselves, and the world that motivate particular episodes of contention? In their chapter on contention and religion, Aminzade and Perry offer many examples of the creative appropriation of familiar religious images, texts, and identities, in the service of popular struggles. Among the most interesting (and ironic) of these examples are the numerous ways in which the Chinese Communists used traditional religious beliefs and practices to help fashion a resonant revolutionary consciousness among movement adherents. This pragmatic appropriation of culturally familiar material apparently even included the perpetuation of the popular belief that Red Army Commander, Zhu De, was the direct descendant of the founder of the Ming Dynasty.

Far from being an unusual occurrence, Aminzade and Perry make it clear that religious texts constitute one of, if not, the most common cultural foundations for a wide variety of nominally secular movements. Indeed, another virtue of the Aminzade and Perry chapter is the authors' persuasive call for a blurring of the stark division between the "secular" and "religious." One of the costs of this particular silence in the literature has been its reinforcement of the traditional social scientific belief in the ubiquity and inevitability of secularization. But as various of their examples make clear – and numerous contemporary observers (Greeley 1995; Smith 1996) are keen to point out – the demise of religion has been greatly exaggerated. The important point for our purposes is simply to note that wherever religious beliefs and practices remain alive and well, you can bet they will continue to serve as important cultural building blocks for all manner of popular struggles. This is not to assert that religious ideas will always – or even most of the time – function as catalysts of protest. On the contrary, the highly variable and contradictory nature of the relationship between religious beliefs and collective action only serves to

229

underscore the central point of this section. It is not the beliefs themselves that stimulate or suppress mobilization, but the ways those beliefs are interpreted and translated into action by specific groups of people.

On the Relationship Between Institutionalized and Contentious Politics: Bringing the State Back In

In our view, the study of politics tends to reify the distinction between the forms of unruly politics that we associate with social movements, revolutions, peasant rebellions, and the like, and the seemingly more routine, forms of institutionalized politics that constitute the "normal" rhythms of political life. Most scholars focus their work on one or the other side of this analytic divide. So we have studies of voting behavior, lobbying, party dynamics, municipal government on the one hand and empirical analyses of movement recruitment, revolutionary violence, framing strategies, and so on on the other. All of these are interesting and important topics. But the sharp distinction between contentious and routine politics that tends to run through all these otherwise unobjectionable topics *is* unfortunate and analytically untenable. For it tends to obscure the dynamic and reciprocal relationships that almost always characterizes the link between routine political processes and episodes of contention. The point is, the latter always occur in an institutionalized political context and typically are set in motion by more routine, political processes. In turn, these episodes have the potential to reshape the formal systems of politics in which they are embedded.

The real problem for us is that research on any given form of contentious politics tends to stress only half of this reciprocal dynamic. In this sense, the various literatures that comprise the field, mirror the more general split in the study of politics. So those studying democratization have tended to either ignore popular movements or to discount them as either irrelevant or an impediment to the "real" action being carried out by entrenched state authority or other elite actors (Bermeo 1997; Collier 1999). By contrast, much of the social movement literature ignores the state and other polity members and focuses its analytic lens only on the actions of insurgents. In the remaining two sections of this thematic summary, we want to redress these two elisions by stressing each of the two halves of what we see as a necessarily reciprocal relationship. In the next section, we will use examples drawn from the chapters to underscore the myriad ways in which popular movements act back to reshape the systems of institutionalized power in which they arise. But here we take up the other half of the equation, urging scholars – especially social movement researchers – to take more seriously the impact of state actors and policies on the timing, forms, and ultimate outcomes of contentious politics.

The State Structuring of the Spatiality of Contention

Among the many virtues of Bill Sewell's chapter on "Space in Contentious Politics," are the numerous examples he offers of the role that state authorities play in shaping the spatial locus of popular protest. Let me revisit this theme, beginning with two examples that Bill touches on in his chapter.

The first such example concerns the unique ecology of the Chinese student prodemocracy movement that took place in the spring of 1989. Drawing heavily on the work of Dingxin Zhao (1998), Sewell argues persuasively that it was the dense concentration of universities in a single district within Beijing that facilitated the rapid and massive mobilization of Chinese students in the early days of the movement. What Sewell does not say, but might well have, is that this ecological concentration reflects not so much independent decisions by the sixty seven universities involved as a centralized state plan for higher education. It may have been that the authorities chose to locate the bulk of Beijing students in a single district for efficiency or perhaps even social control reasons, but, as Zhao notes, in this case, the unique ecology of student life clearly encouraged, rather than impeded, mobilization.

A second way in which state authorities were implicated in the spatial facilitation of the Chinese student movement concerns the semiautonomous status traditionally accorded the universities by the Chinese authorities. By granting the universities a bit freer hand in monitoring and controlling student behavior, state authorities were not in a position to repress the movement on its "home" turf. Thus, like most of their institutional counterparts around the world, Beijing's universities functioned as a kind of state sanctioned "free space" within which students were able to mobilize without much interference from party hardliners.

A second example of the inadvertent creation of "free space" by state authorities involves the role of *de jure* segregation in creating the independent institutional spheres in which the American Civil Rights Movement was nurtured. Though the role of the black church has been rightly noted in this regard (McAdam 1982; Morris 1984; Oberschall 1973), other segregated institutions played an important role as well. The sit-ins, which revived the moribund movement in 1960, were made possible by the relative autonomy enjoyed by the traditional black colleges. And the all important network of NAACP chapters that dotted the South in these years were overwhelmingly staffed by and rooted in several other segregated institutions – most notably funeral parlors, barber shops, and beauty salors (McAdam 1982; Payne 1996). Thus, in one of the more satisfying ironies associated with the civil rights struggle, the segregationist obsession with maintaining the separation of the races has to be credited with contributing significantly to the demise of Jim Crow. By legally defining various institutional spheres as off-limits to whites, state authorities afforded blacks numerous sites in which to organize outside the sphere of white control.

Revolution as a Response to the Routine Generation of Threat

In their chapter on "Threat and Opportunity," Goldstone and Tilly point up the analytic imbalance in the uses to which scholars of contention tend to put the two concepts. It was not always this way. In *From Mobilization to Revolution*, Tilly (1978) assigned equal weight to threat and opportunity as stimulants to collective action. But over the years, threat has given way to opportunity as the analytic sine qua non of most social movement scholars and a good many theorists of revolution. Goldstone and Tilly make a persuasive case that a fuller understanding of contention requires that we redress this imbalance and restore threat to its "rightful" place alongside opportunity in the conceptual vernacular of scholars studying social movements and revolution.

The issue I take up here concerns the source of these "threats." In some cases, these threats would appear to derive from non-state sources, including the kinds of competitive pressures that many associate with the rise of racial and ethnic conflict (Belanger and Pinard 1991; Lieberson 1980; Olzak 1992). But consistent with the theme of this section, the state is properly seen as another important source of the kinds of threats on which episodes of contention often turn. The empirical literature on revolution would appear to offer a good many examples of this dynamic. I will touch on only two.

It is hard to read the history of the American Revolution as stemming from anything so much as the perceived threat posed by a series of economic measures inflicted on the colonists by England during the period

1765–75. Seeking to get the colonies to share more of the cost of their own defense, and to recoup some of the expense involved in the prosecution of the French and Indian War, British authorities levied a series of seemingly innocuous taxes on the colonies beginning with the Stamp Act in 1765. But the imposition of the Stamp Act (as well as later measures) was widely interpreted as an unjust infringement on the rights of British subjects and a serious threat to the economic well being of the colonies. It was this shared sense of injustice and *threat* – certainly more than expanding opportunities – that fueled the developing revolutionary crisis.

Similarly, the 1979 Sandinista Revolution in Nicaragua – to take a very different case – would seem to owe its success more to state imposed "threats," popularly perceived, rather than "opportunities." The significant threats in this case were not to the most disadvantaged segments of Nicaraguan society – who had long been subject to crippling poverty and the arbitrary exercise of state repression – but to segments of the Nicaraguan bourgeoisie with whom the ruling Somoza family had long been allied (Black 1981; Booth 1982). The point is, in its basic contours, the Nicaraguan political economy differed little from other Central American countries (save perhaps Costa Rica), most of whom experienced but survived revolutionary movements akin to the Sandinistas. The clear implication: Gross material inequality may help trigger revolutionary *situations*, but are not sufficient in themselves to produce revolutionary *outcomes*. For that to happen the material/political interests of other elite members of the ruling coalition must be seriously threatened.

By all accounts, the decisive break in this regard came, in Nicaragua, in the aftermath of the massive earthquake that leveled the capital city, Managua, on December 23, 1972 (Black 1981; Booth 1982). Somoza himself described the earthquake as a "revolution of possibilities." He certainly knew what he was talking about; for no one exploited these possibilities more nakedly and with such reckless zeal than Somoza. Somoza cornered the various markets created in the rebuilding of Managua, aggressively denying to all but a few trusted cronies any share of the action. In the end, the Somoza clan exercised monopolistic control over demolition, real estate speculation, road work, and the construction of new homes and commercial buildings, the latter selling at four or five times their original value. Somoza's personal avarice and unwillingness to share the windfall created by the crisis, precipitated another of ultimately greater consequence. Threatened by Somoza's naked bid for monopolistic control of these various economic sectors, several prominent commercial/political groups began, in the early 1970s, to voice tentative opposition to the regime. As the decade wore on, this initial tentative opposition grew broader and more vociferous in response to a series of tactical blunders and threatening actions by the regime. What Goodwin argued in general in his 1994 (757–58) summary article, applies nicely to the specific case of Nicaragua. Writes Goodwin:

First, most of these studies demonstrate how repressive or disruptive state practices . . . may have the unintended consequence of both concentrating or fusing disparate popular grievances and focusing these on these state itself. . . . Second, all of the studies examined . . . suggest that one type of authoritarian regime is especially vulnerable not only to the formation of strong revolutionary movements, but also to actual overthrow by such movements, namely, autonomous corrupt, and repressive personalist dictatorships. By alienating elites and middle strata as well as popular classes, these dictatorships have become the target of broad, multiclass protest movements.

Contentious Politics as a Force for Social Change

In light of the rebirth of ethnic nationalist movements in Eastern Europe and elsewhere in the world, the impact of Islamic fundamentalism on polities from India to Algeria, as well as the more circumspect, but nonetheless consequential, effect of the Christian Right on American politics, to take but a few examples, it would seem obvious that social movements and revolutions constitute potentially important vehicles of social change. And yet, there are many political analysts, especially in political science, who seem to regard contentious politics as little more than the "error term" of political life. While acknowledging, as we have, the central importance of established political institutions and actors to an understanding of social movements and revolutions, we feel compelled to stress the converse as well. Clearly, in our view, such episodes have the potential to reshape or even transform the systems of institutionalized politics in which they occur. Indeed, at any given moment, these systems can be seen as little more than the temporarily stable outcomes of previous contentious episodes.

But it isn't simply the formal political institutions of a society that bear the imprint of social movements and revolutions. In assessing the impact of such episodes, scholars have tended to focus their attention narrowly on political or economic consequences (Burstein et al. 1991; Button 1989; Gamson 1990; Mansbridge 1986). Given the central importance attached to political and economic change by most movements and revolutions, this

is certainly an important topic for investigation. Still resistance to fundamental changes in the political economy of a society is likely to be sufficiently intense as to mute the redistributive effects of all but the most
successful movements. Even a movement as broad based and seemingly
successful as the American Civil Rights Movement failed to effect the fundamental redistribution of political and economic power that it ultimately
sought. Similarly, compared to the myriad cultural changes it appears to
have inspired, the U.S. women's movement has few major national legislative victories to show for its trouble. Finally, though the jury is perhaps
still out, the decomposition of the former Soviet Union has thus far not
been accompanied by the kinds of economic and political outcomes originally envisioned by reformers.

In light of this admittedly selective scorecard, should we conclude that
movements and revolutions have little potential to actually change the
systems in which they develop? No, but, given the entrenched opposition
insurgents are likely to encounter, it may often be the case that the most
significant effects achieved by movements and revolutions have little to do
with the formal political and economic institutions of society. The chapters in this volume contain numerous examples of these often unintended,
but nonetheless highly consequential, effects.

The Demographic/Life-Course Impacts of Soviet Decomposition

Among the most striking (and sobering) of these unintended impacts are
the sharp declines in a host of demographic and life-course indices that
appear to have followed from the breakup of the former Soviet Union.
Reported by Goldstone and McAdam in their chapter on "Contention in
Demographic and Life-Course Context," these various indices paint a
grim picture of life in contemporary Russia, while underscoring the importance, but unpredictable nature, of movements and revolutions as vehicles
of social change.

At the aggregate level, the 1990s have seen a sharp decline in all measures of Russian morbidity and mortality. Most striking in this regard is
the 40+ percent rise in the adult mortality rate between 1980 and 1995
(World Bank 1998:105). Nor does the drop appear to be confined to a particular region or set of subgroups within Russia. Rather it holds for the
country as a whole. The net effect of this change has been to lower Russian
life expectancy, especially in relation to other western industrial countries.
So, for example, in 1996 the natal life expectancy was just sixty six in Russia

as compared to a figure of seventy seven in the United States and United Kingdom (World Bank 1998:105–06).

Another striking shift in Russia since the decomposition of the Soviet Union has been the dramatic decline in the overall birth rate (Heleniak 1995). Between 1985 and 1996 the crude birth rate for all of Russia has been cut nearly in half, from 16.6 births per 1,000 in 1985 to just 8.9 – the lowest rate in the world – in 1996 (Semashko Research Institute 1999). This sharp decline merely confirms what demographers have long known about the link between social stability and birth rates. In situations of manifest political, and especially, economic uncertainty, people are much less willing to bring children into the world. The striking drop in the birth rate over the past decade speaks volumes about the present quality of life (or lack thereof) and shared sense of uncertainty that pervades contemporary Russia.

This generalized sense of uncertainty has also destroyed the kind of anticipatory order needed to sustain high levels of conformity to any kind of normative life course. Accordingly what we see at the aggregate level appears to apply to the individual life course as well. Adherence to any of the broad normative patterns that applied before decomposition have declined sharply. So rates of marriage, family formation, participation in higher education, and so on have dropped significantly in the 1990s. At the same time, rates of alcoholism, suicide, drug addiction and other measures of individual stress and disorganization have risen sharply.

In short, whatever ones ideological or normative take on the former Soviet Union, it is hard to view the present set of circumstances in Russia as representing an improvement on the past, at least in demographic, life-course, and quality of life terms. This sorry story also reminds us of a basic sociological truth; that even a highly restrictive social order is preferable to social disorganization. To the extent that movements and revolutions are capable of producing disorder, we should be careful not to simplistically embrace them as inevitable harbingers of progressive change. Though clearly consequential, the outcomes of contention would appear to be too broad, too varied, and too unpredictable to support such a romanticized view of the phenomenon.

Innovations in Contention

Among the most far-reaching consequences that may result from popular struggle is the modification of the contentious "tool kit" itself. These

236

"innovations in contention" can range from the introduction and spread of a particular repertoire (Traugott 1995) or organizational form (Clemens 1997), to the popularization of a specific ideological frame (Snow and Benford 1992), to the creation of what McAdam and Sewell in their chapter on temporality call a "master template of contention." These templates constitute the broad conceptions or categories of contention within which the more specific repertoires or frames are deployed.

In teasing out the various temporal rhythms evident in the French Revolution and the Civil Rights Movement, McAdam and Sewell credit these struggles with the generation of two of the more enduring of these "master templates." Revisiting an argument familiar to readers of Sewell's work (1990; 1996), the authors make the case that the French experience popularized a general conception and set of shared understandings about "revolution" that held for some 125 years until it was substantially modified by the Russian and subsequent twentieth century revolutions.

Tilly (1995a) and Tarrow (1998b) have made the case that the master template of "social movement" developed in the West – principally Great Britain – in the late eighteenth and early nineteenth centuries. But if the black struggle in the United States did not invent the social movement template, it certainly popularized a broad and coherent variant of the general form. It was the generic "rights movement" with its associated civil rights "master frame" and set of standard action repertoires – specifically the mass march, the sit-in, and the boycott – which fueled the left protest cycle that developed in the United States and Western Europe in the late 1960s and early 1970s. Virtually all of the movements which arose as part of the cycle – the women's movement, the environmental movement, gay rights, animal rights, and so on – have hewed closely to the template developed by black activists in the United States. Even such geographically distant instances of contention as the yellow revolution in the Philippines, the Four Eights Democracy Movement in Burma, and Solidarity in Poland bear more than a passing resemblance to the Civil Rights Movement. So much so that a case could be made for the "rights struggle" as the modal form of contention worldwide. The rights struggle may have arisen in liberal democracies, but through the kinds of diffusion processes described by John Meyer and his colleagues (Meyer et al. 1997) and the creation of international (or transnational) bodies and networks attuned to a "rights discourse" (see Keck and Sikkink 1998), the form is now available to claimants around the globe.

Our more general point is simply that, however modest their immediate substantive impacts, popular struggles may still have an enduring effect through the contentious innovations they pioneer. By granting future generations new "collective identities" around which to mobilize, new frames to animate action, and, most consequentially, new holistic conceptions of contention, activists may achieve a legacy that far outlives the specific struggle in which the innovation was conceived.

Conclusion

The four themes discussed above hardly constitute a theory of contentious politics. Given the diversity of empirical interests and analytic perspectives that the seven of us brought to this collaborative venture, no unified theoretical framework was ever envisioned. Rather the commitment was simply to explore the broad topic of political contention in all its richness and variety. And explore we have through a series of collaborative conversations that have been as analytically demanding, yet open, as any we have experienced.

Out of these conversations has come a renewed appreciation for the complexity of the topic and a clear awareness of the many aspects of the phenomenon that have been understudied by scholars of contention. We have sought to address provisionally a number of these *silences*. But as the project comes to a close, we share more than an awareness of complexity and scholarly inattention. In addition, we find ourselves in agreement on a broad view of contentious politics; one that is considerably richer than one would find in any of the narrower literatures that comprise our scholarly field of vision. It is a view reflected in the four themes that have occupied us here as well as the much broader set of chapters included in the volume. We close by listing the key tenets of this shared perspective:

1. While a boon to those with a penchant for typologies, the mapping of political contention into nominally different forms (for example, revolution, social movement, peasant rebellion, ethnic conflict, and so on) has discouraged the search for dynamic processes that are likely to play a role in the unfolding of virtually all episodes of contention. We strongly suspect that these nominally different phenomena actually comprise a relatively coherent, broad category for study.

2. While hypothesizing broadly similar dynamics across these nominally different forms of contention, we also want to underscore the extraordinary dependence of *any given* movement or revolution on the idiosyncratic mix of culture, history, and politics that shapes it. At first blush it might seem as if this tenet, with its emphasis on the particular, is in conflict with the universalizing spirit of the first. In fact, the two tenets are very compatible. If, for instance, the mobilization of strong and shared emotions is hypothesized to be an important causal force in virtually all instances of contention, an understanding of *how*, *when*, and *why* this mobilization occurred in a given episode is going to depend on a detailed understanding of the cultural and political histories of the parties involved.

3. Without denying that politics is broader than the formal political institutions that one finds in all societies, we nonetheless want to claim a unique and mutually constitutive relationship between institutionalized and contentious politics. Movements and revolutions are born of the perturbations of routine politics, just as they come to be significant forces for change in their own right.

4. In stressing the crucial importance of formal, institutionalized politics to an understanding of the origins, trajectories, and outcomes of contentious politics, we need to broaden our conception of the former to include two sets of relationships that are all too often missing from the analysts kit-bag. These are the links between the central political actors of a given system and: the key economic elites within the polity; and that set of international alignments on which the stability of domestic politics depends. Time and again we see contention set in motion by ruptures in one or both of these sets of relationships.

5. But episodes of contention are not the determinant outcomes of history, culture, and formal institutionalized politics. If they were we would have been more successful in predicting when and where they might occur. For all the attention to context we are urging on the analyst, there is an alchemy to contentious politics that requires equal attention to those critically important moments of cultural creativity in which the cognitive and affective will to break with normative routines is achieved. An understanding of these moments will necessarily mean a closer embrace with social psychology and the study of emotions than has typically been true of the study of contention. It will also require more attention to the whole question of

microfoundations, but without necessarily privileging the rationalist presumption of interest as the basis for collective action.

6. Finally, if political contention is powerfully shaped by the interplay of history, culture and politics as realized in particular "moments of madness," it should be clear that we regard such episodes as indeterminant. That is, the trajectories of movements and revolutions cannot be read off the mix of history, culture, and politics that shape them, nor from the particular cultural moments and understandings that animate their birth. Rather they are ongoing accomplishments that embody the potential for human agency that inheres, but is rarely realized, in social life. As such, they demand much from those who would study them.

Let the conversation continue.

References

Abramian, Ervand. 1993. *Khomeinism: Essays on the Islamic Republic*. Berkeley: University of California Press.

Adams, Paul C. 1996. Protest and the Scale Politics of Telecommunications. *Political Geography* 15:419–41.

Adas, Michael. 1979. *Prophets of Rebellion*. Chapel Hill: University of North Carolina Press.

Adorno, T.W., Else. Frenkel-Brunswick, Daniel Levinson, and R. Nevitt Sanford. 1950. *The Authoritarian Personality*. New York: Harper and Brothers.

Agnew, John. 1987. *Place and Politics: The Geographical Mediation of State and Society*. Boston: Allen and Unwin.

Agulhon, Maurice. 1970. *La République au Village*. Paris: Plon.

Alvarez, Arturo and Sonia E. Escobar. (ed.) 1992. *The Making of Social Movements in Latin America: Identity, Strategy and Democracy*. Boulder, CO: Westview.

Aminzade, Ronald. 1992. "Historical Sociology and Time," *Sociological Methods and Research* 20:456–80.

Anderson, Benedict. 1991. *Imagined Communities: Reflections on the Origin and Spread of Nationalism*. Second edition. London: Verso.

Anwary, Afroza. 1997. *The Dynamics of the Language Movement of East Bengal*. Ph.D. thesis, University of Minnesota, Department of Sociology.

Apter, David E. 1960. "Political Religion in the New Nations." In Clifford Geertz (ed.), *Old Societies and New States*, pp. 57–104. New York: Free Press of Glencoe.

Arjomand, Said. 1988. *The Turban for the Crown: The Islamic Revolution in Iran*. New York: Oxford University Press.

Arjomand, Said. 1993. "Religion and Constitutionalism in Western History and in Modern Iran and Pakistan." In Said Arjomand (ed.), *The Political Dimensions of Religion*, pp. 69–99. Stony Brook, NY: The State University of New York Press.

Ashforth, Adam. 1996. "Of Secrecy and the Commonplace: Witchcraft and Power in Soweto," *Social Research* 63:1183–234.

Baker, Keith Michael. 1990. *Inventing The French Revolution*. New York: Cambridge University Press.

Bales, Robert F. and Philip E. Slater. 1955. "Role Differentiation." In Talcott Parsons and Robert F. Bales (eds.), *Family, Socialization, And Interaction Processes*, pp. 217–46. Glencoe, IL: Free Press.

Barbalet, J. M. 1998. *Emotion, Social Theory, and Social Structure*. Cambridge: Cambridge University Press.

Barnett, Bernice McNair. 1993. "Invisible Southern Black Women Leaders in the Civil Rights Movement: The Triple Constraints of Gender, Race and Class," *Gender & Society* 7(2):162–83.

Beckford, J. A. 1990. "The Sociology of Religion and Social Problems," *Sociological Analysis* 51:1–14.

Beisel, Nicola. 1997. *Imperiled Innocents: Anthony Comstock and Family Reproduction in Victorian America*. Princeton: Princeton University Press.

Beissinger, Mark R. 1996. "Nationalist Violence and the State: Political Authority and Contentious Repetoires in the Former U.S.S.R," *Comparative Politics* 30:401–21.

Beissinger, Mark. 1998. "Event Analysis in Transitional Societies: Protest Mobilization in the Former Soviet Union." In Dieter Rucht, Ruud Koopmans, and Friedhelm Neidhardt (eds.), *Acts of Dissent: The Study of Protest in Contemporary Democracies*. Berlin: Sigma.

Belanger, Sarah and Maurice Pinard. 1991. "Ethnic Movements and the Competition Model: Some Missing Links," *American Sociological Review* 56:446–57.

Benford, Robert D. and Scott A. Hunt. 1992. "Dramaturgy and Social Movements: The Social Construction and Communication of Power," *Sociological Inquiry* 62:36–55.

Berenson, Edward. 1984. *Populist Religion and Left-Wing Politics in France, 1830–1852*. Princeton: Princeton University Press.

Berezin, Mabel. 1999. "Emotions Unbound: Feeling Political Incorporation in the New Europe," paper prepared for the American Sociological Association Meeting, Chicago.

Bermeo, Nancy. 1997. "Myths of Moderation: Confrontation and Conflict during Democratic Transitions," *Journal of Comparative Politics* 27:305–22.

Bezucha, Robert J. 1974. *The Lyon Uprising of 1834: Social and Political Conflict in the Early July Monarchy*. Cambridge, MA: Harvard University Press.

Bhaskar, Roy. 1998 [1979]. *The Possibility of Naturalism: A Philosophical Critique of the Contemporary Human Sciences*, 3rd edition. London: Routledge.

Bien, David B. 1987. "Office, Corps, and a System of State Credit: The Uses of Privilege under the Old Regime." In Keith Michael Baker (ed.), *The French Revolution and the Creation of Modern Political Culture. Vol. 1. The Political Culture and Old Regime*. Oxford: Pergamon.

Billings, Dwight B. 1990. "Religion as Opposition: A Gramscian Analysis," *American Journal of Sociology* 96:1–31.

Black, George. 1981. *Triumph of the People*. London: Zed Press.

Bolton, Charles D. 1972. "Alienation and Action: A Study of Peace Group Members," *American Journal of Sociology* 78:537–61.

References

Booth, John A. 1982. *The End and the Beginning: The Nicaraguan Revolution.* Boulder, CO: Westview Press.

Bossinga, Gail. 1991. *The Politics of Privilege: Old Regime and Revolution in Lille.* New York: Cambridge University Press.

Braungart, Richard G. 1971. "Family Status, Socialization and Student Politics: A Multivariate Analysis," *American Journal of Sociology* 77:108–29.

———. 1984. "Historical and Generational Patterns of Youth Movements: A Global Perspective," *Comparative Social Research* 7:3–62.

Brenner, Neil. 1997. "State Territorial Restructuring and the Production of Spatial Scale: Urban and Regional Planning in the FRG, 1960–1990," *Political Geography* 16(4):273–306.

Brinton, Crane. 1965. *Anatomy of Revolution.* New York: Vintage.

Brooks, Thomas R. 1974. *Walls Come Tumbling Down: A History of the Civil Rights Movement, 1940–1970.* Englewood Cliffs, NJ: Prentice-Hall.

Brubaker, Rogers. 1994. "Nationhood and the National Question in the Soviet Union and Post-Soviet Eurasia: An Institutionalist Account," *Theory and Society* 23:47–78.

Burgess, M. Elaine. 1965. "Race Relations and Social Change." In John C. McKinney and Edgar T. Thompson (eds.), *The South in Continuity and Change,* pp. 337–58. Durham, NC: Duke University Press.

Burns, James MacGregor. 1978. *Leadership.* New York: Harper and Row.

Burstein, Paul, Rachel L. Einwohner, and Jocelyn A. Hollander. 1991. "The Success of Political Movements: A Bargaining Perspective," unpublished paper, University of Washington, Department of Sociology.

Bushnell, John. 1990. *Moscow Grafitti: Language and Subculture.* Boston: Unwin & Hyman.

Button, James W. 1989. *Blacks and Social Change.* Princeton: Princeton University Press.

Calhoun, Craig. 1994. *Neither Gods Nor Emperors.* Berkeley: University of California Press.

Calhoun, Craig. 1995. "'New Social Movements' of the Early Nineteenth Century." In Mark Traugott (ed.), *Repertoires and Cycles of Collective Action,* pp. 173–216. Durham, NC: Duke University Press.

Calhoun, Craig. 1997. *Nationalism.* Minneapolis: University of Minnesota Press.

Carlyle, Thomas. 1849. *On Heroes, Hero-Worship, And The Heroic In History.* New York: John Wiley & Sons.

Carrere d'Encausse, Helene. 1991. *The End of the Soviet Empire: The Triumph of Nations.* Trans. Franklin Philip. New York: Basic Books.

Casanova, Jose, 1994. *Public Religions in the Modern World.* Chicago: University of Chicago Press.

Chan, Anita, Richard Madsen, and Jonathan Unger. 1984. *Chen Village: The Recent History of a Peasant Community in Mao's China.* Berkeley: University of California Press.

Chatterjee, Partha. 1994. *The Nation and Its Fragments.* Princeton: Princeton University Press.

Chen, Nancy N. 1995. "Urban Spaces and Experiences of Gigong." In Deborah S. Davis, Richard Kraus, and Elizabeth J. Perry (eds.), *Urban Spaces in Contemporary China: The Potential for Autonomy and Community in Post-Mao China*, pp. 347–61. New York: Cambridge University Press.

Chen, Lincoln, Friederike Wittgenstein, and Elizabeth McKeown. 1996. "The Upsurge of Mortality in Russia: Causes and Policy Implications," *Population and Development Review* 22:517–30.

Chong, Dennis. 1991. *Collective Action and The Civil Rights Movement*. Chicago: University of Chicago Press.

Clemens, Elisabeth S. 1997. *The People's Lobby: Organizational Innovation and the Rise of Interest Group Politics in the United States, 1890–1925*. Chicago: University of Chicago Press.

Cobban, Alfred. 1964. *The Social Interpretation of the French Revolution*. Cambridge: Cambridge University Press.

Cohn, Norman. 1970. *The Pursuit of the Millennium: Revolutionary Millenarians and Mystical Anarchists of the Middle Ages*. New York: Oxford University Press.

Coles, Robert. 1964. "Social Struggle and Weariness," *Psychiatry* 27:305–15.

Collier, Ruth Berins. 1999. *Paths toward Democracy: The Working Class and Elites in Western Europe and South America*. New York: Cambridge University Press.

Collins, Randall. 1987. "Interaction Ritual Chains, Power, and Property: The Micro-Macro Connection as An Empirically Based Theoretical Problem." In J. C. Alexander et al. (eds.), *The Micro-Macro Link*, pp. 193–206. Berkeley: University of California Press.

Coorey, T. M. and Dennis P. Hogan. 1991. "Marriage in an Institutionalized Life Course: First Marriage among American Men in the Twentieth Century." *Journal of Marriage and the Family* 53:178–90.

Coser, Lewis. 1956. *The Functions of Social Conflict*. New York: Free Press.

Cottle, Thomas J. 1971. *Time's Children*. Boston: Little, Brown, and Company.

Cullen, Robert. 1991. *The Twilight of Empire: Inside the Crumbling Soviet Bloc*. New York: Atlantic Monthly Press.

D'Emilio, John. 1983. *Sexual Politics Sexual Communities*. Chicago: University of Chicago Press.

Darnton, Robert. 1982. *The Literary Underground of the Old Regime*. Cambridge, MA: Harvard University Press.

Davenport, Christian. 1995. "Multi-Dimensional Threat Perception and State Repression: An Inquiry into Why States Apply Negative Sanctions," *American Journal of Political Science* 3:683–713.

della Porta, Donatella and Dieter Rucht. 1991. "Left-Libertarian Movements in Context: A Comparison of Italy and West Germany, 1965–1990." Discussion Paper FS III 91–103. Wissenschaftszentrum Berlin.

DeMartini, Joseph R. 1983. "Social Movement Participation: Political Socialization, Generational Consciousness and Lasting Effects," *Youth and Society* 15:195–223.

Demerath, N. J. III, Gerald Marwell, and Michael Aiken. 1971. *Dynamics of Idealism*. San Francisco: Jossey-Bass.

Diani, Mario and Ron Eyerman. (ed.) 1992. *Studying Collective Action*. Newbury Park, CA: Sage Publications.

References

Dittmer, Lowell. 1974. *Liu Shao-Ch'i And The Chinese Cultural Revolution: The Politics Of Mass Criticism*. Berkeley: University of California Press.

Donnelly, Brenda W. 1987. "The Social Protest of Christian and Nonreligious Groups: The Importance of Goal Choice." *Journal for the Scientific Study of Religion* 26:309–26.

Draper, Alfred. 1981. *Amritsar: The Massacre That Ended the Raj*. London: Cassell.

Dudziak, Mary L. 2000. *Cold War Civil Rights*. Princeton, NJ: Princeton University Press.

Dunlop, John B. 1993. *The Rise of Russia and the Fall of the Soviet Empire*. Princeton: Princeton University Press.

Durkheim, Emile. 1995 [1912]. *The Elementary Forms of Religious Life*. Trans. by Karen Fields New York: Free Press.

Easterlin, Richard. 1980. *Birth and Fortune*. New York: Basic Books.

Eastern Express, October 5, 1995, p. 39.

Eckstein, Susan. (ed.) 1989. *Power and Popular Protest: Latin American Social Movements*. Berkeley and Los Angeles: University of California Press.

Eisenstein, Elizabeth. 1965. "Who Intervened in 1789? A Commentary on the Coming of the French Revolution," *American Historical Review* 70:77–103.

Ekman, P. 1982. *Emotion in the Human Face*. Second Edition. Cambridge: Cambridge University Press.

Elder, Glen. 1978. "Family History and the Life Course," In Tamara K. Hareven (ed.), *Transitions: The Life Course in Historical Perspective*, pp. 17–64. New York: Academic Press.

Elias, Norbert. 1982. *The Civilizing Process*. Volume 1: *The History of Manners*. Trans. by Edmund Jephcott. New York: Pantheon Books.

Elster, Jon. 1998. "Emotions and Economic Theory," *Journal of Economic Literature* 36:47–74.

Erikson, Erik H. 1962. *Young Man Luther: A Study in Psychoanalysis and History*. New York: Norton.

———. 1969. *Ghandi's Truth: On the Origins of Militant Nonviolence*. New York: Norton.

Esty, Dan, Jack A. Goldstone, Ted R. Gurr, Barbara Harff, Pamela T. Surko, Alan N. Unger, and Robert Chen. 1998. "The State Failure Project: Early Warning Research for US Foreign Policy Planning." In John L. Davies and T. R. Gurr (eds.), *Preventive Measures: Building Risk Assessments and Crisis Early Warning Systems*, pp. 27–38. Boulder, CO: Rowman and Littlefield.

Eyerman, Ron and Andrew Jamison. 1991. *Social Movements: A Cognitive Approach*. State College, PA: The Pennsylvania State University Press.

Fairclough, Adam. 1995. *Martin Luther King, Jr*. Athens, GA: University of Georgia Press.

Fantasia, Rick. 1988. *Cultures of Solidarity: Consciousness, Action, and Contemporary American Workers*. Berkeley: University of California Press.

Fendrich, James M. 1977. "Keeping the Faith or Pursuing the Good Life: A Study of the Consequences of Participation in the Civil Rights Movement," *American Sociological Review* 42:144–57.

——. 1993. *Ideal Citizens.* Albany, NY: State University of New York Press.

Fendrich, James M. and Alison T. Tarleau. 1973. "Marching to a Different Drummer: Occupational and Political Correlates of Former Student Activists," *Social Forces* 52:245–53.

Fendrich, James M. and Robert W. Turner. 1989. "The Transition from Student to Adult Politics," *Social Forces* 67:1049–57.

Fernandez, Roberto and Doug McAdam. 1988. "Social Networks and Social Movements: Multiorganizational Fields and Recruitment to Mississippi Freedom Summer," *Sociological Forum* 3:357–82.

Ferree, Myra Marx. 1992. "The Political Context of Rationality: Rational Choice Theory and Resource Mobilization." In Aldon Morris and Carol McClurg Mueller (eds.), *Frontiers in Social Movement Theory*, pp. 29–52. New Haven, CT: Yale University Press.

Feuer, Lewis. 1969. *The Conflict of Generations: The Character and Significance of Social Movements.* New York: Basic Books

Fielder, Fred E. 1967. *A Theory Of Leadership Effectiveness.* New York: McGraw-Hill.

Fields, Karen E. 1982. "Charismatic Religion as Popular Protest: The Ordinary and the Extraordinary in Social Movements," *Theory and Society* 11:321–61.

Forman, James. 1972. *The Making of Black Revolutionaries.* New York: Macmillan.

Francisco, Ronald A. 1996. "Coercion and Protest: An Empirical Test in Two Democratic States," *American Journal of Political Science* 40:1179–204.

Frazier, E. Franklin. 1957. *Black Bourgeoisie.* New York: The Free Press.

Freeman, Jo. 1973. "The Origins of the Women's Liberation Movement," *American Journal of Sociology* 78:792–811.

Freud, Sigmund. 1965. *Group Psychology and the Analysis of the Ego.* Trans. by James Strachey. New York: Bantam Books.

Furet, Francois. 1971. "Le Catichisme Rivolutionnaire," *Annales: Economies, Sociétés, Civilisations* 26:255–89.

Furet, François. 1981 [1978]. *Interpreting the French Revolution.* Cambridge: Cambridge University Press.

——. 1989. "Jacobinism." In François Furet and Mona Ozouf (eds.), *A Critical Dictionary of the French Revolution*, pp. 704–15. Cambridge: Harvard University Press.

Gamson, Joshua. 1991. "Silence, Death, and the Invisible Enemy: AIDS Activism and Social Movement 'Newness.'" In Michael Burawoy et al. (eds.), *Ethnography Unbound*, pp. 35–57. Berkeley: University of California Press.

Gamson, William A. 1990. *The Strategy of Social Protest.* Second Edition. Belmont, CA: Wadsworth.

——. 1991. "Commitment and Agency in Social Movements," *Sociological Forum* 6:27–50.

——. 1992a. *Talking Politics.* New York: Cambridge University Press.

——. 1992b. "The Social Psychology of Collective Action." In Aldon D. Morris and Carol McClurg Mueller (eds.), *Frontiers in Social Movement Theory*, pp. 53–76. New Haven, CT: Yale University Press.

References

————. 1995. "Constructing Social Protest." In Hank Johnston and Bert Klandermans (eds.), *Social Movements and Culture*, pp. 85–106. Minneapolis: University of Minnesota Press.

Gamson, William and David Meyer. 1996. "The Framing of Political Opportunity." In Doug McAdam, John D. McCarthy, and Mayer N. Zald (eds.), *Comparative Perspectives on Social Movements: Political Opportunities, Mobilizing Structures, and Cultural Framings*, pp. 275–90. Cambridge: Cambridge University Press.

Gamson, William, Bruce Fireman, and Steven Rytina. 1982. *Encounters With Unjust Authority*. Homewood, IL: Dorsey Press.

Garrett, Clarke. 1985. "Popular Religion in the American and French Revolutions." In Bruce Lincoln (ed.), *Religion, Rebellion, Revolution*, pp. 69–88. New York: St. Martin's Press.

Gartner, Scott Sigmund and Patrick M. Regan. 1996. "Threat and Repression: The Non-Linear Relationship Between Government and Opposition Violence," *Journal of Peace Research* 33:273–88.

Giddens, Anthony. 1976. *New Rules of Sociological Method: A Positive Critique of Interpretative Sociologies*. London: Hutchinson.

————. 1979. *Central Problems in Social Theory: Action, Structure and Contradiction in Social Analysis*. Berkeley and Los Angeles: University of California Press.

————. 1984. *The Constitution of Society: Outline of a Theory of Structuration*. Berkeley and Los Angeles: University of California Press.

Gieger, Susan. 1997. *Tanu Women*. Portsmouth, NH: Heineman.

Gilligan, Carol. 1982. *In a Different Voice*. Boston: Harvard University Press.

Giugni, Marco. 1998. "Was It Worth the Effort? The Outcomes and Consequences of Social Movements," *Annual Review of Sociology* 24:371–93.

Godechot, Jacques. 1965. *France and the Atlantic Revolution of the Eighteenth Century, 1770–1799*. Trans. by Herbert H. Rowen. New York: Free Press.

Golden, Miriam A. 1997. *Heroic Defeats: The Politics of Job Loss*. New York and Cambridge: Cambridge University Press.

Goldfield, Michael. 1987. *The Decline of Organized Labor in the United States*. Chicago: University of Chicago Press.

Goldstone, Jack A. 1991. *Revolution and Rebellion in the Early Modern World*. Berkeley and Los Angeles: University of California Press.

————. 1994. "Is Revolution Individually Rational?: Groups and Individuals in Revolutionary Collective Action," *Rationality and Society* 6:139–66.

————. 1996. "Theories of Revolution and the Revolutions of 1989 in the USSR and Eastern Europe: The Past and the Future." In Alexander J. Groth (ed.), *Revolution and Political Change*, pp. 491–508. Aldershot: Dartmouth Publishers.

————. 1997. "Population Growth and Revolutionary Crises." In John Foran (ed.), *Theorizing Revolutions*, pp. 102–20. London: Routledge.

————. 1998a. "Social Movements or Revolutions? On the Evolution and Outcomes of Collective Action." In Marco Giugni, Doug McAdam, and Charles Tilly (eds.), *Democracy and Contention*, pp. 125–45. Boulder, CO: Rowman and Littlefield.

———. 1998b. "The Soviet Union: Revolution and Transformation." In Mattei Dogan and John Higley (eds.), *Elites, Crises, and the Origins of Regimes,* pp. 95–123. Lanham, MD: Rowman and Littlefield.

Gong, Xiaoxia, personal communication, November 2, 1995.

Goodwin, Jeff. 1994. "Toward a New Sociology of Revolutions," *Theory and Society* 23:731–66.

———. 1997. "The Libidinal Constitution of a High-Risk Social Movement: Affectual Ties and Solidarity in the Huk Rebellion, 1946–54," *American Sociological Review* 62:53–69.

Goodwin, Jeff and James M. Jasper. 1999. "Caught in a Winding, Snarling Vine: The Structural Bias of Political Process Theory," *Sociological Forum* 14(1):27–54.

Gould, Debbie. 2000. "Emotions, Ambivalence, and the Emergence of Militant AIDS Activism," Paper presented at the Social Science History Association conference, October 26–29, 2000, Pittsburgh, PA.

Gould, Roger. 1993. "Collective Action and Network Structure," *American Sociological Review* 58:182–96.

———. 1995. *Insurgent Identities: Class, Community, and Protest in Paris from 1848 to the Commune.* Chicago: University of Chicago Press.

Gouldner, Alvin. 1979. *The Future of Intellectuals and Rise of the New Class.* New York: Oxford University Press.

Granovetter, Mark. 1973. "The Strength of Weak Ties," *American Journal of Sociology* 78:1360–80.

Greeley, Andrew. 1995. *Religion as Poetry.* New Brunswick, NJ and London: Transaction Publishers.

Gueniffey, Patrice and Ran Halévy. 1989. "Clubs and Popular Societies." In François Furet and Mona Ozouf (eds.), *A Critical Dictionary of the French Revolution,* pp. 458–73. Cambridge, MA: Harvard University Press.

Guirin, Daniel. 1946. *La Lutte des Classes: Sous la Premire Ripublique, Bourgeois et Bras-nus.* Paris: Gallimard.

Gurr, Ted R. 1971. *Why Men Rebel.* Princeton: Princeton University Press.

Gurr, Ted R. (ed). 1980. *Handbook of Political Conflict.* New York: Free Press.

———. 1986. "The Political Origins of State Violence and Terror: A Theoretical Analysis." In Michael Stohl and George Lopez (eds.), *Governmental Violence and Repression: An Agenda for Research,* pp. 45–71. New York: Greenwood Press.

Gwassa, Gilbert. 1972. "Kinjikitile and the Ideology of Maji Maji." In Terence Ranger and I. N. Kimambo (eds.), *The Historical Study of African Religion,* pp. 202–17. London: Heineman.

Haines, Herbert H. 1988. *Black Radicals and the Civil Rights Movement, 1954–1970.* Knoxville: University of Tennessee Press.

Hall, John R. 1978. *The Ways Out: Utopian Communal Groups in an Age of Babylon.* London: Routledge & Kegan Paul.

Hampson, Norman. 1963. *A Social History of the French Revolution.* Toronto: University of Toronto Press.

Hannigan, John A. 1990. "Apples and Oranges or Varieties of the Same Fruit? The New Religious Movements and the New Social Movements Compared," *Review of Religious Research* 31:246–58.

References

Hannigan, John A. 1991. "Social Movement Theory and the Sociology of Religion: Toward a New Synthesis," *Sociological Analysis* 52:311–31.

Hart, Janet. 1996. *New Voices In the Nation*. Ithaca, NY: Cornell University Press.

Harvey, David. 1989. *The Condition of Postmodernity*. Cambridge, MA and Oxford: Blackwell.

Heberle, Rudolf. 1951. *Social Movements: An Introduction to Political Sociology*. New York: Appleton-Century-Crofts.

Heleniak, Timothy. 1995. "Economic Transition and Demographic Change in Russia, 1989–1995," *Post-Soviet Geography* 36:446–58.

Heng, Liang and Judith Shapiro. 1983. *Son of the Revolution*. New York: Vintage Books.

Herbert, Steve. 1996. "The Geopolitics of the Police: Foucault, Disciplinary Power and the Tactics of the Los Angeles Police Department," *Political Geography* 15:47–59.

Herod, Andrew. 1997. "Labor's Spatial Praxis and the Geography of Contract Bargaining in the U.S. East Coast Longshore Industry, 1953–89," *Political Geography* 16:145–69.

Hersey, Paul and Kenneth H. Blanchard. 1982. *Management of Organizational Behavior, Utilizing Human Resources*, 4th edition. Englewood Cliffs, NJ: Prentice-Hall.

Hertzman, Clyde, Shona Kelly, and Martin Bobak (eds.). 1996. *East-West Life Expectancy Gap in Europe: Environmental and Non-Environmental Determinants*. Dordrecht: Kluwer.

Hinton, William. 1983. *Shenfan*. New York: Random House.

Hobsbawm, Eric J. 1959. *Primitive Rebels: Studies in Archaic Forms of Social Movements in the 19th and 20th Centuries*. Manchester: University of Manchester Press.

Hochschild, A. R. 1979. "Emotion Work, Feeling Rules, and Social Structure," *American Journal of Sociology* 85:551–75.

Hochschild, Arlie. 1983. *The Managed Heart: The Commercialization of Human Feeling*. Berkeley: University of California Press.

Hoffer, Eric. 1951. *The True Believer: Thoughts on the Nature of Mass Movements*. New York: New American Library.

Hoover, Dean and David Kowalewski. 1992. "Dynamic Models of Dissent and Repression," *Journal of Conflict Resolution* 36:150–82.

Huang, Jinhai. April 5, 1977. Testimony in Shanghai Municipal Archives.

Hunt, Lynn. 1984. *Politics, Culture, and Class in the French Revolution*. Berkeley: University of California Press.

———. (ed.) 1989. *The New Cultural History*. Berkeley: University of California Press.

Hurd, Madeleine. 2000. "Class, Masculinity, Manners, and Mores: Public Space and Public Sphere in Nineteenth-Century Europe," *Social Science History* 24: 75–110.

Iliffe, John. 1979. *A Modern History of Tanganyika*. New York: Cambridge University Press.

Jackson, Maurice, Eleanora Petersen, James Bull, Sverre Monsen, and Patricia Richmond. 1960. "The Failure of an Incipient Social Movement," *Pacific Sociological Review* 3:35–40.

Jackson, Steven, Bruce Russett, Duncan Snidal, and David Sylvan. 1978. "Conflict and Coercion in Dependent States," *Journal of Conflict Resolution* 22:627–57.

Jaggar, Alison M. 1989. "Love and Knowledge: Emotion in Feminist Epistemology." In Alison M. Jaggar and Susan R. Bordo (eds.), *Gender/Body/Knowledge*, pp. 145–71. Rutgers University Press.

Jasper, James M. 1997. *The Art of Moral Protest*. Chicago: University of Chicago Press.

———. 1998. "The Emotions of Protest: Affective and Reactive Emotions in and Around Social Movements," *Sociological Forum* 13:397–424.

Johnston, Hank. 1993. "Religio-Nationalist Subcultures under the Communists: Comparisons from the Baltics, Transcaucasia and Ukraine," *Sociology of Religion* 54:237–55.

Jones, Colin. 1991. "A Bourgeois Revolution Revivified: 1789 and Social Change." In Colin Lucas (ed.), *Rewriting the French Revolution*, pp. 69–118. New York: Oxford University Press.

Jones, Kathleen B. 1993. *Compassionate Authority: Democracy and the Representation of Women*. London: Routledge.

Jones, Landon Y. 1980. *Great Expectation*. New York: Ballantine Books.

Jones, Susan Mann and Philip Kuhn. 1978. "Dynastic Decline and the Roots of Rebellion." In D. Twitchett and J. K. Fairbank (eds.), *The Cambridge History of China*, Vol. 10: *Late Ch'ing, 1800–1911, Part 1*, pp. 107–62. New York: Cambridge University Press.

Jordan, David P. 1996. *Transforming Paris: The Life and Labors of Baron Haussmann*. Chicago: University of Chicago Press.

Juergensmeyer, Mark. 1993. *The New Cold War: Religious Nationalism Confronts the State*. Berkeley: University of California Press.

Kaniki, M. H. Y. 1979. "The End of the Colonial Era." In Kaniki (ed.), *Tanzania Under Colonial Rule*, pp. 344–87. London: Longman.

Kaplan, Temma. 1997. *Crazy for Democracy: Women in Grassroots Movements*. New York: Routledge.

Karklins, Rasma and Roger Petersen. 1993. "Decision Calculus of Protesters and Regimes: Eastern Europe 1989," *Journal of Politics* 55:588–614.

Katz, Friedrich. 1998. *The Life and Times of Pancho Villa*. Stanford, CA: Stanford University Press.

Katzenstein, Mary. 1979. *Ethnicity and Equality: The Shiv Sena Party and Preferential Politics in Bombay*. Ithaca and London: Cornell University Press.

Kautsky, John H. 1967. *Political Change in Underdeveloped Countries: Nationalism and Communism*. New York: John Wiley & Sons.

Keck, Margaret E. and Kathryn Sikkink. 1998. *Activists beyond Borders: Transnational Advocacy Networks in International Politics*. Ithaca, NY: Cornell University Press.

Kelly, Robin D. G. 1991. "The Religious Odyssey of African Radicals: Notes on the Communist Party of South Africa, 1921–34," *Radical History Review* 51:5–24.

References

Kemper, Theodore. 1978. *A Social Interactional Theory of Emotions*. New York: John Wiley & Sons.

Kennedy, Michael L. 1982. *The Jacobin Clubs in the French Revolution: The First Years*. Princeton: Princeton University Press.

Kertzer, David. 1988. *Ritual, Politics and Power*. New Haven, CT and London: Yale University Press.

Khawaja, Marwan. 1993. "Repression and Popular Collective Action: Evidence from the West Bank," *Sociological Forum* 8:47–71.

Klandermans, Bert and Suzanne Staggenborg (eds.). Forthcoming. *Methods in Social Movement Research*. Minneapolis: University of Minnesota Press.

Kim, Hyojoung. 2000. "Shame, Anger, and Love in Collective Action: Emotional Consequences of Suicide Protest in South Korea, 1970–1997," Paper presented at the Social Science History Association conference, October 26–29, 2000, Pittsburgh, PA.

Klandermans, Bert, Hanspeter Kriesi and Sidney Tarrow (ed.). 1988. *From Structure to Action: Comparing Social Movement Research Across Cultures. International Social Movement Research*, 1. Greenwich, CT: JAI.

Klapp, Orrin. 1969. *Collective Search for Identity*. New York: Holt, Rinehart, and Winston.

Kleidman, Robert. 1993. *Organizing for Peace*. Syracuse, NY: Syracuse University Press.

Knight, Alan. 1986. *The Mexican Revolution*. 2 Vols. Cambridge: Cambridge University Press.

Kobben, J. F. 1960. "Prophetic Movements as an Expression of Social Protest," *International Archives of Ethnography* 49:117–64.

Kochman, Thomas. 1981. *Black and White Styles in Conflict*. Chicago: University of Chicago Press.

Koenker, Ernest B. 1965. *Secular Salvations: The Rites and Symbols of Political Religions*. Philadelphia: Fortress Press.

Kornhauser, William. 1959. *The Politics of Mass Society*. New York: The Free Press.

Kriesi, Hanspeter, Ruud Koopmans, Jan Willem Duyvendak, and Marco G. Giugni. 1995. *The Politics of New Social Movements in Western Europe*. Minneapolis: University of Minnesota Press.

Kruse, Corwin. 1995. "Frame Alignment, Emotion, and Micro-Mobilization in Movements of Conscience." Paper presented at the Annual Meeting of the American Sociological Association, Washington, DC.

Kurtz, Lester. 1995. *Gods in the Global Village: The World's Religions in Sociological Perspective*. Thousand Oak, CA: Pine Forge Press.

Kurzman, Charles. 1996. "Structural Opportunity and Perceived Opportunity in Social Movement Theory: The Iranian Revolution of 1979," *American Sociological Review* 61:153–70.

Lan, David. 1985. *Guns and Rain: Guerrillas and Spirit Mediums in Zimbabwe*. Berkeley: University of California Press.

Lane, David. 1996. "The Gorbachev Revolution: the Role of the Political Elite in Regime Disintegration," *Political Studies* 44:1–23.

251

Lane, David and Cameron Ross. 1994. "The Social Background and Political Allegiance of the Political Elite of the Supreme Soviet of the USSR: The Terminal Stage, 1984 to 1991," *Europe-Asia Studies* 46:437–63.

Lane, David and Cameron Ross. 1998. "The Russian Political Elites, 1991–1995: Recruitment and Renewal." In John Higley, Jan Pakulski, and Wlodzimierz Wesolowski (eds.), *Postcommunist Elites and Democracy in Eastern Europe*, pp. 34–66. London: Macmillan.

Lang, Kurt and Gladys Lang. 1961. *Collective Dynamics*. New York: Crowell.

Lanternari, Vittorio. 1963. *The Religions of the Oppressed*. Trans. by L. Sergio. New York: Alfred A. Knopf.

Lanternari, Vittorio. 1985. "Revolution and/or Integration in African Socio-Religious Movements." In Bruce Lincoln (ed.), *Religion, Rebellion, Revolution*, pp. 117–41. New York: St. Martin's Press.

Laslett, Barbara. 1990. "Unfeeling Knowledge: Emotion and Objectivity in the History of Sociology." *Sociological Forum* 5:413–33.

Laslett, Barbara and Barrie Thorne. 1997. "Life Histories of a Movement: An Introduction." In Barbara Laslett and Barrie Thorne (eds.), *Feminist Sociology: Life Histories of a Movement*, pp. 1–27. New Brunswick, NJ: Rutgers University Press.

Lasswell, Harold. 1948. *Power and Personality*. New York: Viking Press.

Laumann, Edward O. and Franz U. Pappi. 1976. *Networks of Collective Action: A Perspective on Community Influence Systems*. New York: Academic Press.

Layton, Azza Salama. 2000. *International Politics and Civil Rights Policies in the United States, 1941–1960*. New York: Cambridge University Press.

Le Bon, Gustave. 1960. *The Crowd: A Study of the Popular Mind*. New York: Viking Press.

Lefebvre, Georges. 1971 [1949]. *The Coming of the French Revolution*. Trans. by R. R. Palmer. Princeton, NJ: Princeton University Press.

Lefebvre, Georges. 1973 [1932]. *The Great Fear of 1789*. Trans. by J. White. New York: Vintage Booxs.

Lefebvre, Henri. 1991 [1974]. *The Production of Space*. Trans. by Donald Nicholson-Smith. Oxford: Blackwell.

Legum, Colin and Geoffrey Mmari. 1995. *Mwalimu: The Influence of Nyerere*. London: James Currey Ltd.

Levine, Daniel. 1985. "Religion and Politics in Comparative and Historical Perspective," *Comparative Politics* 9:95–122.

Leon, David A. and Vladimir M. Shkolnikov. 1998. "Social Stress and the Russian Mortality Crisis," *Journal of the American Medical Association* 279:790–91.

Levine, Daniel. 1990. "Popular Groups, Popular Culture, and Popular Religion," *Comparative Studies in Society and History* 32:718–64.

Lewis, John Wilson. 1968. *China in Crisis*, Ping-ti Ho and Tang Tsou (eds.), Chicago: University of Chicago Press.

Lewy, Guenter. 1974. *Religion and Revolution*. New York: Oxford University Press.

Liebman, Robert C. and Robert Wuthnow. 1983. *The New Christian Right*. New York: Aldine Publishing Co.

References

Li Kaifu (ed.). 1992. *Xingshi fanzui anli congshu – fangeming zui* (Compilation of Criminal Cases – Counterrevolutionary Crimes). Beijing: Chinese Procuracy Press.

Li, Jianyu. July 3, 1992. Interview with Li Xun in Shanghai (private transcript).

Li, Zhisui. 1994. *The Private Life of Chairman Mao: The Memoirs of Mao's Personal Physician*. London: Chatto & Windus.

Lichbach, Mark Irving. 1987. "Deterrence or Escalation?: The Puzzle of Aggregate Studies of Repression and Dissent," *Journal of Conflict Resolution* 31:266–97.

———. 1995. *The Rebel's Dilemma*. Ann Arbor, MI: University of Michigan Press.

Lieberson, Stanley. 1980. *A Piece of the Pie: Black and White Immigrants Since 1890*. New York: Free Press.

Lincoln, Bruce. 1985. *Religion, Rebellion, Revolution*. New York: St. Martin's Press.

———. 1989. *Discourse and the Construction of Society*. New York: Oxford University Press.

Listowel, Judith. 1965. *The Making of Tanganyika*. London: Chatto & Windus.

Liu Shaoqi. 1938. "Jianchi Huabei kangzhanzhong de wuzhuang budui" (Strengthen North China's armed forces in the War of Resistance), *Jiefang* (Liberation) 43:51–2.

Lofland, John. 1969. *Deviance and Identity*. Englewood Cliffs, NJ: Prentice-Hall.

Lofland, John. 1981. "Collective Behavior: The Elementary Forms." In Morris Rosensberg and Ralph H. Turner (eds.), *Social Psychology: Sociological Perspectives*, pp. 411–46. New York: Basic Books.

Lutz, Catherine and Geoffrey M. White. 1986. "The Anthropology of Emotions," *Annual Review of Anthropology* 15:405–36.

Lutz, Catherine. 1986. "Emotion, Thought, and Estrangement: Emotion as a Cultural Category," *Cultural Anthropology* 1:287–309.

Lyman, Peter. 1981. "The Politics of Anger: On Silence, Resentment, and Political Speech," *Socialist Review* 11:55–74.

MacFarquhar, Roderick. 1974 (1997 2nd Edition). *The Origins of the Cultural Revolution, 3 Volumes*. New York: Columbia University Press.

Madsen, Richard. 1984. *Morality and Power in A Chinese Village*. Berkeley: University of California Press.

Malthus, Thomas R. 1993. *An Essay on the Principle of Population*. Edited by Geoffrey Gilbert. Oxford and New York: Oxford University Press.

Mannheim, Karl. 1952. "The Problem of Generations." In Paul Kecskemeti (ed. and trans.) *Essays on the Sociology of Knowledge*, pp. 276–322. London: Routledge & Kegan Paul.

Mansbridge, Jane J. 1986. *Why We Lost the ERA*. Chicago: University of Chicago Press.

Markoff, John. 1997. *The Abolition of Feudalism: Lords, Peasants, and Legislators in the French Revolution*. University Park: Pennsylvania State University Press.

Marks, Monique. 1996. "Onward Marching Comrades: The Career of the Charterist Youth Movement in Diepkloof, Soweto." Paper presented to the Workshop on Social Movements and Social Change in South Africa, University of Natal, Durban.

Marks, Robert. 1984. *Rural Revolution in South China: Peasants and the Making of History in Haifeng County, 1570–1930*. Madison: University of Wisconsin Press.

Marston, Sallie. 2000. "The Social Construction of Scale," *Progress in Human Geography* 24:219–42.

Marthiez, Albert. 1928 [1922]. *The French Revolution*. Trans. by Catherine Alison. New York: Grosset and Dunlap.

Marwell, Gerald, Michael Aiken, and N. J. Demerath. 1987. "The Persistence of Political Attitudes Among 1960s Civil Rights Activists," *Public Opinion Quarterly* 51:359–75.

Marwell, Gerald, and Pamela Oliver. 1993. *The Critical Mass in Collective Action: A Micro-Social Theory*. Cambridge: Cambridge University Press.

Marx, Anthony. 1998. *Making Race and Nation. A Comparison of the United States, South Africa, and Brazil*. New York: Cambridge University Press.

Massey, Doreen. 1994. *Space, Place, and Gender*. Minneapolis: University of Minnesota Press.

Maynes, Mary Jo. 1995. *Taking the Hard Road*. Chapel Hill: University of North Carolina Press.

Mazlish, Bruce. 1976. *The Revolutionary Ascetic: Evolution of A Political Type*. New York: Basic Books.

Mazrui, Ali A. 1972. "The Sacred and the Secular in East African Politics," *Dini na Mila* 61:1–16.

McAdam, Doug. 1982 (1999, 2nd Edition). *Political Process and the Development of Black Insurgency, 1930–1970*. Chicago: University of Chicago Press.

———. 1983. "Tactical Innovation and the Pace of Insurgency," *American Sociological Review* 48:735–54.

———. 1986. "Recruitment to High-Risk Activism: The Case of Freedom Summer," *American Journal of Sociology* 92:64–90.

———. 1988. *Freedom Summer*. New York: Oxford University Press.

———. 1989. "The Biographical Consequences of Activism," *American Sociological Review* 54:744–60.

———. 1994. "Social Movements and Culture." In Joseph R. Gusfield, Hank Johnston, and Enrique Larana (eds.), *Ideology and Identity in Contemporary Social Movements*, pp. 36–57. Philadelphia, PA: Temple University Press.

———. 1996. "Conceptual Origins, Current Problems, Future Directions." In Doug McAdam, John D. McCarthy, and Mayer N. Zald (eds.), *Comparative Perspectives on Social Movements: Political Opportunities, Mobilizing Structures, and Cultural Framings*, pp. 23–40. New York: Cambridge University Press.

———. 1999. "Revisiting the U.S. Civil Rights Movement: Toward a More Synthetic Understanding of the Origin of Contention." Introduction to 2nd edition of *Political Process and the Development of Black Insurgency, 1930–1970*, pp. vii–xlii. Chicago: University of Chicago Press.

McAdam, Doug, John D. McCarthy, and Mayer N. Zald. 1988. "Social Movements." In Neil J. Smelser (ed.), *Handbook of Sociology*, pp. 695–737. Newbury Park, CA: Sage Publications.

References

————— (eds.). 1996. *Comparative Perspectives on Social Movements: Political Opportunities, Mobilizing Structures, and Cultural Framings.* Cambridge: Cambridge University Press.

McAdam, Doug and Ronnelle Paulsen. 1993. "Specifying the Relationship between Social Ties and Activism," *American Journal of Sociology* 99:640–67.

McAdam, Doug, Sidney Tarrow, and Charles Tilly. 1996. "To Map Contentious Politics," *Mobilization* 1:17–34.

—————. 1997. "Toward and Integrated Perspective on Social Movements and Revolution." In Marc Lichbach and Alan Zuckerman (eds.), *Comparative Politics: Rationality, Culture, and Structure*, ch. 6. New York and Cambridge: Cambridge University Press.

—————. 2001. *The Dynamics of Contention.* New York: Cambridge University Press.

McAdam, Doug, Nella Van Dyke, Allison Munch, and Jim Shockey. 1998. "Social Movements and the Life-Course." Unpublished paper, Department of Sociology: University of Arizona.

McAllister Groves, Julian. 1995. "Learning to Feel: The Neglected Sociology of Social Movements," *The Sociological Review* 43:435–61.

McCarthy, John D., Clark McPhail, and Jackie Smith. 1996. "Images of Protest: Estimating Selection Bias in Media Coverage of Washington Demonstrations, 1982, 1991," *American Sociological Review* 61:478–99.

McCarthy, John D. and Mayer N. Zald. 1973. *The Trend of Social Movements in America: Professionalization and Resource Mobilization.* Morristown, N.J.: General Learning Press.

McNeill, William H. 1995. *Keeping Together in Time: Dance and Drill in Human History.* Cambridge, MA: Harvard University Press.

Meisner, Maurice. 1986. *Mao's China and After.* New York: Free Press.

Melucci, Alberto. 1985. "The Symbolic Challenge of Contemporary Movements," *Social Research* 52:789–816.

—————. 1995. "The Process of Collective Identity." In Hank Johnston and Bert Klandermans (eds.), *Social Movements and Culture.* Minneapolis: University of Minnesota Press.

Melucci, Alberto. 1996. *Challenging Codes: Collective Action in the Information Age.* Cambridge and New York: Cambridge University Press.

Merton, Robert. 1984. "Socially Expected Durations: A Case Study of Concept Formation in Sociology." In W. Powell and R. Robbins (eds.), *Conflict and Consensus*, pp. 262–83. New York: Free Press.

Meyer, John W., David John Frank, Ann Hironaka, Evan Shofer, and Nancy Brandon Tuma. 1997. "The Structuring of a World Environmental Regime, 1870–1990," *International Organization* 51:623–51.

Michels, Robert. 1959. *Political Parties: A Sociological Study of the Oligarchical Tendencies of Modern Democracy.* New York: Dover.

Midlarsky, Manus (ed.). 1986. *Inequality and Contemporary Revolutions.* Denver, CO: Graduate School of International Studies, University of Denver.

Millar M. and Tesser A. 1986. "Effects of Affective and Cognitive Focus on the Attitude-Behavior Relation," *Journal of Personality and Social Psychology* 51:270–6.

Miller, Byron. 1994. "Political Empowerment, Local-Central State Relations and Geographically Shifting Opportunity Structures: Strategies of the Cambridge, MA, Peace Movement," *Political Geography* 13:393–406.

———. 1997. "Political Action and the Geography of Defense Investment: Geographical Scale and the Representation of the Massachusetts Miracle," *Political Geography* 16:171–85.

Miller, Robert William. 1968. *Martin Luther King, Jr.: His Life, Martyrdom and Meaning to the World*. New York: Weybright and Talley.

Mills, Wright C. 1959. *The Sociological Imagination*. London: Oxford University Press.

Moaddel, Mansoor. 1993. *Class, Politics, and Ideology in the Iranian Revolution*. New York: Columbia University Press.

Modell, John F. 1989. *Into One's Own: From Youth to Adulthood in the United States, 1920–1975*. Berkeley: University of California Press.

Molotch, Harvey, William Freudenburg, and Krista Paulsen. 1998. "History Repeats Itself, but How? City Character, Urban Tradition, and the Accomplishment of Place."

Mooney, James. 1991. *The Ghost-Dance Religion and the Sioux Outbreak of 1890*. Lincoln, NE: University of Nebraska Press.

Moore, Barrington, Jr. 1966. *Social Origins of Dictatorship and Democracy*. New York: Beacon.

Morgen, Sandra. 1995. "It Was the Best of Times, It Was the Worst of Times: Emotional Discourse in the Work Cultures of Feminist Health Clinics." In Myra Marx Ferree and Patricia Yancey Martin (eds.), *Feminist Organizations*, pp. 234–47. Philadelphia, PA: Temple University Press.

Morris, Aldon D. 1984. *The Origins of the Civil Rights Movement: Black Communities Organizing for Change*. New York: Free Press.

Mousnier, Roland. 1970. *Peasant Uprisings in Seventeenth Century France, Russia, and China*. New York: Harper and Row.

Myrdal, Gunnar. 1970. "America Again at the Crossroads." In Richard P. Young (ed.), *Roots of Rebellion: The Evolution of Black Politics and Protest Since World War II*, pp. 13–46. New York: Harper and Row.

Naquin, Susan. 1976. *Millenarian Rebellion in China: The Eight Trigrams Uprising of 1813*. New Haven, CT: Yale University Press.

———. 1981. *Shantung Rebellion: The Wang Lun Uprising of 1774*. New Haven, CT: Yale University Press.

Nash, June. 1989. "Religious Rituals of Resistance and Class Consciousness in Bolivian Tin-Mining Communities." In Susan Eckstein (ed.), *Power and Popular Protest: Latin American Social Movements*, pp. 182–202. Berkeley: University of California Press.

National Archives of Tanzania, Accession 540, 17c. African National Congress, 1960–61.

Neitz, Mary Jo. 1993. "Inequality and Difference: Feminist Research in the Sociology of Religion." In William H. Swatos, Jr. (ed.), *A Future for Religion*, pp. 164–84. Beverly Hills, CA: Sage Publication.

References

Noonan, Rita K. 1995. "Women Against the State: Political Opportunities and Collective Action Frames in Chile's Transition to Democracy," *Sociological Forum* 10:81–111.

Notzon, Francis C., Yuri M. Komarov, Sergei P. Ermakov, Chrisopher T. Sempos, James S. Marks, and Elene V. Sempos. 1998. "Causes of Declining Life Expectancy in Russia," *Journal of the American Medical Association* 279:793–800.

Nyerere, Julius. 1967. "The Race Problem in East Africa." In Julius Nyerere (ed.), *Freedom and Unity*, pp. 22–9. New York: Oxford University Press.

O'Donnell, Guillermo and Philippe Schmitter. 1986. "Tentative Conclusions about Uncertain Democracies." In Guillermo O'Donnell, Philippe Schmitter, and Laurence Whitehead (eds.), *Transitions from Authoritarian Rule*, part IV. Baltimore, MD: The John Hopkins University Press.

Oates, Stephen B. 1982. *Let the Trumpet Sound: The Life of Martin Luther King, Jr.* New York: Harper and Row.

Oberschall, Anthony. 1973. *Social Conflict and Social Movements*. Englewood Cliffs, NJ: Prentice-Hall.

Offe, Claus. 1985. "New Social Movements: Challenging the Boundaries of Institutional Politics," *Social Research* 52:817–68.

———. 1990. "Reflections on the Institutional Self-Transformation of Movement Politics: A Tentative Stage Model." In Russell Dalton and Manfred Kuechler (eds.), *Challenging the Political Order*, pp. 232–50. Oxford and New York: Oxford University Press.

Oliver, Pamela. 1984. "If You Don't Do It, Nobody Will: Active and Token Contributors to Local Collective Action," *American Sociological Review* 49:601–10.

Olivier, Johan L. 1990. "Causes of Ethnic Collective Action in the Pretoria Witwatersrand and Triangle, 1970 to 1984," *South African Sociological Review* 2:89–108.

———. 1991. "State Repression and Collective Action in South Africa, 1970–84," *South African Journal of Sociology* 22:109–17.

Olzak, Susan. 1992. *The Dynamics of Ethnic Competition and Conflict*. Stanford: Stanford University Press.

Opp, Karl-Dieter, Peter Voss, and Christiane Gern. 1995. *Origins of a Spontaneous Revolution: East Germany 1989*. Ann Arbor: University of Michigan Press.

Orum, Anthony M. 1972. *Black Students in Protest*. Washington, DC: American Sociological Association.

Osa, Maryjane. 1996. "Pastoral Mobilization and Contention: The Religious Foundations of the Solidarity Movement in Poland." In Christian Smith (ed.), *Disruptive Religion*, pp. 67–85. London: Routledge.

———. 1997. "Creating Solidarity: The Religious Foundations of the Polish Solidarity Movement," *Eastern European Politics and Society* 11(2):339–65.

Overmyer, Daniel L. 1976. *Folk Buddhist Religion: Dissenting Sects in Late Traditional China*. Cambridge, MA: Harvard University Press.

Oxford English Dictionary. 1971. Compact edition. Oxford: Oxford University Press.

Ozouf, Mona. 1988 [1976]. *Festivals and the French Revolution*. Trans. by Alan Sheridan. Cambridge, MA: Harvard University Press.

Ozouf-Marignier, Marie-Vic. 1989. *La formation des départements: La représentation du territoire français à la fin du 18e siècle*. Paris: École des Hautes Études en Sciences Sociales.

Pagan, Eduardo Obregon. 2000. "Geopolitics and the Zoot Suit Riot, 1943," *Social Science History* 24:223–56.

Pagnucco, Ron. 1996. "A Comparison of the Political Behavior of Faith-Based and Secular Peace Groups." In Christian Smith (ed.), *Disruptive Religion*, pp. 205–22. London: Routledge.

Paige, Jeffery M. 1975. *Agrarian Revolution*. New York: Free Press.

Pareto, Vilfredo. 1935. *The Mind And Society*, Ed. by Arthur Livingston. New York: Harcourt Brace.

Passerini, Luisa. 1996. *Autobiography of a Generation, Italy 1968*. Hanover, NH: Wesleyan University Press.

Payne, Charles. 1990. "'Men Led, but Women Organized': Movement Participation of Women in the Mississippi Delta." In Guida West and Rhoda Blumberg (eds.), *Women And Social Protest*, pp. 156–65. New York: Oxford University Press.

———. 1996. *I've Got the Light of Freedom*. Berkeley: University of California Press.

Perry, Elizabeth J. and Ellen V. Fuller. 1991. "China's Long March to Democracy," *World Policy Journal* 8(4):663–85.

Perry, Elizabeth J. and Li Xun. 1997. *Proletarian Power: Shanghai in the Cultural Revolution*. Boulder, CO: Westview Press.

Pfaff, Steven. 1996. "Collective Identity and Informal Groups in Revolutionary Mobilization: East Germany in 1989," *Social Forces* 75:91–118.

Pierce, Jennifer. 1995. *Gender Trials*. Berkeley: University of California Press.

Pinard, Maurice and Richard Hamilton. 1989. "Intellectuals and the Leadership of Social Movements," *Research in Social Movements, Conflict and Change*. (11):73–107.

Pinkney, David H. 1958. *Napoleon III and the Rebuilding of Paris*. Princeton, NJ: Princeton University Press.

Piven, Frances Fox and Richard A. Cloward. 1992. "Normalizing Collective Protest." In Aldon D. Morris and Carol McClurg Mueller (eds.), *Frontiers in Social Movement Theory*, pp. 301–25. New Haven, CT: Yale University Press.

Plummer, Brenda Gayle. 1996. *Rising Wind: Black Americans and U.S. Foreign Affairs, 1935–1960*. Chapel Hill, NC: The University of North Carolina Press.

Ponella, Cletus. 1996. "Government Urged to Condemn Obscene Pictures," *Sunday Observer* December 29.

Popkin, Samuel. 1979. *The Rational Peasant*. Berkeley: University of California Press.

Porter, Susie S. 2000. "'And That It Is Custom Makes It Law': Class Conflict and Gender Ideology in the Public Sphere, Mexico City, 1880–1910," *Social Science History* 24:111–48.

Potelchina, Irinaad and Vladimir Belykh. 1994. "Life Loses Value in St. Petersberg," *World Press Review* 41:15–16.

References

Pratt, Cranford. 1976. *The Critical Phase in Tanzania: 1945–1968.* New York: Cambridge University Press.

Price, Robert M. 1991. *The Apartheid State in Crisis. Political Transformation in South Africa, 1975–1990.* New York: Oxford University Press.

Pye, Lucian W. 1976. *Mao Tse-Tung: The Man in the Leader.* New York: Basic Books.

——. 1988. *The Mandarin and the Cadre: China's Political Cultures.* Ann Arbor: Center for Chinese Studies, The University of Michigan.

Raines, Howell. 1983. *My Soul Is Rested.* New York: Penquin Books.

Ranger, Terence O. 1967. *Revolt in Southern Rhodesia, 1896–1897.* Portsmouth, NH: Heinemann.

Rasler, Karen. 1996. "Concessions, Repression, and Political Protest in the Iranian Revolution," *American Sociological Review* 61:132–52.

Ray, Raka. 1999. *Fields of Protest: Women's Movements in India.* Minneapolis: University of Minnesota Press.

Reiff, Janice L. 2000. "Rethinking Pullman: Urban Space and Working-Class Activism," *Social Science History* 24:7–32.

Rejai, Mostafa and Kay Phillips. 1979. *Leaders of Revolution.* Beverly Hills, CA: Sage Publications.

Réimpression de l'Ancien Moniteur. 1858. Paris: Plon.

Remington, Thomas. 1990. "Regime Transitions in Communist Systems: The Soviet Case," *Soviet Economy* 6:160–90.

Remnick, David. 1994. *Lenin's Tomb: The Last Days of the Soviet Empire.* New York: Vintage.

Rindfuss Ronald R., Craig G. Swicegood, and Rachel A. Rosenfeld. 1987. "Disorder in the Life Course: How Common and Does It Matter?" *American Sociological Review* 52:785–801.

Robertson, Roland. 1989a. "A New Perspective on Religion and Secularization in the Global Context." In Jeffrey K. Hadden and Anson Shupe (eds.), *Secularization and Fundamentalism Reconsidered,* pp. 63–75. New York: Paragon House.

——. 1989b. "Globalization, Politics and Religion." In James Beckford and Thomas Luckmann (eds.), *The Changing Face of Religion,* pp. 10–23. Beverly Hills, CA: Sage Publications.

——. 1991. "Globalization, Modernization and Postmodernization: The Ambiguous Position of Religion." In Roland Robertson and William Garrett (eds.), *Religion and Global Order,* pp. 281–91. New York: Paragon House.

Robinson, Geroid T. 1967. *Rural Russia Under the Old Regime.* Berkeley: University of California Press.

Robnett, Belinda. 1996. "African-American Women in the Civil Rights Movement, 1954–1965: Gender, Leadership, and Micro-Mobilization," *American Journal of Sociology* 101(6):1661–94.

Robnett, Belinda. 1997. *How long? How long? African American Women in the Struggle for Civil Rights.* New York: Oxford University Press.

Rosaldo, Michelle Z. 1984. "Toward an Anthropology of Self and Feeling." In Richard A. Shweder and Robert A. Levine (eds.), *Culture Theory: Essays on Mind, Self, and Emotion,* pp. 137–57. New York: Cambridge University Press.

Rosenbach, William E. and Robert Taylor (eds.). 1993. *Contemporary Issues in Leadership*. Boulder, CO: Westview Press.

Rosenthal, Anton. 2000. "Spectacle, Fear, and Protest: A Guide to the History of Urban Public Space in Latin America," *Social Science History* 24:33–74.

Routledge, Paul. 1996. "Critical Geopolitics and Terrains of Resistance," *Political Geography* 15:509–31.

Rucht, Dieter, Ruud Koopmans, and Freidhelm Neidhardt (ed.). 1998. *Acts of Dissent: New Developments in the Study of Protest*. Berlin: Sigma.

Rudé, George. 1959. *The Crowd in the French Revolution*. Oxford: Oxford University Press.

Rudolf, Susane Hoeber, and James Piscatori (ed.). 1997. *Transnational Religion and Fading States*. Boulder, CO: Westview Press.

Rueschemeyer, Dietrich, Evelyne Huber Stephens, and John D. Stephens. 1992. *Capitalist Development and Democracy*. Chicago: University of Chicago Press.

Rupp, Leila J. and Verta A. Taylor. 1987. *Survival in the Doldrums: The American Women's Rights Movement, 1945 to the 1960s*. New York: Oxford University Press.

Rutten, Roseanne. 1996. "Popular Support for the Revolutionary Movement CPP-NPA: Experiences in a Hacienda in Negros Occidental, 1978–1995." In Patricio N. Abinales (ed.), *The Revolution Falters: The Left in Philippine Politics After 1986*, pp. 101–53. Ithaca: Cornell University Southeast Asia Program Publications.

Sahlins, Marshall. 1981. *Historical Metaphors and Mythical Realities*. Ann Arbor: University of Michigan Press.

———. 1985. *Islands of History*. Chicago: University of Chicago Press.

Salehi, M. M. 1996. "Radical Islamic Insurgency in the Iranian Revolution of 1978–1979." In Christian Smith (ed.), *Disruptive Religion: The Force of Faith in Social Movement Activism*, pp. 47–63. New York: Routledge.

Sanneh, Lamin. 1991. "Religion and Politics: Third World Perspectives on a Comparative Religious Theme," *Daedalus* 120:203–18.

Sashkin, Marshall and William E. Rosenbach. 1993. "A New Leadership Paradigm." In *Contemporary Issues In Leadership*, pp. 87–108. Boulder, CO: Westview.

Sashkin, Marshall and William R. Lassey. 1983. "Theories of Leadership: A Review of Useful Research." In William R. Lassey and Marshall Sashkin (eds.), *Leadership And Social Change*, 3rd edition, pp. 91–106. San Diego, CA: University Associates.

Satter, David. 1998. "Black Russia: the Mob Makes a Bid to Rule Russia," *National Review* December 21, 28.

Scheff, Thomas J. 1992. "Rationality and Emotion: Homage to Norbert Elias." In James S. Coleman and Thomas Fararo (eds.), *Rational Choice Theory: Advocacy and Critique*, pp. 101–19. Beverly Hills, CA: Sage.

Scheff, Thomas J. 1994. *Bloody Revenge*. Boulder, CO: Westview Press.

Schoffeleers, Matthew. 1991. "Ritual Healing and Political Acquiescence: The Case of the Zionist Churches in Southern Africa," *Africa* 60:1–25.

Searles, Ruth and J. Allen Williams, Jr. 1962. "College Students' Participation in Sit-ins," *Social Forces* 40:215–20.

References

Selbin, Eric. 1993. *Modern Latin American Revolutions*. Boulder, CO: Westview Press.

Semashko Research Institute, Russian Academy of Medical Sciences, Moscow. 1999. Department of Comprehensive Studies of Population Health and Social Hygienic Monitoring website (http:members.tripod.com/~Tokourov/birttabl.htm).

Sewell, Jessica. 1998. "Taking It to the Streets: The Importance of Space to Feminist Action." Paper presented to the National Women's Studies Association Meeting, Seneca Falls, NY.

Sewell, Jessica. Forthcoming. "Selling Suffrage: Shop Windows and Politics in the 1911 California Women's Suffrage Campaign Vol. 9." In Allison K. Hoagland and Kenneth Breisch (eds.), *Perspectives in Vernacular Architecture*. Frankfort, KY: University of Kentucky Press.

Sewell, William, Jr. 1990. "Collective Violence and Collective Loyalties in France: Why the French Revolution Made a Difference," *Politics and Society* 18:527–52.

———. 1992. "A Theory of Structure: Duality, Agency, and Social Transformation," *American Journal of Sociology* 98:1–29.

———. 1996. "Historical Events as Transformations of Structures: Inventing Revolution at the Bastille," *Theory and Society* 25:841–81.

———. Forthcoming. "The French Revolution and the Emergence of the Nation Form." In Michael Morrison and Melinda Zook (eds.), *Revolutionary Currents: Transatlantic Ideology and Nationbuilding, 1688–1821*.

Sherkat, Darren E. and T. Jean Blocker. 1997. "Explaining the Political and Personal Consequences of Protest," *Social Forces* 75:1049–76.

Shorter, Edward and Charles Tilly. 1971. *Strikes in France, 1830–1968*. Cambridge: Cambridge University Press.

Shott S. 1979. "Emotion and Social Life: A Symbolic Interactionist Analysis," *American Journal of Sociology* 84:1317–34.

Slavin, Morris. 1986. *The Making of an Insurrection: Parisian Sections and the Gironde*. Cambridge: Harvard University Press.

Simmel, Georg. 1955. *Conflict*. Trans. by Kurt H. Wolff. New York: Free Press.

Simonds, Wendy. 1995. "Feminism on the Job: Confronting Opposition in Abortion Work." In Myra Marx Ferree and Patricia Yancey Martin (eds.), *Feminist Organizations*, pp. 248–60. Philadelphia, PA: Temple University Press.

Skocpol, Theda. 1979. *States and Social Revolutions: A Comparative Analysis of France, Russia, and China*. Princeton, NJ: Princeton University Press.

Skrentny, John David. 1998. "The Effect of the Cold War on African-American Civil Rights: America and the World Audience, 1945–1968," *Theory and Society* 27:237–85.

Slavin, Morris. 1986. *The Making of an Insurrection: Parisian Sections and the Gironde*. Cambridge, MA: Harvard University Press.

Smesler, Neil. 1962. *Theory of Collective Behavior*. London: Routledge and Kegan Paul.

Smith, Christian. 1991. *The Emergence of Liberation Theology*. Chicago: University of Chicago Press.

Smith, Christian (ed.). 1996. *Disruptive Religion: The Force of Faith in Social Movement Activism*. New York: Routledge.

Smith, Deborah A. and Rebecca J. Erickson. 1997. "For Love or Money? Work and Emotional Labor in a Social Movement Organization," *Social Perspectives on Emotion* 4:317–46.

Smith, Neil. 1992. "Geography, Difference, and the Politics of Scale." In Joe Doherty, Elspeth Graham, and Mo Malek (eds.), *Postmodernism and the Social Sciences*, pp. 57–79. New York: St. Martin's Press.

———. 1993. Homeless/Global: Scaling Places. In Jon Bird, Barry Curtis, Tim Putnam, George Robertson, and Lisa Tickner (eds.), *Mapping the Futures: Local Cultures, Global Change*, pp. 87–119. London: Routledge.

Snow, David A. and Robert D. Benford. 1988. "Ideology, Frame Resonance, and Participant Mobilization." In Bert Klandermans, Hanspeter Kriesi, and Sidney Tarrow (eds.), *From Structure to Action: Social Movement Participation Across Cultures*, pp. 197–217. Greenwich, CT: JAI Press.

Snow, David A. and Robert D. Benford. 1992. "Master Frames and Cycles of Protest," In Aldon D. Morris and Carol McClurg Mueller (eds.), *Frontiers in Social Movement Theory*, pp. 133–55. New Haven, CT: Yale University Press.

Snow, David A., Dan M. Cress, Liam Downey, and Andrew W. Jones. 1998. "Disrupting the 'Quotidian': Reconceptualizing the Relationship Between Breakdown and the Emergence of Collective Action," *Mobilization* 3:1–22.

Snow, David A. and E. Burke Rochford, Jr. 1983. "Structural Availability, the Alignment Process, and Movement Recruitment." Paper presented at the Annual Meetings of the American Sociological Association, August, Detroit, Michigan.

Snow, David A., E. Burke Rochford, Jr., Steven K. Worden, and Robert D. Benford. 1986. "Frame Alignment Processes, Micromobilization, and Movement Participation," *American Sociological Review* 51:464–81.

Snow, David A., Louis A. Zurcher, Jr., and Sheldon Ekland-Olson. 1980. "Social Networks and Social Movements: A Microstructural Approach to Differential Recruitment," *American Sociological Review* 45:787–801.

Snyder, David and Charles Tilly. 1972. "Hardship and Collective Violence in France: 1830–1960," *American Sociological Review* 37:520–32.

Soboul, Albert. 1962. *Les Sans-culottes Parisiens en l'an II; Mouvement Populaire et Gouvernement Révolutionnaire, 2 juin 1793–9 Thermidor an II*. Paris: Librairie Clavreuil.

———. 1964. *The Parisian Sans-Culottes and the French Revolution*. Trans. by Gwynne Lewis. Oxford: Oxford University Press.

Sohrabi, Nader. 1995. "Historicizing Revolutions: Constitutional Revolutions in the Ottoman Empire, Iran, and Russia, 1905–1908," *American Journal of Sociology* 100:1383–447.

Soja, Edward W. 1989. *Postmodern Geographies: The Reassertion of Space in Critical Social Theory*. London: Verso.

Sorkin, Michael (ed.). 1993. *Variations on a Theme Park: The New American City and the End of Public Space*. New York: Hill and Wang.

Staeheli, Lynn A. 1994. "Empowering Political Struggle: Spaces and Scales of Resistance," *Political Geography* 13:387–92.

References

Staeheli, Lynn A. and Meghan S. Cope. 1994. "Empowering Women's Citizenship," *Political Geography* 13:443–60.

Stark, Rodney and Kevin J. Christiano. 1992. "Support for the American Left, 1920–24: The Opiate Thesis Reconsidered," *Journal for the Scientific Study of Religion* 31:62–75.

Steadman, Ian. 1994. "Toward Popular Theater in South Africa." In Liz Gunner (ed.), *Politics and Performance: Theatre, Poetry, and Song in Southern Africa*, pp. 11–34. Johannesberg: Witwatersrand University Press.

Stearns, Peter N. 1993. "Girls, Boys, and Emotions: Redefinitions and Historical Change," *The Journal of American History* 80:36–74.

Stearns, Peter N. 1993. "History of Emotions: The Issue of Change." In Michael Lewis and Jeannette Havilands (eds.), *Handbook of Emotions*, pp. 17–28. New York: Guilford Press.

Steinberg, Philip E. 1994. "Territorial Formation on the Margin: Urban Anti-Planning in Brooklyn," *Political Geography* 13:461–76.

Stephens, Hugh H. 1968. *The Political Transformation of Tanganyika, 1920–67*. New York: Frederick Praeger.

Stokes, Gale. 1993. *The Walls Came Tumbling Down: The Collapse of Communism in Eastern Europe*. New York: Oxford University Press.

Swidler, Ann. 1986. "Culture in Action: Symbols and Strategies," *American Sociological Review* 51:273–86.

Szasz, Andrew. 1994. *EcoPopulism: Toxic Waste and the Struggle for Environmental Justice*. Minneapolis: University of Minnesota Press.

Tagama, Herald. 1997. "The Story of Nyerere's Magic Wand," *New African* February 24.

Tamason, Charles. 1980. "From Mortuary to Cemetery: Funeral Riots and Funeral Demonstrations in Lille, 1779–1870," *Social Science History* 4(1):15–31.

Tang, Wenlan, Interview, May 17, 1992.

Tarrow, Sidney. 1989. *Democracy and Disorder: Protest and Politics in Italy, 1965–1975*. Oxford and New York: Oxford University Press.

———. 1995. "Mass Mobilization and Elite Exchange: Democratization Episodes in Italy and Spain," *Democratization* 2:221–45.

———. 1998. *Power in Movement*. 2nd edition. Cambridge: Cambridge University Press.

———. 1998a. "The Very Excess of Democracy': State Building and Contentious Politics in America." In Anne Costain and Andrew McFarland (eds.), *Social Movements and American Political Institutions*, pp. 20–38. Boulder, CO: Rowman and Littlefield.

———. 1998b. *Power in Movement*, 2nd edition. New York: Cambridge University Press.

———. 1999. "Paradigm Warriors: Regress and Progress in the Study of Contentious Politics," *Sociological Forum* 14:71–7.

Taylor, Verta. 1989. "Social Movement Continuity: The Women's Movement in Abeyance," *American Sociological Review* 54:761–75.

———. 1995. "Watching for Vibes: Bringing Emotions into the Study of Feminist Organizations." In Myra Marx Ferree and Patricia Yancey Martin (eds.), *Feminist Organizations: Harvest of the New Women's Movement*, pp. 223–33. Philadelphia, PA: Temple University Press.

———. 1996. *Rock-A-Bye Baby*. London: Routledge.

———. 1997. "The Revolution from Within: Emotions and Identity in Women's Self-Help Movements." Paper prepared for "Self, Identity, and Social Movements" Conference. Indianapolis: Indiana University–Purdue University.

Taylor, Verta and Nancy Whittier. 1995. "Analytical Approaches to Social Movement Culture: The Culture of the Women's Movement." In Hank Johnston and Bert Klandersmans (eds.), *Social Movements and Culture*, pp. 163–87. Minneapolis: University of Minnesota Press.

Thoits, Peggy A. 1989. "The Sociology of Emotions," *Annual Review of Sociology*. 15:317–42.

Tilly, Charles. 1964. *The Vendée*. Cambridge, MA: Harvard University Press.

———. 1977. "Getting It Together in Burgundy," *Theory and Society* 4:479–504.

———. 1978. *From Mobilization to Revolution*. Reading, MA: Addison-Wesley.

———. 1982. "Britain Creates the Social Movement." In James Cronin and Jonathan Schneer (eds.), *Social Conflict and the Political Order in Modern Britain*, pp. 21–51. New Brunswick, NJ: Rutgers University Press.

———. 1983. "Speaking Your Mind Without Elections, Surveys, or Social Movements," *Public Opinion Quarterly* 47:461–78.

———. 1986. *The Contentious French*. Cambridge, MA: Harvard University Press.

———. 1992. *Coercion, Capital and European States, AD 990–1992*. Oxford: Blackwell.

———. 1993. *European Revolutions, 1492–1992*. Oxford: Blackwell.

———. 1995a. "Contentious Repertoires in Britain, 1758–1834." In Mark Traugott (ed.), *Repertoires and Cycles of Collective Action*, pp. 15–42. Durham, NC: Duke University Press.

———. 1995b. *Popular Contention in Great Britain, 1758–1834*. Cambridge, MA: Harvard University Press.

———. 1998. "Social Movements and (All Sorts of) Other Political Interactions – Local, National, and International – Including Identities. Several Divagations from a Common Path, Beginning With British Struggles Over Catholic Emancipation, 1780–1829, and Ending With Contemporary Nationalism," *Theory and Society* 27:453–80.

Tilly, Charles and Chris Tilly. 1998. *Work Under Capitalism*. Cambridge, MA: Harvard University Press.

Tilly, Charles, Louise Tilly, and Richard Tilly. 1975. *The Rebellious Century, 1830–1930*. Cambridge, MA: Harvard University Press.

Tilly, Louise A. 1972. "La Révolte Frumentaire, Forme de Conflit Politique en France," *Annales: Economies, Sociétés, Civilisations* 27:731–57.

Tiryakian, Edward A. 1988. "From Durkheim to Managua: Revolutions as Religious Revivals." In Jeffrey C. Alexander (ed.), *Durkheimian Sociology: Cultural Studies*, pp. 44–65. New York: Cambridge University Press.

———. 1995. "Collective Effervescence, Social Change and Charisma: Durkheim, Weber and 1989," *International Sociology* 10:269–81.

References

Traugott, Marc. 1995a. "Barricades as Repertoire: Continuities and Discontinuities in the History of French Contention." In Marc Traugott (ed.), *Repertoires and Cycles of Collective Action*, pp. 43–56. Durham, NC: Duke University Press.

———. (ed.). 1995b. *Repertoires and Cycles of Collective Action*. Durham, NC: Duke University Press.

———. 1995c. "Capital Cities and Revolution," *Social Science History* 19:147–68.

Tsebelis, George and John Sprague. 1989. "Coercion and Revolution: Variations on a Predator-Prey Model," *Mathematical and Computer Modeling* 12:547–59.

Tucker, Robert C. 1961. *Philosophy and Myth in Karl Marx*. Cambridge: Cambridge University Press.

Turner, Lowell. 1998. *Fighting for Partnership: Labor and Politics in Unified Germany*. Ithaca and London: Cornell University Press.

Turner, Ralph T. and L.M. Killian. 1972. *Collective Behavior*, 2nd edition. Englewood Cliffs, NJ: Prentice Hall.

Turner, Terrence. 1991. "Representing, Resisting, Rethinking: Historical Transformations of Kayapo Culture and Anthropological Consciousness." In George W. Stocking, Jr. (ed.), *Colonial Situations: Essays on the Contextualization of Ethnographic Knowledge*. Volume 7 of *History of Anthropology*, pp. 285–313. Madison: University of Wisconsin Press.

U.S. Bureau of the Census. 1975. *Historical Statistics of the United States, Colonial Times to 1970*. Bicentennial Edition, Parts 1 and 2. Washington, DC: U.S. Government Printing Office.

Urban, Michael, Vyacheslav Igrunov, and Sergei Mitrokhin. 1997. *The Rebirth of Politics in Russia*. New York: Cambridge University Press.

Voss, Kim. 1993. *The Making of American Exceptionalism: The Knights of Labor and Class Formation in the Nineteenth Century*. Ithaca and London: Cornell University Press.

Vovelle, Michel. 1976. *Religion et Revolution: La Dechristianisation de l'An II*. Paris: Hachette.

Wallace, Anthony. 1956. "Revitalization Movements," *American Anthropologist* 58:264–81.

Walsh, Edward and Rex Warland. 1983. "Social Movement Involvement in the Wake of a Nuclear Accident: Activists and Free Riders in the TMI Area," *American Sociological Review* 48:764–81.

Wang, Shaoguang. 1995. *Failure of Charisma: The Cultural Revolution in Wuhan*. New York: Oxford University Press.

Wasielewski, Patricia. 1985. "The Emotional Basis of Charisma," *Symbolic Interaction* 8:207–22.

Weber, Max. 1954. *The Theory of Social and Economic Organization*, Edited by Talcott Parsons. New York: Free Press.

Weiner, Myron (ed.). 1993. *International Migration and Security*. Boulder, CO: Westview.

West, Martin. 1975. "The Shades Come to Town: Ancestors and Urban Independent Churces." In Michael Whisson and Martin West (eds.), *Religion and Social Change in Southern Africa*, pp. 185–206. David Philip: Capetown, South Africa.

Whalen, Jack and Richard Flacks. 1989. *Beyond the Barricades: The Sixties Generation Grows Up.* Philadelphia: Temple University Press.

White, Ralph K. and Ronald Lippitt. 1960. *Autocracy and Democracy: An Experimental Inquiry.* New York: Harper and Row.

Whitmeyer, Joseph M. and Rosemary Hopcroft. 1996. "Community, Capitalism, and Rebellion in Chiapas," *Sociological Perspectives* 39(4):517–39.

Wickham-Crowley, Timothy. 1992. *Guerillas and Revolution in Latin America.* Princeton, NJ: Princeton University Press.

Wiltfang, Greg and Doug McAdam. 1991. "Distinguishing Cost and Risk in Sanctuary Activism," *Social Forces* 69:987–1010.

Witwer, David. 2000. "Unionized Teamsters and the Struggle over the Streets of the Early Twentieth-Century City." *Social Science History* 24:183–222.

Wolf, Eric. 1969. *Peasant Wars of the Twentieth Century.* New York: Harper & Row.

Wolfe, Bertram David. 1964. *Three Who Made A Revolution: A Biographical History.* New York: Dell.

Wolfenstein, Victor E. 1967. *The Revolutionary Personality: Lenin, Trotsky, Ghandi.* Princeton, NJ: Princeton University Press.

———. 1969. *Personality And Politics.* Belmont, CA: Dickenson.

Womack, John. 1969. *Zapata and the Mexican Revolution.* New York: Knopt.

The World Bank. 1998. *World Development Indicators.* Washington, DC: The World Bank.

World Press Review 41:15–16.

Worsley, Peter. 1968. *The Trumpet Shall Sound: A Study of "Cargo" Cults in Melanesia.* New York: Schocken Books.

Wright, Marcia. 1995. "Maji Maji: Prophecy and Historiography." In David M. Anderson and Douglas H. Johnson (eds.), *Revealing Prophets: Prophecy in Eastern African History.* London: James Currey.

Wuthnow, Robert. 1980. "World Order and Religious Movements." In Albert Bergesen (ed.), *Studies of the Modern World System,* pp. 57–75. New York: Academic Press.

Yarnold, Barbara M. 1991. *The Role of Religous Organizations in Social Movements.* New York: Praeger.

Zald, Mayer N. 1982. "Theological Crucibles: Social Movements in and of Religion," *Review of Religious Research* 23:317–36.

Zhao, Dingxin. 2001. *The Power of Tiananmen: State-Society Relations, and the 1989 Beijing Student Movement.* Chicago: University of Chicago Press.

———. 1999. "Ecologies of Social Movements: Student Mobilization during the 1989 Prodemocracy Movement in Beijing," *American Journal of Sociology* 103:1493–529.

Zolberg, Aristide R. 1972. "Moments of Madness," *Politics and Society* 2:183–207.

Zukin, Sharon. 1992. *Landscapes of Power: From Detroit to Disney World.* Berkeley: University of California Press.

Index

activism. *See also* American
   biographical availability, new left,
   recruitment and, 195, 197t8.1
   faith and, 161, 168, 171
   individual level of, 17
   youth disposition to, 195–6
Afghan War, 204
Africa, 8, 9. *See also* South Africa
   Christian-Muslim conflict in, 175
   commemorative events in, 166–7
   dead, witchcraft and, 161
   overlapping of secular with religion
      in, 170
   nationalism in, 34n6, 41–2
   religion, moral authority and, 161–
      3
   religious resurgence in, 176–7
   rituals, religious symbols and, 165–
      6
   sacred legitimations, politics and,
      155–6
Afro-Americans
   emergence of middle class for, 92–3
   emotions, reasoning, gender and,
      40–1
   migration of, 91–2
   voting for, 92–3
Agnew, John, 11, 56n4
AIDS, 35
Alinsky, Saul, 33–4
alliances, 22
altruism, 35

American Revolution, 148–9, 153,
      232–3. *See also* Washington,
      George
Amritsar Massacre, 51
Anderson, Benedict, 83
Anderson, Marion, 32, 123
anger, 19, 33, 41, 49, 110, 130
   confrontations and, 16, 20
   containing of, 35
   injustice and, 26, 31n5, 31–2
   recruitment and, 24
   shame about, 16
   women and, 39
animal rights, 40, 116
Apter, David, 9
aristocracy, 95, 98–9
authoritarian states. *See also* Stalin
   repression, concessions and, 188,
      192–3
authority, baiting of, 44

baby boomers, 208–9
   counterculture and, 218–19
   efficacy of, 212–13
   generational identification of, 211–
      12
   higher education growth with,
      209f8.1, 209–10
   life-course deviations with, 215–20
   population growth of, 208–9
   prosperity and, 210–13
   risk taking, optimism and, 210–11

Bangladesh, 42
Bastille, 79–80, 83–4, 98, 102–6,
120–1
Biedenkopf, *land* Prime Minister, 3
biographic impact
new left and, 215–17
biographical availability, 195, 197t8.1
Birth and Fortune, 217
Bishop, Maurice, 130, 149, 151
Black Panthers, 98
Black Power, 28–9, 97, 110, 208
bocage, 61
Bolivia, 131, 160, 170
Bolshevik Revolution, 114
Bonaparte, Napoleon, 106
Bosnia-Herzegovina, 43
boundary, group, 43–4
bourgeoisie, 94–5, 98–9, 233
fleeing of, 149–50
Britain, 170
Cromwell and, 154
Brown vs. Topeka Board of Education,
124
Buddhists, 160
Burma, 116–17
bystander politics, 35
emotions for, 24

capitalism
electronically mediated markets of,
115–16
industrial, 90
international, 67
rise of, 94
Carbonari, 87
Carmichael, Stokely, 97, 110
Castro, Fidel, 130–2, 148–51, 153, 191
Castro, Raul, 130, 148–9
Catholic church, 149
charisma, 129–30, 133
prudential, 142
China, 8, 9. *See also* Tiananmen
Square
Bolshevik model of revolution for,
114
commemorative events in, 166–7

conservatives (mandarin) in, 139–40
Cultural Revolution in, 132, 134–40,
165–6
duality of political culture of, 133
institutionalizing revolution in, 154
Mao *vs.* Liu and, 133–6
national holidays in, 164–5
nonfreedom of religion in, 155–6,
165
"One Strike Three Antis"
Campaign in, 139–40
organizing of peasants in, 60–1
overlapping of secular with religion
in, 168
pilgrimages in, 167, 167n2
rebellion from religious suppression
in, 163
rebels in, 137–9
rebels *vs.* conservatives in village
structure in, 136–8
religion, limited repression and, 159
religious resurgence in, 176–7
repression, opportunity and, 181–2
rituals, religious symbols and, 165–
6, 229
Scarlet Guards of, 139–40
see-saw revolutionary success of,
132–42
space, student insurgency of April
27, 1989 in, 71–6, 231
Taiping Rebellion of, 168–9
terror in, 140–1
white and red areas of, 134
Yan'an roundtable and, 136
civil rights, 32, 33, 37, 51, 67–8, 235.
See also Afro-Americans
cultural epochs in contention,
master template and, 116–17, 237
desegregation through, 65, 93, 123–
4
Greensboro Sit-in and, 107–8, 111,
120
hostility to, 28–9, 69
important events of, 123–4
Ku Klux Klan and, 44
long-term change process and, 91–4

ministers in, 38
Mississippi Freedom Democratic Party (MFDP) and, 108–12
Montgomery Bus Boycott and, 107–8, 110–11, 120, 123–4
organization of, 111
overlapping of secular with religion in, 164, 172
political economics of, 91–2
post World War II and, 93–4, 123–4
protest cycles of, 96–8, 101
protest, repression, and concessions in, 191–2
radical aging for, 97–8
radicalizing of, 29
safe space for, 69–70, 231
shift in, 28
transformative events and, 107–12, 123–4
women organizing in, 142
clergy, 61–2
Cobban, Alfred, 95
Coles, Robert, 29
collective action
motivation of, 90–1,
repertoires of, 112–13
collective behavior
crowd behavior and, 20
collective effervescence, 58, 73, 75, 164
collective interpretation, 226–7
events, unsettled times and, 227–9
religion and, 229–30
Committee of Public Safety, 85–6, 99, 121
Committee on Civil Rights, 93, 123–4
Committees of Correspondence, 59
communication
instantaneous globalized, 115–16
Jacobin club and, 84–6
liaison men and, 74–5
modern, 79
repression and dissemination of, 58–9
communism
religion, utopian future and, 168

Communist Party
Afghan War problem for, 201
collapse of, 206
corruption in, 201
education, overqualification and, 199–200
concessions
repression and, 186–94, 187f7.1
confrontations
fear, anger and, 16, 20
Congress of South African Trade Union (COSATU), 179
contention
broadening of, 8
construction to, 226–30
decline/demobilization of, 44–7
development/sustenance of, 39–44
emergence of, 30–8
innovations in, 236–8
institutionalized, 32–3
repertoires of, 63
social construction in, 226–30
spatiality and, 11
transgressive, 7
contentious politics
definition of, 7, 55
emotions in, 8
episodic nature of, 7
as force for social change, 234–8
perspectives for, 238–40
social movement studies of, 6–8, 12–13
spatialities of power and, 70–1
state-centric understanding of, 23
Cordelliers Club, 81
cotton economy, 91–2
counterculture, 218–19
Cress, Dan, 36
Cuba, 130–2, 148–50
concessions, repression and, 191
democracy and, 132, 150
cultural epochs in contention, 112–13, 237
civil rights as master template of, 116–17, 237

French Revolution as master
template of, 113–16
cultural shifts, 32
culturalists, 25, 127, 226–8, 239–40
bottom up approach of, 119n2
cognitive processes and, 22
emotions and, 19n2, 19–20
cultures
multiple emotion of, 50
cycles of contention. *See* protest cycles
cynicism, 49
demobilizing through, 45

Dalai Lama, 159
decision making
emotionality, rationality and, 18, 49
Declaration of the Rights of Man and
Citizen, 83
democracy
repression, concessions and, 188,
192
revolution and, 130, 132, 150–1
Democracy and Disorder, 96
Democratic National Convention, 109
Democratic Party, 109, 112
demographics, 6, 12. *See also* life-
course
collapse of Soviet Union and
outcomes of macro, 205–6
collapse of Soviet Union and
outcomes of micro, 206–7
decomposition of Soviet Union and
macro, 198–203
decomposition of Soviet Union and
micro, 203–5
macro concerns of, 196
new left and outcomes of macro,
217–20
new left and process of macro, 208–
13
population and, 196
Soviet Union decomposition, life-
course in, 235–6
Deng, Xiaoping, 182
depression, 26
despair, 44–5, 46, 49

disgust, 26
doldrums, 100n1
Donnelly, Brenda, 171
Downey, Liam, 36

East Germany
spread of work actions/negotiations
in, 12–13
unemployment in, 1
Easterlin, Richard, 217–18
Eastern Europe, 115–16, 164, 183
education
growth of U.S. higher, 209f8.1,
209–10
improvement in Soviet, 198–9
Soviet Union and over, 198–201
Eisenstain, Elizabeth, 95
Elias, Norbert, 16, 26
embarrassment, 26
emotions, 6, 239. *See also* anger;
despair; fear; feeling rules; grief;
guilt; hope; pride; shame
alliance and, 22
appeals to, 47
coexistence of different, 27
collective identity through
investment of, 22
commitment, risk and, 17, 21, 24
cultural aspects of, 19n2, 19–20,
23
definition of, 18–20
delimiting topic of, 15–16
demobilizing, 44–5
dependency of, 46–7
feminist movement and, 26, 39
future research for, 47–9
gain from studying of, 16–18
individual activism motivated by, 17
leadership and, 24–5, 34–6
life of movement and mobilization
of, 27–30
management skills of, 25
Mao's, 135–7
mass communications and, 48–9
micro-level and sociology of, 26,
26n4

motivation of action by, 4, 14n1,
14–17, 224–5
movements and variability of, 27–30
observation impeded by, 24
outlaw, 25
physiological aspects of, 19
race and, 40–1
rationality and, 18, 20–3, 48
reactive *vs.* affective, 20
rituals, mobilization and, 41–3
socialization of, 8–9, 39–41
structural change through, 16
structuralists and, 20
thought/affect value of, 18–19
women's acuity of, 34
empathy, 40. *See also* sympathy
environment, 10
ethnography, 50
event research. *See also* protest event
research events. *See*
transformative events

fear, 110
among authorities, 34n6
and anger, 39
confrontations and, 16
dampening of, 33
death and, 73
demobilizing through, 45
initial, 75
motivating value of, 17, 31, 36,
224–5
rejection/ostracism and, 37–8
repression/backlash and, 35–6
uncertainty heightening of, 17
feeling rules, 25, 27, 40, 49, 173
feminism. *See* women's movement
feudal polity, 68, 99
Feuillant society, 85
Forman, James, 109–10
framing process, 119, 127, 165, 184–5
Free Speech Movement, 65
Freedom Summer Project (1964), 28–
9, 43, 70, 211, 213–14, 215,
218
free-rider problem, 17, 224

French Revolution, 8, 10–11, 33, 41,
152
attempted insurrections after, 86–7
August 10, 1792 in, 81
the Bastille and, 79–80, 83–4, 98,
102–6, 120–1
Committee of Public Safety and,
85–6
cultural epochs in contention,
master template and, 113–16
education, overqualification and,
200
equality *vs.* despotism in, 77–8
four class revolutions in, 98–9
fraternization in, 82
Great Fear, 106, 182
insurrection in, 81–3
Jacobin club, communication and,
59, 84–6, 153
lack of social mobility and, 200
long-term change process and, 94–
6
municipal revolution of, 84
National Assembly and, 79–81, 84,
98–9, 103–6, 121
new national political scale from,
83–4
October Days of, 80
Paris people/mobs and, 76n7, 76–7,
79–81, 103–5
Paris primacy in, 80–4
Paris primacy lost in, 86
policing by sections in, 81, 83
protest cycles of, 96–8
purging of Girondins in, 76, 81
radicalizing of, 99–100, 100n1
religion and, 157, 164
repression, opportunity and, 182
revisionist political causes of, 95
section's mobilization of
demonstrations in, 82
socioeconomic causes of, 94–5
spatial dynamics of, 57n5, 75–88
special events of, 106
Terror of, 76, 81, 86, 99
Thermidor and, 99, 106

transformative events and, 102–7
Vendée Revolt and, 61–2
Furet, Francois, 95, 100

Gamson, William, 14n1, 31
gay/lesbian movement, 35, 116
Geiger, Susan, 42, 142
gender
  divisions in, 46
  emotions, race and, 40–1
  faith-based groups and, 173
  male *vs.* female academia and, 22–3
  use of, 35
geographers
  concrete space and, 53–4
German Federal Republic, 3
Giddens, Anthony, 54–5, 57
Girondins, 81, 120
global opinion, 192
global organization
  state development taken over by, 175
globalization
  cultural, 175–6
Goldstone, Jack, 118
Gorbachev, 181
Gorbachev, Mikhail, 33, 186, 191, 198, 201, 203
Gorbachev reforms, 33
Gould, Debbie, 35
grass-roots organizations, 60, 136
  women, 142, 153
Great Fear, 106, 182
Greensboro Sit-in, 107–8, 111, 120
Gregory, Dick, 38
Grenada, 130–1, 149, 151
grief, 19, 35
grievances, 21
group solidarity, 58
groups, 184
Groves, Julian McAllister, 40
Guerin, Daniel, 99–100
guerrilla, 61, 68

Guevara, Che, 131, 148, 153
guilt, 16, 26, 35, 41
  commitment and, 24
  mobilizing value of, 45

Hamer, Fannie Lou, 109
Harding, Susan, 33
Harvey, David, 60
Hinton, William, 137
holidays, national, 164–5
hope, 33, 49, 110, 211
  mobilizing value of, 31–2, 36
  prospects for change and, 31, 33
  recruitment and, 24, 47
Hu, Yaobang, 71

identity formation, 50
IG Metall, 1–2, 4, 6
Indians, 168, 183
indigenous communities, 67
individuals, 184
injustice, 26
  collective action against, 34
  framing of, 31
  threat of, 233
insurgents, 55–6
insurrection. *See also* revolution
  attempted, 86–7
  French Revolution and, 81–3
integration, 97
intimidation, 79
Iranian revolution, 159–60, 164, 168, 176, 190–1
  Islamic model of, 114–15
  repression, concessions and, 189, 190–1
  repression, opportunity and, 182
irrationality, 21, 23, 48
  emotions and, 23
isotopism, 78, 78n9

Jacobin club
  communication through, 59, 84–6, 153
Jaggar, James, 24–5, 34
Jasper, James, 14n1, 20, 37

Index

Johnson, Lyndon, 109, 111–12
Jones, Andrew W., 36
Juergensmeyer, Mark, 176

Kenya, 153
Kertzer, David, 9
Kim, Hyojoung, 41
King, Martin Luther Jr., 96, 107, 120,
    129–30, 215
Korea, 69–70
Korean War, 210
Kruse, Corwin, 47
Ku Klux Klan, 44, 107

labor movement, 1, 3–4, 32, 90, 101,
    122, 192
labor unions, 67, 69, 179
Latin America
    religious resurgence in, 176–7
leadership dynamics, 6
    actualizing potential with, 2
    autocratic *vs.* democratic, 131
    background of, 129
    bridge building with, 148, 150,
        152–3
    charismatic and rational
        (organizational), 129, 133
    charismatic (visionary), 126–7, 129–
        30, 142, 148, 166
    China see-saw revolutionary success
        and, 132–42
    contingency/situational approach to,
        127–8
    definition of, 126
    democracy, revolution and, 130,
    elite and, 126–7, 239
    emotions with, 24–5, 34–6
    failure in, 130–1, 149, 153
    framing process of, 127, 165
    independent aspect of, 128
    institutional building with, 148–51
    institutionalize charismatic
        leadership with, 126–7
    mandarin and rebel, 133–7, 141
    manipulation of incentives by, 128
    men *vs.* women, 142

    people-oriented, 130–2, 152
    personality influence on, 225–6
    postrevolutionary, 148–51, 153–4
    revolutionary leaders in Americas
        and, 147–52
    revolutionary military *vs.* politics in,
        153
    self-effacing and self-aggrandizing,
        131–2, 152
    skills of, 4, 10
    success/failure dependent on, 128,
        133, 141, 151–2, 154
    Tanganyikan independence turning
        points and, 143–7
    task-oriented, 129–32, 152–3
    women, grass-roots organization
        and, 153
Lefebvre, Georges, 84, 94, 98
Levine, Daniel, 165
liaison men, 74–5
liberation
    cognitive, 30–1, 41
life-course, 9, 12
    alternative patterns of, 218–20
    deviations of normative, 215–17
    emergence and decline/outcome of,
        197, 197t8.1
    new left and impact on, 215–17
    new left and macro outcomes on,
        217–20
    new left recruitment and micro,
        213–15
    political contention and, 195–7,
        197t8.1
    Soviet Union decomposition in,
        235–6
Liu, Shaoqi, 133–6, 140, 141, 154,
    165
location, 56n4, 56–7
London Corresponding Society, 59
long-term change process, 90–1
    civil rights and, 91–4
    delimiting of, 113
    French Revolution and, 94–6
    master template and, 122

transformative events, protest cycles
and, 117–20
Louis XIV, 77
Lutz, Katherine, 49

Madsen, Richard, 136
Malcolm X, 129–30
Mannheim, Karl, 195–6
manuals, 50
Mao, Zedong, 132, 149, 153–4, 225
alleged son on, 167n2
as prophet, 165–7
as rebel, 133–7, 139, 141
marches
enemy territory, 44
meaning of space for, 65
recruitment for, 73
space vs. numbers in, 58, 74–5
Marx, Karl, 90, 168
masculinity, 22
master template, 113, 116–17, 237. See
also cultural epochs in contention
long-term change process, and
birth/death of, 122
transformation events, protest cycles
and, 120–2
McCain, Franklin, 108
McNeill, William, 42
membership
threat of rejection from, 37–8
Mexican Revolution, 87
Meyer, John, 237
Michels, Robert, 126–7
micro-macro linkages, 12, 26, 26n4,
47–8, 196–7, 197t8.1, 223–4. See
also demographics
individual emotions, motivation of
action and, 224–5
personality as causal force and, 225–
6
Mills, C. Wright, 213
Mississippi Freedom Democratic Party
(MFDP), 108–12
mobilization. See also protest cycles
cause of, 12
demobilization and, 44–7

emotions, collective action and,
14n1, 14–17
group boundaries and, 43–4
leadership, emotions and, 34–6
ritual, emotions and, 41–4
university, 210, 214, 221, 231
Montgomery Bus Boycott, 96–7, 101,
107–8, 110–11, 120
moral authority
new social movements and, 171–3,
176
religion and, 161–2
political power vs., 110
movements. See social movements
Mozambique, 42
Muster, Manfred, 2, 4
Myrdal, Gunnar, 94

Napoleon, Bonaparte, 154
National Assembly, 79–81, 84, 98–9,
103–6, 121
National Convention, 81–2, 85
national identity, 83–4, 87
National Labor Relations Board
(NLRB), 67
nationalism, 48
ethnic, 234
faith-based, 168, 171, 176
Soviet Union and, 201–3, 205
Nazi Germany, 17, 225
neoliberals, 174–5
networks, social, 72–3
New Deal, 93
new left, American, 116
baby boom affect on, 208–13, 217–
19
definition of, 208
hope/risk taking and, 211
life-course patterns and macro
outcomes on, 217–20
macrodemographic process in rise
of, 208–13
micro life-course impact on, 215–17
micro life-course process in
recruitment to, 213–15
opportunities in, 221

prosperity influence on, 210–13
recruitment to, 213–15
Nicaragua, 130, 149, 164, 233–4
democracy in, 150–1
Nixon, Richard, 112
nonviolence, 97, 115–17, 171
Nyerere, Julius, 11, 34n6, 153
conviction and fine of, 146–7
national (independence) elections
and, 143–6
religious symbols and, 166

observation
emotions as impediment to, 24
opportunities, 6, 12, 36
action and, 180
emotions and, 22
increase of, 182–4
new left, 221
political, 32–3
religion and, 174
religious *vs.* secular, 159–60
repression as motivation for, 181,
193, 233
Soviet Union, 220–1
success formula of, 184–5
Ortega, Daniel, 149–51
organizers
communication of, 59
socializing recent members by,
40

Pagnucco, Ron, 171
paradigms, 8, 12
Pareto, Vilfredo, 126
Paris
density of population of, 77
Haussman's rebuilding of, 62
lost of primacy for, 86
moving of government to, 80
people/mobs of, 76n7, 76–7, 79–81,
103–5
primacy in revolution for, 80–4
proximity to power in, 78–9
sections of, 81–2
Parks, Rosa, 110–11
Payne, Charles, 38

peasants, 98–9, 196
people
sovereign power of, 81–2
People's Daily, 71, 73
People's University, 74
personality. *See also* leadership
dynamics, 225–6
Philippines, 16, 37, 47, 115, 164
physiology
emotions and, 19
pity, 35, 40
Poland, 159, 164, 176
police, 68–9, 74, 81, 83
political generation, 195
Political Geography, 52n3
political power
moral power *vs.*, 110
political scale, 83–4
pollution, Soviet Union, 202, 205
population
baby boom and, 208–13
educational improvement of, 198–9
growth of, 196, 208–9
rural to urban shift of, 91–2, 198–9
urban, 42
positivists, 54
Prague, 71
pride, 40, 41, 44
anger *vs.*, 35
commitment and, 24
injustice and, 26
as master emotions, 22
recruitment and, 47
shame replaced by, 21
proletariat, 114
protest cycles, 96, 101, 195
active/broader, 30
civil rights and, 96–8
French Revolution, 96–8
transformative events, long-term
change process and, 117–20
transformative events, master
template and, 120–2
protest event research, 102, 124–5

protest groups
  as abnormal, 21
  threat, opportunity, concessions and,
    184–92, 187f7.1, 193
public politics, 7
public sphere, 122
Pye, Lucian, 133

qigong masters, 162

race
  divisions in, 46
racism, 29
  colonial, 143–4
  post World War II and, 93–4
radical flank effect, 16, 34n6
rational choice theory, 21
rationalists, 127, 224, 225, 240
rationality
  emotions and, 18, 20–3
  irrationality *vs.*, 48
  Liu's, 135–6
  socializing of members and, 40
recruitment, 47
  biographical availability, activism
    and, 195, 197t8.1
  emotions for, 24
  marches and, 73
regret, 19
relationships, 15
religion, 6–7, 9. *See also* Iranian
  revolution
  Africa's sacred legitimations, politics
    and, 155–6
  China's nonfreedom of, 155–6
  contentious politics of, 158
  definition of, 156
  faith, activism and, 160–1, 168, 171,
    173
  institutional legitimacy of, 159
  limitation of repression on, 159–
    60
  movements of, 174
  overlapping of secular movements
    with, 163–4, 168–70, 229–30
  rebellion from suppression of, 163
  revolution and, 157–8, 177–8

ritual calendar, protests and, 159–60
rituals, religious symbols and, 165–
  7, 229
  sacred, secular and, 65–6, 156
  science, moral authority and, 171–3,
    176
  stabilizing role of, 157
  supernatural realm of, 160–3, 177
  sustained commitment by, 174
  tax-exempt status of, 159
  transcendental ontology based
    movement and, 160–2, 174
  types of, 157, 177
repertories, 63, 112–13
repression, 11. *See also* threat
  addiction to, 188, 193
  concessions and, 186–94, 187f7.1
  limitation of, 159–60
  mounting protest with increased,
    190
  opportunities from, 179–81
  opportunities lost due to, 181–2
resentment, 46
resignation, 49
  demobilizing through, 45
revolution, 240
  Bolshevik model of, 114
  constitutional model of, 113–14
  culturalist bottom up approach to,
    119n2
  democracy and, 130, 132, 150–1
  demographic macro concerns of,
    196–7
  faith source of, 168, 171
  international pressure in, 117–18
  Islamic modal of, 114–15
  leadership dynamics for, 126–7, 147–
    52
  military *vs.* politics in, 153
  modern concept of, 79–80
  people power, 115–17
  political psychology of, 135
  re-defining of, 103–4, 113
  religion and, 157–8, 176–8
  repression and, 189
  situation *vs.* outcome for, 233

Index

sociology of, 22
stages of, 10
Revolution and Rebellion in the Early Modern World, 117
riots, 62–3
rituals
  emotions, mobilization and, 41–4
  religion and, 159–60, 165–7, 229
Robertson, Roland, 176
Robespierre, 85, 99, 105, 106, 132, 153
Roosevelt, Eleanor, 32, 123
Roosevelt, Franklin, 92–4
routinization, 45
rules
  breakers *vs.* makers of, 138, 141
rural areas, 42, 61–2
  built environment for, 61–2
rural population, 42
Russia, 154, 186. *See also* Soviet Union
  health problems in, 205–7
  identification issues in, 206–7
  inflation in, 207
  organized crime in, 207
  repression and, 154, 190–1
  revolution and, 114–15
  Tsar decomposition of, 197–8

Sahlins, Marhall, 102
Sandanistas, 149–51, 233
sans-culotte movement, 81–2, 86, 94–5, 100
scale jumping, 67–8
science
  religion, moral authority and, 171–3, 176
secularization, 156, 176
Selbin, Eric, 130
Sewell, Jessica, 63
Sewell, William Jr., 30, 33, 193
shame, 16, 26, 35, 41, 49
  and anger, 39
  as master emotions, 22
  mobilizing value of, 45
  pride replacement of, 21
  recruitment and, 24

Siemens, 1–4
silk-weavers, 69–70
Skocpol, Thelda, 117
Smith, Christian, 161, 169
Snow, David, 36, 119
Soboul, Albert, 94, 99–100
social appropriation, 37
social history, 26n4
social movements, 5, 9. *See* new left, American
  alternative emotion rules of, 25
  biographical impact on, 195
  built environment constraint on, 61–2
  classical paradigm for, 12
  commemorative events in, 166–7
  comparative methods for, 11
  conservative aging of, 97
  contentious politics as force for, 234–8
  counseling *vs.*, 25
  cultural shifts and, 32
  decline/demobilization of, 44–7
  definition of, 7
  development/sustenance of, 39–44
  emergence of, 30–8
  entering/exiting of, 28, 39
  framing process of, 119, 127
  marches by, 44, 58, 73–5
  moral authority and new, 172–3
  motivation, collective action and, 90–1
  overlapping of secular with religion in, 163–4, 168–70, 172–3
  personal feelings and goals of, 24, 27
  political process of, 91, 117, 127
  popularization of, 45–6
  radical aging of, 97–8, 99–100
  recruitment into, 12, 213–15
  religion, identity transforming for, 169–70
  repression as motivation of, 179–81
  routinization of, 45
  safe space and, 69–70, 72, 75
  social appropriation in, 37

spatial agency and, 55–6
subgroups of and intramovement within, 27–8
sustained commitment by religion to, 162–3, 174
theories of, 3–6, 127–8
transforming events in, 33, 100–12, 118–24
variable emotional investment in, 27
social partnerships, 1, 3
Social Science History, 52n3
socialization, emotional, 39–41
sociology
emotions and, 8–9
religion and, 158, 158n1
Sohrabi, Nader, 114
Somoza, 150, 233
South Africa
repression in, 179–81, 186
supernatural, religion and, 161
threat, opportunity, concessions and, 191–2
Southern Christian Leadership Conference, 215
Soviet Union. *See also* Russia
Afghan War and, 204
Central Asian decline in, 202
collapse of "Soviet man" for, 205
Communist Party, education and, 199–200
Democratic Russia movement in, 201
education, and overqualification in, 198–200
failure of countercoup in, 204
health problems in, 202–3, 205–7, 235–6
lack of social mobility in, 199–200
loyalty from prosperity for, 203
macrodemographic outcomes of collapse of, 205–6
macrodemographic process in decomposition of, 197–203, 235–6
microdemographic outcomes of collapse of, 206–7
microdemographic process and decomposition of, 203–5
nationalism in, 201–3, 205
opportunities/threats in, 220–1
post World War II generation in, 203–5
rural to urban population for, 198–9
Russification of, 201–3
shift in Communist Party/Supreme Soviet of, 200–1
static workforce in, 199
technical/professional movement against, 200–1, 205
youth culture in, 203–4
space
abstract conceptions of, 53
built environment and, 61–2, 72, 75–6
Chinese student insurgency and, 71–5, 231
civil rights and, 69–70, 231–2
concrete conceptions of, 53–4
contention, repression and, 11
copresence and, 57–60, 61, 62, 73, 78–9, 83
definition of, 52–3
dynamics of, 87
French Revolution, Paris and, 75–88
inequality of, 77–8
location and differentiation of, 56n4, 56–7
meaning and, 64–6
numbers *vs.* control of, 58, 74–5
power of, 68–70, 81
routines and, 62–4, 73, 82–3
safe (free), 69–70, 72, 75, 83, 231–2
scale of, 66–8
state structure of, 55, 58, 68, 231–2
structure of, 55–6, 67
strategy of, 82
time-distance of, 60–1, 78–9
Spanish Civil War, 43
spatial agency, 55–6, 74, 75, 88
spatial imagination, 87
Sproul Hall Plaza, 65

Index

Stalin, Joseph, 132, 154
state, 23, 239
  change, and institution of, 235
  concessions *vs.* repression of,
    187f7.1, 187–92
  guerrillas, supply lines and, 61
  policing by, 68–9, 74
  perceived weakness of, 189
  social movements influenced by,
    230–1
  space and, 55, 58, 68, 231–2
  suppress of information by, 58–9
  threat and, 184–6, 232–4
States and Social Revolution, 117
strain, 36
strike
  warning, 1–3
structuralists, 20, 127, 225, 226–7
Student Nonviolent Coordinating
  Committee (SNCC), 28–9, 98,
  109–12, 208
superiority, 46
Swindler, Ann, 227–9
symbols
  defilement of, 42–4
  religious, 165–7, 229
sympathy, 24, 35
syncretism, 177n4

Tanganyikan nationalist movement,
  34n6, 42, 132
  elections and, 144–6
  leadership, turning points and, 143–
    7
  racial nationalism in, 144–5, 147
  racial parity and, 144
  Tabora decision in, 146
  women in, 142
Tarrow, Sidney, 96, 102, 112, 171,
  237
Taylor, Verta, 14n1, 26, 41
temporality, 6, 8, 239
  cultural epochs in contention and,
    10–11, 100, 112–17, 120–2, 237
  doldrums and, 100n1
  lack of study of, 90

  long-term change process and, 30,
    90–6, 117–20, 122
  other rhythms emphasized in, 89
  protest cycles and, 30, 96–101, 117–
    22
  subjective, 100–1n1
  transformative events and, 10–11,
    100–12, 118–25
The Coming of the French Revolution,
  98
Thermidor, 99, 106
threat, 12. *See also* repression
  current, 185, 186, 188
  emotions and, 22
  increase of, 182–3
  injustice with, 233
  meaning, membership and, 37
  non action as, 183
  to the quotidian, 36–7
  religion and, 159, 163, 174
  repressive, 185, 186
  state control over, 184–5, 232–4
Three Mile Island, 36–7
Tiananmen Square, 70–2, 74–5, 110,
  115, 174, 182, 190
  meaning of, 65–6
Tilly, Charles, 90, 112–13, 237
time-space compression, 60
transformative events, 33, 100–2
  civil rights and, 107–12, 123–4
  French Revolution and, 102–7
  long-term change process and, 118–
    20, 123
  protest cycles, master template and,
    118–22
  unsettled times and, 227–9
Truman, Harry, 92–4
Turner, Lowell, 1–2

Uganda, 143
unions. *See* labor unions
United Democratic Front (UDF),
  179
United States, 8. *See also* American
  revolution; new left, American
  activism, faith and, 161, 171

universities
  mobilizing structure of, 210, 214,
    221, 231
  proximity of Chinese, 72, 74, 231
  safe space of, 72, 231
urban areas
  Black migration to, 92–3
  built environment for, 61–2
  disorders of, 31
  population of, 42
  Soviet migration to, 198–9

Vendée Revolt, 61–2
Versailles, 77, 80
victories, small measured, 33–6
violence
  riots *vs.* revolutionary, 104–6

Walsh, Edward, 36
Wang, Hongwen, 139
Warland, Rex, 36
Washington, D.C.
  Mall of, 65–6
Washington, George, 131, 148–9, 153
Watchtower movement
  Latter Day Saints, 170

Weber, Max, 9, 126–7, 129, 142, 166,
    228
White, Geoffray, 49
Whites
  detachment/emotions of, 40–1
women
  acuity of emotions by, 34, 40
  emotions, feminist movement and,
    26, 39
  grass-roots organization and, 142,
    153
  grieving mothers and, 35
  organizing by, 142
  protests against Nazis by, 17,
    225
  suffrage for, 63, 100–1n1
women's movement, 23, 39, 42, 65,
    116, 235
  emotional discourses of, 26

Yelstin, Boris, 204, 207
youth
  activism and, 195–6
Youth-Parent Socialization Panel
    Study, 216

CPSIA information can be obtained at www.ICGtesting.com
Printed in the USA
LVOW13s2025090314

376594LV00001B/22/P